Tropical Apocalypse

New World Studies

J. Michael Dash, *Editor*

Frank Moya Pons and
Sandra Pouchet Paquet,
Associate Editors

Tropical Apocalypse

Haiti and the Caribbean End Times

Martin Munro

University of Virginia Press
Charlottesville and London

University of Virginia Press

Printed in the United States of America on acid-free paper

First published 2015

9 8 7 6 5 4 3 2 1

Library of Congress Cataloging-in-Publication Data
Munro, Martin
Tropical apocalypse : Haiti and the Caribbean end times / Martin Munro.
pages cm. — (New world studies)
Includes bibliographical references and index.
ISBN 978-0-8139-3819-6 (cloth : alk. paper) — ISBN 978-0-8139-3820-2 (pbk. : alk. paper) — ISBN 978-0-8139-3821-9 (e-book)
1. Haitian literature—20th century—History and criticism. 2. Haiti—In literature. 3. Apocalypse in literature. 4. Apocalypse in motion pictures. 5. Haiti—Social conditions. 6. Religion—Haiti. 7. Psychic trauma—Caribbean Area. 8. Literature and history—Caribbean Area. I. Title. II. Title: Haiti and the Caribbean end times.
PQ3940.M863 2015
840.9′97294—dc23

2015007794

Contents

Acknowledgments

I AM VERY grateful to Cathie Brettschneider and everyone at the University of Virginia Press for their support and professionalism. I have benefited greatly over the years from the guidance and example of Celia Britton and Michael Dash. Thanks and love as always to Cheralyn, Conor, and Owen. Sections of the book have been published as the following articles: "The Apocalyptic Creole, from Dessalines to the Chimères," *Diaspora: A Journal of International Affairs* 17.1 (Spring 2008 [2013]): 105–20; "Exile, Return, and Mourning in *Cahier d'un retour au pays natal* and *L'Énigme du retour*," *Irish Journal of French Studies* (2013): 87–109. My thanks to the editors of those journals for allowing me to reproduce the work here. Also, grateful thanks to Peter Doig for the use of his work on the book's cover.

Tropical Apocalypse

Introduction

When the earthquake struck Haiti on January 12, 2010, amid the chaos of fallen buildings, dead bodies, and general panic, citizens of Port-au-Prince were heard to cry that it was the "fin du monde," the end of the world. To many, it was an apocalyptic moment, a cataclysmic end, but without the promise contained in biblical versions of the apocalypse of a new and better beginning. This was therefore a very particular apocalypse, one that had been prepared for, indeed prophesied to some degree in religious and political discourse, the arts, and culture more generally for decades, perhaps centuries. For Haitian and broader Caribbean history were founded on the apocalyptic meeting of Europeans and Amerindians—the latter being quickly exterminated by the former. Subsequent Haitian and Caribbean history has been shaped by the no less apocalyptic reality of plantation slavery and colonialism, and their enduring legacies. This book is about that history, and the quite singular apocalypse that has long been part of Haitian and Caribbean reality. It is written in a sense in the shadow of the earthquake, which stands as the terrible conclusion to Haiti's centuries-long apocalyptic history. The apocalypse in this context relates to the biblical sense of the final destruction of the world, the end of the present age, and to the meaning of the Ancient Greek term *apocálypsis,* which refers to a revelation, the uncovering of something hidden. Apocalypse is in this sense something of a polyvalent term, one that is used at times symbolically, as a narrative tool to think of human and societal relationships to time and place; at others, the apocalypse is a means of understanding the lived reality and narrating of disaster; while at others still, it is an ideologically charged concept, related to long-standing conceptions of Haiti as a failed, ill-starred nation, for example in political or religious discourse, where it may be used to justify Western economic, military, and political interventions. In some cases, Haitian authors refute these representations of Haiti and present distinctly anti-apocalyptic narratives of time, place, and nature. More commonly, however, the apocalyptic narrative is generated as it were from the inside, as a means of understanding (and surviving) the particular movements of history that have created the disasters of the present.

History seems to create a particular relationship with death that is expressed in the Haitian proverb "Nou mouri déjà, nou pa pè santi"—we are already dead, we don't fear the odor of death. In a sense, the world and life came to enslaved Africans through death, the deadening nonexistence of the plantation. Such a conception of death (and life) is not that far removed from the apocalyptic thought of modern-day evangelicals and explains to some extent the stoic fatalism—often interpreted as innate "resilience"—that underlies much of the history of the Haitian people, and in particular their reactions to the 2010 earthquake. It is this polyvalent quality that characterizes Haitian apocalyptic narratives, and that distinguishes them from, for example, the "southern apocalyptic imaginary," defined in a recent work as "a field of reference, drawn from the cosmology of southern evangelical Protestantism, that maps the apocalyptic possibilities of cataclysm, judgment, deliverance, and even revolution onto the landscape of the region" (Hoefer 4). While, as chapter 4 of this book shows, evangelical Protestantism is a significant element in propagating apocalyptic ideas in contemporary Haiti, the other chapters demonstrate the range and complexity of Haiti's apocalyptic imaginary, and show that the Haitian and Caribbean apocalypse has its own particular meanings and paradoxes, for instance in the ways in which the state functions (or does not function), and most notably in the sense that the apocalypse has endured for centuries, and that the end times have no apparent end.

While it was a national, localized event, the Haitian earthquake may be read as a particularly devastating instance in a contemporary, global moment that seems to throw up new apocalyptic scenarios almost by the day: tsunamis, hurricanes, floods, food crises, riots, financial markets collapsing. In his recent work *Living in the End Times,* Slavoj Žižek offers a vision of the contemporary globalized world on the cusp of an apocalyptic breakdown. This moment is heralded by the prominence of what he calls his "four riders of the apocalypse," which are: "the ecological crisis, the consequences of the biogenetic revolution, imbalances within the system itself (problems with intellectual property; forthcoming struggles over raw materials, food and water), and the explosive growth of social divisions and exclusions" (x). For Žižek, the coming apocalypse is inevitable, but is something that the world ignores and tries "desperately" to not think about (xi). To explain this general reticence to face up to the apocalyptic truth, he uses the psychologist Elisabeth Kübler-Ross's well-known scheme of the five stages of grief: denial, anger, bargaining, depression, and acceptance (xi).[1] One can see, he says, the same five figures in the way the world's "social consciousness" thinks of the forthcoming apocalypse (xi). The first reaction, he says, is one of "ideological denial: there is no fundamental disorder"; the second "is exemplified by explosions of anger at the injustices of the new world order"; the third "involves attempts at bargaining ('if we change things here and there, life could perhaps go on as before')," and when the bargaining fails, "depression and withdrawal set in"; finally, after passing through this "zero-point, the subject no longer perceives the situation as a threat, but as the chance of a new beginning, or as Mao Zedong put it: 'There is great disorder under heaven, the situation is excellent'" (xi–xii). In other words, Žižek sees finally in the coming apocalypse an opportunity to do away with the old order and to create what he calls an "emancipatory subjectivity" (xii). As such, this apocalypse has, at least potentially, a redemptive quality; it is a narrative with a teleology and built-in process that takes the subject and the society from one state considered to be undesirable to another that is seen as being ideal, almost utopian in its emancipatory potential for the individual living freely in the "germs of a communist culture" (xii).

The Four Riders of the Caribbean Apocalypse

This book is less about the global apocalypse that Žižek envisions than the apocalyptic history and actuality of a region—the Caribbean—that one might say was born out of the apocalypse, and whose subsequent history has turned in further apocalyptic cycles, in which nature and human agency conspire to create a quite particular experience of time and place. The birth of the modern Caribbean was brought about in conditions that both recall and modify Žižek's characterization of the "four riders of the apocalypse." There are no doubt more than four harbingers of the apocalypse in the Caribbean, but it is instructive to work with Žižek's model as this allows the present inquiry to ultimately zoom out as it were and place the apocalyptic Caribbean in relation to the broader world.

In both cases, there is an ecological crisis that is an almost inevitable consequence of the economic system: in the Caribbean, this ecological disaster dates back to the earliest days of European colonization, and is exacerbated by the region's susceptibility to natural disasters.[2] On many islands, contacts with Europeans led to the near decimation of the indigenous Amerindian population, while the forests were cut down and the land cleared for European crops and livestock by the early 1600s. In the French colony of Saint-Domingue, colonists wrote in the eighteenth century of the environmental damage caused by plantation agriculture. Planters complained to the French government that the only wood they could use for building was found on mountain summits, and while Versailles proposed a reforestation program, colonists were more concerned with the profits they could reap quickly in sugar and coffee than with the less lucrative business of growing timber. By the end of the century, planters had already observed how deforestation had led to a drastic decrease in rainfall, which in turn lowered the levels of nearby rivers (Garrigus 116–17). Thus was set in motion a cycle of environmental decay that makes Haiti an extreme case of the ecological crisis of the Caribbean, a crisis felt to varying degrees in all the islands of the region. Genocide and ecocide were complementary projects in the Caribbean, as Derek Walcott writes in *Omeros:* "Seven Seas would talk/bewilderingly that man was an endangered/species now, a spectre, just like the Aruac/or the egret, or parrots screaming in terror/when men approached, and that once men were satisfied/with destroying men they would move on to Nature" (300).

The second rider of the Caribbean apocalypse—slavery—is intimately connected to the first, and is something of an undead ghost from the past that haunts every apocalyptic turn in Caribbean history. Slavery was instituted once the native populations had become, as Walcott says, specters, eradicated from the landscape that was itself changing and deteriorating rapidly. Among its many effects was the creation of societies structured by death: slavery was a system that killed, through disease, malnutrition, overwork, and violence. White planters were far from immune to the deadly instability of plantation societies: epidemics of tropical diseases decimated the white population, to the extent that in Kingston, Jamaica, from 1722 to 1774 there were nearly 18,000 funerals and only 2,669 baptisms (Brown 2). In Jamaica and other plantation societies, the whites' accumulation of property and wealth and the renewal of family and social networks as well as the slaves' conception and representation of their own existences in cultural forms "stemmed in significant ways from high mortality and the lingering presence of the dead" (ibid. 4). It is this "lingering," deathly presence that is perhaps slavery's most enduring legacy, and which is felt still in the apocalyptic present, where the codes and sanctions of slavery always "resurface and find new places to inhabit" (Dayan 194). In particular, the notion that people could be possessed and owned by others and exist as human chattels to be "passed around, damaged, or consumed" in effect eliminated the very idea of personhood for the enslaved (ibid. 195). In such a situation, because the living never truly live, "The dead do not die. They haunt the living, both free and unfree, African and European [and] still speak in the present landscape of terror and ruin" (ibid.).

The present landscape is indeed haunted by the undead memory of slavery, by great swathes of people living a kind of "social death" (Patterson 22), and by colonially inherited systems of law, governance, and society that reproduce in commuted form figures that live, as slaves did, by and through the body, and in a self-destructive cycle that leads such figures to seek social and historical revenge through inflicting damage not on the elites but on those that resemble them the most directly. It is no coincidence that when such post-slavery figures assembled themselves into organized groups in Haiti they adopted or were given names that evoke their haunting, undead qualities: the Tontons macoutes and the Chimères. The former, the notorious private militia of the Duvalier presidents, were named after the Creole bogeymen figures who would kidnap errant children in the night and keep them in their knapsacks, while the latter, the organized gangs hired from the urban slums to support Jean-Bertrand Aristide and the Lavalas party, are named after shadowy monsters, or else composite mythological beings, only partially human. In both cases, the names indicate the ghostly nature of the militiamen and suggest that they are manifestations of the unfinished past, phantoms born of the enduring legacy of slavery in the Caribbean.

The third rider of the Caribbean apocalypse is a consequence of the second, and relates directly to one of Žižek's categories, what he calls "the explosive growth of social divisions and exclusions" (x). In this regard, the Caribbean has a long history; slavery and colonialism instituted color and class hierarchies that to a large extent continue to shape social structures. These inherited structures are exacerbated and indeed bolstered by contemporary local and global economic dynamics that further widen the divides in Caribbean standards of living. Those working in the global economy are increasingly living almost in a different world from those in the sprawling slums that blight even the most prosperous Caribbean countries. Stark economic differences are reflected in the organization of space, in the growth in gated communities—secluded colonies of the relatively wealthy, and signs of the fear and mistrust that are born of the radical differences in standards of living between communities within single Caribbean nations.[3] It is the entrenched social divisions as much as the redundancy of postcolonial regimes that have created what David Scott calls the "dead-end present," the sense that despite, or indeed because of, the "earnestly progressive ideologies" of early Caribbean postcolonial regimes—"radical nationalisms, Marxisms, Fanonian liberationisms, indigenous socialisms"—the various anticolonial projects across the region have stalled radically (*Conscripts* 1). In many ways, the "free community of valid persons" envisioned by the Guyanese poet Martin Carter seems as distant and unattainable as at any time in modern Caribbean history (qtd. in ibid. 2). In Scott's withering critique, the perpetuation of social divisions and exclusions is due to the "acute paralysis of will and sheer vacancy of the imagination, the rampant corruption and vicious authoritarianism, the instrumental self-interest and showy self-congratulation" that have characterized governance in the postcolonial Caribbean (ibid.). Almost everywhere, he adds, perhaps recognizing the apocalyptic direction in which many Caribbean societies are headed, the anticolonial utopias have "gradually withered into postcolonial nightmares" (ibid.).

The fourth rider of the Caribbean apocalypse is the crisis of criminality that pervades virtually every society in the region. This crisis is closely related to political failings, and is as much a question of the failure of the state and of the law as it is a matter of criminality per se. Caribbean people are no more naturally inclined to criminality than anyone else, but there exists in many places a potent and dangerous mix of social and economic division, unemployment, low salaries, limited access to education, weak state institutions, corrupt and ineffectual policing, and other factors that have combined to make the Caribbean the site of a crisis that touches every level of society, and which led for example to the declaration of a state of emergency in Trinidad in 2011. Security is one of the boom businesses in the Caribbean, as the wealthy seek to protect their property and families with personal guards, themselves hired from the poor and paid a minimum wage that barely covers their food and living costs in economies with spiraling inflation. It appears significant too that one of the most common crimes across the Caribbean is kidnapping, an act that seems to have historical resonances, and to underscore the importance in Caribbean history of owning and appropriating bodies, stealing them, and using them as a form of currency.[4]

Each of these four riders of the Caribbean apocalypse is closely connected to the others, both in a cause-and-effect way and in a more complex circular, reciprocal relationship that perpetuates the apocalyptic cycle. The ecological crisis is a direct result of slavery, which left a legacy of social division and color and class complexes, which fuels the wave of criminality, which is also a result of the ecological crisis, which has led in many countries to urbanization and the creation of the urban slums in which criminality thrives. Add to this external factors such as the global financial crisis and the rising cost of food, and natural factors such as the region's susceptibility to earthquakes, droughts, floods, and other events, and one has a particularly precarious situation, and a sense that the region stands at the edge of an apocalyptic abyss that is deeper and more long-standing than the one envisioned by Žižek for the Western world. One feels indeed that the Caribbean has been at or around this point since the earliest days of colonialism and that in some ways it has been living its own version of the end times for centuries.

Caribbean Literature and the Apocalypse

It is no surprise therefore that one finds in Caribbean literature, and regional culture more generally, images of the apocalypse and strands of millenarian thought that reflect quite directly the historical reality of the region. One might say that the most important issue in the development of Francophone Caribbean literature in particular has been the conceptualization of the region as "a site for romantic fantasies of liberation or more precisely of redemptive or revolutionary apocalypse" (Dash, "Postcolonial Eccentricities" 33–34).[5] In Aimé Césaire's work, for instance, the Caribbean is often presented as the negative pole of the "triangular circuit" (83); while Europe has power and resources and Africa has culture and history, the Caribbean for Césaire is kind of void, an apocalyptic site that is marked by absence and emptiness. One senses with Césaire that he lived still in the apocalyptic history instigated in the earliest days of slavery and colonialism. "What remains for you from former times," he asks in one poem, before offering his own response: "Exploded sky flayed curve/of flogged slaves' backs/grief treasurer of the trade winds/shut book of spells forgotten words/I question my mute past" (255). The apocalyptic islands are thus characterized by silence and forgetting; and yet at the same time and in that very silence history is everywhere perceptible.[6]

One could say that Césaire's epic work, *Cahier d'un retour au pays natal,* is shaped around an apocalyptic movement that bears some comparison to Žižek's adapted model of the five stages of grief: denial, anger, bargaining, depression, and acceptance (xi). While Žižek writes of an impending apocalypse, Césaire's has already taken place and is ongoing. This is why Césaire, at least in this poem, in a sense skips the denial stage: the reality around him makes it impossible to deny that the apocalypse has occurred and that its effects are still being felt. Thus, Césaire's poem begins with anger, and with images of the Caribbean that suggest strongly the poet's apocalyptic vision: he writes of the "hungry Antilles, the Antilles pitted with smallpox, the Antilles dynamited with alcohol," of letting free "monsters," of a historical and contemporary "disaster" and, more obliquely, of the "putrefying force of crepuscular surroundings, surveyed night and day by a cursed venereal sun" (35).

Again, because the apocalypse has already taken place, there is little sense of Césaire addressing the next stage of Žižek's model of grief: bargaining. There is to be no bargaining with a history that has already occurred. Instead, the speaker seems to lapse at times into the next stage, depression, which is due at once to the historical and contemporary forces that have brought about the apocalypse, and to the inertia and apathy of the people. The crowd he writes of is "detoured from its cry of hunger, of poverty, of revolt, of hatred," and appears to him "so strangely chattering and mute" (ibid.), and the speaker seems caught at times in a similar state of depressed, voiceless inertia. Toward the end of the poem, Césaire moves strikingly into the final stage of Žižek's model: acceptance. In one memorable sequence, he seems to go beyond hatred, depression, and the other stages of grief to a state of acceptance that suggests a kind of healing:

> I accept . . . I accept . . . totally, without reservation . . .
> my race that no ablution of hyssop mixed with lilies could purify
> my race pitted with blemishes
> my race a ripe grape for drunken feet
> my queen of spittle and leprosy
> my queen of whips and scrofula
> . . . .
> I accept. I accept. (73)

This acceptance of history and race in effect prepares the way for the final, triumphant images of the speaker and his country "standing now, . . . hair in the wind, my hand puny in its enormous fist and now the strength is not in us but above us" (77). The poem closes with the word *verrition,* which as Dash argues, means "to scrape clean or sweep away" and contains the words *vérité* (truth) and *vert* (green), "suggesting a fresh, green truth that explodes from this fiery conflagration" ("Postcolonial Eccentricities" 38).

In effect, Césaire arrives at a point similar to that foreseen by Žižek, who writes that after passing through the "zero-point" of anger and depression, the subject no longer views his situation as a threat, "but as the chance of a new beginning" (xii). In Césaire's case, this new beginning is the result of a process whose apocalyptic nature exists in the poem's imagery, its movement through its various stages, and in the underlying idea that the new beginning must follow the end of the previous order. "What can I do?" he asks at one point in the poem, before replying, "One must begin somewhere. Begin what? The only thing in the world worth beginning: The End of the world of course" (55).[7]

Similar images of apocalyptic endings and beginnings appear in the work of many of the other major figures in Caribbean writing; indeed it could be argued that "the apocalyptic aesthetic" is "the most fundamental practice of twentieth-century French Caribbean literature" in particular (Joseph 28). Derek Walcott, like Césaire, writes of the legacies of apocalyptic history and asks: "who in the New World does not have a horror of the past, whether his ancestor was torturer or victim? Who, in the depth of conscience, is not silently screaming for pardon or for revenge?" (*What the Twilight Says* 39). Walcott's "Adamic" perspective on Caribbean history, one that "neither explains nor forgives history," and which abandons any desire to find redemption or justification in history, is essentially a response to (and also one way out of) the common problem of the perceived lack of history, for when he does look back he, like the others, sees in "the seeded entrails of the slave" a "new nothing, a darkness" (ibid.). Amnesia, Walcott says "is the true history of the New World" (ibid.). These factors create what he sees as the essentially bitter tone in New World poetry: "In such poetry there is a bitter memory and it is the bitterness that dries last on the tongue. It is the acidulous that supplies its energy. The golden apples of the sun are shot with acid. The taste of Neruda is citric, the Pomme de Cythère of Aimé Césaire sets the teeth on edge, the savour of Perse is of salt fruit at the sea's edge. . . . For us in the archipelago the tribal memory is salted with the bitter memory of migration" (41). Walcott sees in all great New World poets a rejection of "ethnic ancestry" and a faith in "elemental man," a kind of post-apocalyptic figure with his memory erased, a "second Adam," as he names it, who will mark a beginning similar to that envisioned by Césaire, and the "re-creation of the entire order" (40).

In a similar vein, Antonio Benítez-Rojo considers the plantation, the New World apocalyptic site par excellence, to have been, he says, "the womb of my otherness," in other words the matrix from which was born the "new" in the New World ("Three Words Toward Creolization" 54). The plantation is Benítez-Rojo's "old and paradoxical homeland," whose foundation he imagines in positively apocalyptic terms as "the big bang of the Caribbean universe, whose slow explosion throughout modern history threw out billions and billions of cultural fragments in all directions—fragments of diverse kinds that, in their endless voyage, come together in an instant to form a dance step, a linguistic trope, the line of a poem, and afterward repel one another to re-form and pull apart once more, and so on" (ibid.). In Benítez-Rojo's version, no doubt the most utopian of those considered here, the apocalyptic moment produces therefore a great energy, in which he sees almost exclusively new birth, new cultural forms, and a source of endlessly creative reproduction.

Indeed, Benítez-Rojo goes even further by arguing that the apocalypse is an alien concept to the Caribbean. Writing of the Cuban missile crisis of 1962, Benítez-Rojo contends that with the world at the edge of a nuclear catastrophe the Cubans defused the moment by refusing to consider it in apocalyptic terms. This was a revelatory moment for Benítez-Rojo; he identifies it as the time he reached "the age of reason" (*The Repeating Island* 10). The children of Havana had been evacuated and a "grave silence" had fallen over the streets and the sea (ibid.). While the state bureaucracy searched for news on the radio or issued communiqués, two "old black women" passed by Benítez-Rojo's balcony, walking "in a certain kind of way" (ibid.). While he cannot describe precisely this way of walking, he says that there was "a kind of ancient and golden powder between their gnarled legs, a scent of basil and mint in their dress, a symbolic, ritual wisdom in their gesture and their gay chatter" (ibid.). Watching the two women, Benítez-Rojo says, he knew "at once that there would be no apocalypse" (ibid.). "The swords and the archangels and the beasts and the trumpets and the breaking of the last seal were not going to come," he writes, "for the simple reason that the Caribbean is not an apocalyptic world; it is not a phallic world in pursuit of the vertical desires of ejaculation and castration" (ibid.). The notion of the apocalypse, he argues, is "not important" in Caribbean culture, but is a product of "ideological propositions" articulated in Europe and which the Caribbean shares "only in declamatory terms, or, better, in terms of a first reading" (ibid.). The culture of the apocalypse is, he argues, a culture of the land, of Europeans for whom the sea is a "forgotten memory" (11). The culture of the Caribbean, in contrast, is not terrestrial but "aquatic": "a sinuous culture where time unfolds irregularly and resists being captured by the cycles of clock and calendar. . . . A chaos that returns, a detour without a purpose" (ibid.).

While there is something seductive in Benítez-Rojo's evocation of the Caribbean as an anti-apocalyptic site, the region's history often tells a different story: there have been many instances of dictators creating, to use Benítez-Rojo's own term, "phallic" worlds, and of political systems based on apocalyptic systems of for or against, honor or blood, death or glory. Also, important aspects of Caribbean culture, not least the literary and theoretical texts discussed here, bear the imprint of apocalyptic thought, which is as Dash says "more deeply ingrained in Caribbean thought than Benítez-Rojo is willing to concede" ("Postcolonial Eccentricities" 35). It seems finally something of a conceptual leap for Benítez-Rojo to take from the apparent insouciance of two elderly women in a time of crisis a sweeping theory of Caribbean culture.[8] The fact that they are identified as black women suggests too that there is a kind of internal exoticism at play, that Benítez-Rojo is projecting onto them qualities and ways of thinking that he believes he sees, but which must to some extent be a product of his own imagination and the social and cultural distance that exists between the women and him, a distance that is suggested by his looking down on them from his balcony, as a spectator.[9]

Nevertheless, Benítez-Rojo's reconsideration of the apocalyptic vision of the Caribbean is indicative of a broader movement in regional thought in the post-Negritude era, which in general terms places the emphasis more on lived experience than on mystical conjurations of the past, and this in turn led to less markedly apocalyptic versions of Caribbean reality, at least in works of literature.[10] In the French Caribbean, for example, following Césaire, there was a decisive movement away from apocalyptic poetry to engaged, phenomenological thought and more markedly realist fiction.[11] Frantz Fanon was largely responsible for this shift, notably in *Peau noire, masques blancs,* in which he trenchantly critiques Negritude's mystical, African elements, and also more implicitly its apocalyptic strain, figured in the following quotation in the reference to the apocalyptic Césairean tropes of explosive, sudden changes and absolute truths. "The explosion will not take place today," he announces in this text. "I do not come armed with decisive truths. My consciousness is not traversed by essential flashes of lightning" (25).[12] Fanon further distances himself from Negritude's apocalyptic strain in his indirect critique of Jean-Paul Sartre's famous essay "Orphée noir," published in 1948, four years before *Peau noire, masques blancs.* Fanon denounces Sartre's

Hegelian interpretation of Negritude as the antithesis to the thesis of white supremacy—"an anti-racist racism" in Sartre's famous phrase, a step toward the synthesis of the universal and the "human." Tellingly, Fanon also critiques Sartre's argument that Negritude's raison d'être is to finally "destroy itself," being only a passage and not a final destination, the means and not the end (107–8). In this sense, Fanon is wary of imposing an apocalyptic teleology onto black Caribbean intellectualism. To truly know the Caribbean, Fanon argues, one must be able to "lose oneself in the absolute," for "consciousness engaged in experience ignores, must ignore the essences and the determinations of its being" (108). This phrase, which indicates the philosophical influence of Merleau-Ponty and phenomenology, shows that for Fanon a proper understanding of Caribbean consciousness must be firmly grounded in the analysis of experience, in the study of what *is,* not of what is putatively missing or lost.[13] In thus resetting the conditions for valid intellectual inquiry into the Caribbean, Fanon not only marked a break with the racial essentialism of Negritude, he also, inadvertently perhaps, set out the future shape and direction of French Caribbean writing, which was to make a decisive turn toward the recording and interpretation of lived experience. The radical shift to prose—chiefly novels, memoirs, and short stories—in the post-Negritude era can be attributed in part to the increasing emphasis on lived experience in that period. With poetry largely related in the literary imagination as a mystical means of reconnecting with the mythical African past, prose became the favored means of investigating the "real," the everyday, and the personal (which is always nevertheless closely related with the collective). As René Ménil argues, much like Fanon, "The mystery of our impossible history lies not in the absurdity of our past but in the incoherence and inconsistency of our present social consciousness. The prerequisite to any history of Martinique is the study of our consciousness as it exists today" (47). Consequently, too, the apocalyptic element in Caribbean thought faded for at least several decades, as authors consciously distanced themselves from Negritude and its explosive version of Caribbean history and being. René Depestre said farewell to Negritude and to revolution, acts that to him marked "the death of a dream," which "ensured the return to poetic and novelistic good health; the end of Manicheanism; a free view on the complexity of life in society; the possibility for the body and the mind to be in harmony in any situation."[14] Daniel Maximin effectively expresses the spirit of the post-Negritude period when he writes of the "feeling of despair that we share over dreams of ruins and total apocalypse" (22). As Chris Bongie argues, it was in the post-Negritude period that was founded the “postmodern vision [which] takes at its point of departure the collapse of the heroic dreams of modernism—and of the aesthetic and political revolutions and/or resolutions that such dreams promised” (354).[15]

Edouard Glissant’s reading of history is perhaps the least apocalyptic of all the major writers of his and the preceding generation. Glissant shares to some extent Benítez-Rojo’s idea that the plantation was the birthplace of the dynamic, creolizing culture of the New World, though Glissant’s vision of Caribbean history is considerably more muted. Glissant to a certain degree writes against and in dialogue with Césaire, so that one finds with Glissant at once the deliberate deflation of his predecessor’s explosive mysticism and the residue of Césaire’s apocalyptic vision of history. One could say that the main thrust of Glissant’s writing involves “a desperate attempt to free himself from the epistemic violence of apocalyptic discourse,” and constitutes “the creative indeterminacy of a post-apocalyptic poetics” (Dash, “Postcolonial Eccentricities” 34, 40). Rather than as an explosion or big bang, Glissant reads Caribbean history as an inwardly directed “implosion” that creates silence and absence rather than the cacophonous creation that Benítez-Rojo suggests (*Caribbean Discourse* 66). It is also significant that Glissant addresses to a large extent the particular history of the French Caribbean, the territories still linked politically to France, and as such is less drawn to ideas of apocalyptic endings and dramatic new beginnings than to the complexities of a compromised identity and an incomplete liberty.

This is not to say that Glissant is less sensitive than other Caribbean intellectuals to the terrible reality of the slave trade. On the contrary, slavery appears as an ineradicable memory that informs all of his work. “The French Caribbean,” Glissant writes, “is the site of a history characterized by ruptures and that began with a brutal dislocation, the slave trade.” Consequently, he says, in the French Caribbean “historical consciousness could not be deposited gradually and continuously like a sediment . . . but came together in the context of shock, contraction, painful negation, and explosive forces” (ibid. 61–62). The imagined memory of the slave ship is particularly enduring. “Imagine vomit,” he writes, “naked flesh, swarming lice, the dead slumped, the dying crouched” (*Poetics of Relation* 5). “Imagine, if you can, the swirling red of mounting to the deck, the ramp they climbed, the black sun on the horizon, vertigo, this dizzying sky plastered to the waves” (ibid. 5–6). This history is for Glissant apocalyptic, as he imagines the deported Africans “worn down, in a debasement more eternal than apocalypse” (ibid. 6).

The boat takes the slave to the edge of an abyss, and yet in its belly there is also a kind of birth: the boat is "a womb, a womb abyss[,] . . . pregnant with as many dead as living under sentence of death" (ibid.). The abyss is to Glissant a "tautology," in that the ocean finally meets the shore, "gently collapsing in the end into the pleasures of the sand," which makes "one vast beginning, but a beginning whose time is marked by these balls and chains gone green" (ibid.). The slave is thus born into Relation, a form of non-hierarchical exchange with the other, and a somewhat salutary consequence of the Middle Passage. Relation is "totality in evolution," an order of human and cultural contacts that is "continually in flux and whose disorder one can imagine forever" (133). Contemporary human truths, for Glissant, are not be found in an apocalyptic "lightning strike," but rather in a more muted process of repetition and "difficult approximation" (*L'intention poétique* 48). The lightning strike is, he says, "the art of blocking the obscure in its revealing light," while accumulation is that of "consecrating the everyday in its duration, finally recognized" (ibid.). Thus Glissant, unlike Césaire but something like Walcott and Benítez-Rojo, sees in apocalyptic history the start of something new that will come to characterize Caribbean societies, and indeed puts them at the forefront of the broader world's movement into similar relations; as modernity expands and spreads, it brings into being the kinds of relations that Glissant sees as the paradoxical beginnings of modern Caribbean societies. There is in Glissant's later exploration of key concepts such as Relation, chaos, creolization, and the rhizome a sense of exhilaration at the "breakup of the old, singular system of domination and its replacement by a world view based on diversity and unpredictability" (Britton 179). "The whole world," Glissant writes in a well-known phrase, "is becoming archipelagized and creolized" (*Traité du tout-monde* 179). He sees in modern mass communications "unimagined possibilities for sharing and equality," and a means for the continued "liberation of the imagination" (*Poetics of Relation* 108–9). And although this creates a "multiply dispersed zone," which leads to a sense of "vertigo," this he insists, "is not the vertigo preceding apocalypse and Babel's fall. It is the shiver of a beginning, confronted with extreme possibility" (109). Thus, Glissant's interpretations of both history and the present do not so much reject outright the notion of the Caribbean apocalypse as see in it the potential birth of something new: in trouble and chaos he sees the emergence of new ways of being and relating, in the Caribbean and across the entire world.

And yet, for all his remarkable conceptual inventiveness and intricacy of thought, Glissant seems to some extent out of step with the apocalyptic turn both in Caribbean lived reality and in certain key works of Caribbean criticism. The effects of the four riders of the Caribbean apocalypse have been compounded by a series of natural disasters, food crises, and financial catastrophes that have struck the region since the turn of the millennium. The people and places of the world may indeed be interconnected more than ever before, but in economic and social terms this means that the small economies of the Caribbean, already overly reliant on external produce, are particularly susceptible to downward shifts in global markets and upward slides in inflation. This lack of control over national economies, and therefore national destiny, is surely one of the postindependence realities that have led David Scott to declare that "we live in tragic times" (*Conscripts* 2). For Scott, Caribbean anticolonialism depended on a certain way of "telling the story" of the past, present, and future of the region (ibid.). His suggestion is that anticolonial versions of telling this story have been emplotted in the distinctive narrative form of romanticism. That is, they have tended to be "narratives of overcoming, often narratives of vindication[,] . . . and to tell stories of salvation and redemption" (8). The futures envisioned by these romantic narratives have been focused on a "certain (utopian) horizon toward which the emancipationist history is imagined to be moving" (ibid.). In the light of what he calls the "global and historico-political and cognitive shifts" of recent decades Scott calls into question the critical salience of this narrative form, and turns to tragedy as a narrative that may offer a more appropriate means of interrogating the troubled present (ibid.). The tragic mode typically engages with moments of "historical upheaval or civilizational rupture," when new kinds of subjects are "thrown upon the historical stage," individuals that embody the great "conundrums and divisions of their age" (12). A tragic vision of history moreover questions whether reason can be separated from myth, and the past disentangled from the present. Perhaps most importantly, tragedy casts doubt on the view of human history as "moving teleologically and transparently toward a determinate end, or as governed by a sovereign and omnisciently rational agent" (ibid.). As such, the relationship between past, present, and future is never a romantic one "in which history rides a triumphant and seamlessly progressive rhythm, but a broken series of paradoxes and reversals in which human action is ever open to unaccountable contingencies—and luck" (13).

The sense of a tragic, dystopian Caribbean present is further suggested in the visual art project undertaken in 2011 by the journal *Small Axe*, entitled "The Visual Life of Catastrophic History." The project is a response to the coming to prominence of the theme of catastrophe in a number of domains of critical thought and artistic practice. The reasons offered for interest in disasters are largely familiar: the "wars without end" unleashed by "emperor-like sovereigns"; the personal and social effects of systemic financial collapse; the destructive force of natural events such as tsunamis, hurricanes, and earthquakes; and the "terrible spectacle" of the most vulnerable people fleeing in fear "the total power of men and gods" (133). Together, these calamities create the "pervasive haunting sense" that we are living in "a perpetual state of emergency, not only in the very midst of seemingly uncontrollable disaster but also in a constant *expectation* of disaster" (133). And, in stark contrast to the romantic vision of history and time critiqued by Scott, such a scene of catastrophe is marked by a temporal block, the effect of which is to make the future almost impossible to envision in terms other than as a continued disaster. This is what the project statement means when it refers to the "paralyzing *futurelessness* of catastrophe" (134, emphasis original).

Within this global scenario of disaster, the Caribbean is "a measureless scene of catastrophe," a site particularly prone and susceptible to calamities, to various natural disasters and social and political atrocities (134). The statement further argues that the Caribbean was "*inaugurated* in catastrophe" (ibid., emphasis original): the Spanish colonial enterprise that led to the swift extermination of native peoples. Subsequent Caribbean history is conceived of in the statement as a series of catastrophes that range from the capture, transportation, and enslavement of Africans to the indentureship of Chinese and East Indians. "In fundamental ways," the statement proposes, "the Caribbean has never overcome this founding colonial catastrophe," the reverberations of which have shaped to a considerable extent the postcolonial history of the region to the present day in the form of economies driven by "external imperatives," societies structured with "tiny rapacious elites" at one end and "impoverished masses" at the other, and "cynical, unresponsive governments given to authoritarian rule and corruption" (ibid.).

While tragedy and catastrophe are not quite synonymous with each other or with apocalypse, it is not too far a critical and conceptual leap to see these turns toward tragic and catastrophic interpretations as essentially connected to, or as critical stages that anticipate, the apocalyptic criticism and aesthetic that this book examines and pursues. Indeed, in focusing, as the chapters of this book do, on the particular case of Haiti, one is almost compelled to switch from the tragic or catastrophic to the apocalyptic. For Haiti, as the *Small Axe* statement argues, is perhaps the "*limit*-instance" of catastrophic history, of a "hard experience familiar to *all* our Caribbean" (134, emphases original).

Haiti Apocalypse Now

Following the earthquake of January 12, 2010, the Haitian filmmaker Arnold Antonin released a short film entitled *Haiti Apocalypse Now.* The title is well chosen, for the film captures some of the terrible chaos that swept through Port-au-Prince on that dreadful day: bodies are everywhere, twisted, crushed, or otherwise destroyed while the living negotiate in shock the apocalyptic reality into which they have been thrown. As the journalist Jonathan Katz writes, the year following the earthquake "began with the end of days" (263). Perhaps more than any other single event in the recent catastrophic history of the Caribbean, the 2010 earthquake encourages an apocalyptic interpretation of the present, and of the past that led to such a calamity. It moreover renders the conception of future time all the more difficult. While it may be too much to say that the post-earthquake nation exists in a state of "futurelessness," it seems almost impossible to think of the future as anything other than, at best, a slow and tortuous movement beyond the apocalyptic event. As such, there appears in the Haitian narrative of apocalypse to be little prospect of a final redemption, the stage that follows the "zero-point" that Žižek talks of, which brings in his version, "the chance of a new beginning" (xii). In this sense, and in many other crucial ways, the Haitian apocalypse is a quite singular phenomenon.

In this regard, Myriam J. A. Chancy's work is a key critical point of reference. Chancy situates her work on the Haitian apocalypse in relation to a broader sense of imminent disaster, the belief that the world at large is "gravitating toward destruction" (*Framing Silence* 136).[16] The importance of Haitian literature, she says, is that it reveals that "the Third World is undergoing its own forms of apocalypse" (137). For the Third World and its inhabitants, she says, "the apocalypse is already underway" (ibid.). Haiti stands again as an extreme case in this ongoing apocalypse: at the mercy of an economic system beyond its control, it "lives by dying, supplying . . . the First World with its lifeblood" (138). Haitian writers are unlike those from the global North who have addressed the questions of the apocalypse (she references Derrida in particular), in that they do not take nuclear war as an apocalyptic "absolute referent" (140). Instead, the apocalypse is already there, and exists in part in the annihilation of memory that is a key element of Haitian and Caribbean historical experience. Haitians' first encounter with the apocalypse occurred, Chancy says, in the Middle Passage, and even after independence Haiti did not free itself from the colonial ideology that "has kept Haitians in a state of oppression since the 1400s" (143). In the twentieth century, Haitian apocalyptic thought took perhaps its most damaging and enduring turn with the emergence of the *noiristes* and their absolutist ideas of race, color, class, and culture. As Chancy argues, the election of François Duvalier in 1957 as president of Haiti in effect inaugurated a new apocalypse for Haiti, one that more than fifty years later continues to cast a shadow on the present, the end time without end.

This book complements Chancy's work on the apocalypse in its initial focus on the Duvalier dictatorships as the founding moment of the modern apocalypse in Haiti.[17] It considers the dictatorships in terms of a further apocalyptic implosion that manipulates the past, specifically the history of the revolution, in order to alter the present and determine the shape of the future. Chapter 1, "The Duvaliers and Apocalyptic Memory," proposes that, in many ways, Haiti is still living the Duvalier apocalypse, and considers, as do the other chapters, the use of apocalypse as a rhetorical figure in works of Haitian literature. Apocalyptic memory is the guiding critical concept, and is something of a paradoxical term in that it evokes some of the temporal contradictions with which many contemporary authors contend. Specifically, what does it mean to have an apocalyptic memory, when apocalypse refers most apparently to endings, and is itself normally part of an eschatological model of time and history that would foreclose any sense of the future? As such, the authors studied in this chapter write in something of a non-future, about events that certainly took place, but which have not until now featured largely in creative works. To write of such events in the present is to evoke an apocalyptic memory—a recollection of a time that was marked by endings, and was inscribed as the chapter shows in the apocalyptic ideology and even in the very structure of the state—and to live still in that sense of an ongoing ending. Writing becomes in this sense a temporally significant act, in that the invocation of apocalyptic memory seems to disrupt the feeling of living in an endless end time, for that concept itself relies on a form of collective and individual amnesia, a sense that the past should not, even cannot be called to mind, such is the terror associated with it. As such, the authors discussed in this chapter work as it were anti-apocalyptically, against forgetting, and in favor of memory, the recovery of which in the present appears as perhaps the most effective means of disrupting the apocalyptic narrative that is one of the Duvaliers' most lasting legacies. The recovery of memory is further related in the chapter and throughout the book to the original Greek meaning of the word *apocalypsis*—to unveil, or uncover. To remember is to reveal that which has been obscured, and in each case the exploration of apocalyptic memory unveils personal and societal truths that time has obscured and which only now, decades following the dictatorships, emerge from memory and are brought into plain sight.

The chapter begins by evoking the terror released on Haiti by the Duvaliers: the violent, obsessive repression of any dissent. The violence had a "quality of phantasm" that is the foundation for Chancy's belief that Haiti is living through an apocalypse (145). The chapter builds on Chancy's critique through analyses of Raoul Peck's film *L'homme sur les quais* and close readings of key literary works published in the twenty-first century—Edwidge Danticat's *The Dew Breaker* (2004), Kettly Mars's *Saisons sauvages* (2010), and Evelyne Trouillot's *La mémoire aux abois* (2010). Danticat's work seems to break several taboos in its evocation of an exiled Haitian family, haunted by the crimes committed by the father during the Duvalier era. The novel flits between Haiti and Brooklyn, between the silenced past of the "dew breaker" and the present in a way that evokes questions of memory, forgiveness, and redemption. *Can* one ever forgive a torturer? *Should* an individual or a nation forgive? Or are they condemned to relive the sins of the past, even in exile? In a sense Danticat's work prepares the way for that of Mars and Trouillot, in that both revisit the Duvalier era and offer singular responses to the questions evoked in *The Dew Breaker.* Published in 2010, Kettly Mars's novel is read here as a prime example of the mature and daring rethinking of the history of recent times. I argue that, in its treatment of the Duvalier era, Mars's novel is at once a critique of the dictatorship and a provocative statement on the allure of power, the entanglement of sex and politics, and the people's complicity in their own subjugation. Evelyne Trouillot's novel is similarly provocative and imaginative in its critique of the Duvaliers. The originality of her work largely resides in her focus on Simone Duvalier, the wife of the dictator. The novel is a kind of mute dialogue between Simone Duvalier and a Haitian nurse, and takes place in a Parisian hospital, long after the end of the dictatorship. As such, the novel explores the memory of the dictatorship, and how trauma survives and haunts the present. To what extent, the chapter finally asks, is the memory of the Duvalier apocalypse still alive, and what role can the arts play in recuperating that memory?

Chapter 2, "Utopian Ends: Aristide and the Apocalypse," explores the presidency and legacy of Jean-Bertrand Aristide, and considers his particular contribution to the sense that Haiti is living in an ongoing apocalypse. The chapter traces the rise and fall of the former president and his Lavalas party, and the prophetic, apocalyptic aspects of his public discourse. This is not therefore apocalypse as memory, but as foreseeing, a future-oriented political narrative that carries the apparent promise of a radical break with the past, but which has ultimately a cyclical quality, and brings about a repetition in many senses of the past from which it ostensibly sought to free itself. Arguing that the Haitian arts, and literature in particular, offer some of the most penetrating critiques of the Aristide period, the chapter engages with key works, such as Raoul Peck's film *Moloch tropical* (2009), Lyonel Trouillot's novel *Rue des pas perdus* (1996), and Gary Victor's *A l'angle des rues parallèles* (2000), all of which offer distinctly apocalyptic visions of Aristide's Haiti. The novels in particular reveal one of the fascinating elements in Haitian apocalyptic literature: that, in contrast to Christian apocalyptic narratives, there is often little distinction made between the good and the evil in Haitian writing. Opposing political forces are often presented as being fundamentally alike, so that there is little sense of natural or divine justice imposing itself at the end of the conflict. Rather, these confrontations are worldly affairs, governed by a different set of rules in which the most violent, the most wicked, often prevail. The chapter argues that it is no coincidence that the theme of the apocalypse should reappear so prominently around the turn of the millennium, in that such a moment seems to incite simultaneously the fear and hope for the end of a historical period and for deliverance into a new time in which the people would be finally freed from the phantoms of the past. This is I argue apocalyptic writing without the eschatological promise of a new age to come. All that is foreseen is the continuation of a cycle that stretches back to colonial times, which stand as the initial apocalyptic moment, an historical shock so violent that it continues to disrupt the present, rendering impossible any sense of history (as in many religious versions of the apocalypse) as a linear progression from one age to the next. What we see in Trouillot's and Victor's novels of the Aristide era is a people and a nation caught in a self-perpetuating cycle that confuses and confounds any straightforward understanding of ethics and morality. As such, the works studied in chapter 2 differ from those considered in chapter 1 in that the works on Duvalier are anti-apocalyptic in their attempts to recover memory and thereby negate the amnesia that perpetuates the sense of living in the end times, while the works on Aristide are written more or less contemporaneously with that political period and as such are less about memory than the lived experience of the Aristide era. There is little sense of narrative distance in the works on Aristide; rather these are remarkable, immediate documents of a political period that is lived as a newly apocalyptic moment, indeed an even more intensely apocalyptic time in the ways in which Aristide's own apocalyptic discourse clashes with the ideological and physical residues of Duvalierism. There is also little of the apocalyptic unveiling that one finds in the works on Duvalier, or at least what is unveiled is profound confusion, an apocalyptic experience, again without the eschatological promise of an imminent ending. In turn, the contemporaneous nature of these works has significant effects on narrative style, and one finds here, paradoxically perhaps, not directly realist accounts of a very real, lived experience, but various forms of narrative indirection—Peck's allegorical style, Victor's surreal, magical realist form, and Trouillot's mélange of narrative styles, the alternation between various narrative voices that suggests the insufficiency of one particular perspective or narrative form to communicate the experience of the present, apocalyptic moment.

Chapter 3, "The Chimères and the Haitian Antihero," analyzes the figure of the Haitian antihero in history, literature, and film. Drawing on the ideas of Maximilien Laroche, who has written on the figure of the antihero in Haitian literature, the chapter argues that the figure's classic movement from resistance to self-sacrifice is an apocalyptic one. I further argue that self-sacrifice for the nation is inscribed in its earliest history, in the deaths of Toussaint Louverture, Jean-Jacques Dessalines, and Henri Christophe, and in the national slogan "Vivre libre ou mourir"—live free or die. The chapter considers recent manifestations of this antiheroic figure, notably in Lyonel Trouillot's *Bicentenaire* (2004) and Yanick Lahens's *La couleur de l'aube* (2009). Crucially, too, the chapter considers the history and representation of the Chimères, Aristide's militia hired from the urban slums, who appear in literary and cinematic works as apocalyptic figures, grotesque, nihilistic re-figurations of the Tontons macoutes. The chapter shows that in Lahens's novel there is a fascinating play between the antihero protagonist and the Chimères. The paradoxes of Haitian politics complicate the question of ethics so that it is difficult to judge if the antihero is completely on the "right side." Drawn to a politics of liberation, the novel's antihero ends up for a time on the same side as the Chimères, with whom he has much in common. Specifically, they are all part of the apocalyptic narrative that makes the city the site of a battle to the end. The armed thugs are as much apocalyptic figures as the antihero figure is. A crucial component of the novel's apocalyptic narrative is that the killer needs a victim, while the self-condemned victim needs a killer; the one completes and validates the other. Representations of the Chimères in literary works by Lahens and Lyonel Trouillot are compared and contrasted to those in the films *Ghosts of Cité Soleil* (2006) and *Haïti, la fin des Chimères?* (2004). As such, the chapter revisits the complex question of evaluating and explaining the differences in representations of Haiti by Haitian and non-Haitian writers and filmmakers. In effect, the Chimère figures often appear as incomplete, composite beings—brothers are like two halves of a full being, their identities in some senses split in two, dualistic parts. What they have in common is however the fundamental emptiness and despair that is the lot of what may be termed the apocalyptic subject, those living at the economic, psychological, and existential limits. In terms of form, the works studied in this chapter tend toward a more realist representation, notably in the films, but also in the fiction, which, in relation to the works on Aristide in chapter 2, engages more directly with the lived experiences of the urban poor. Instead of the allegory and magical realism of Peck and Victor, one finds here various forms of psychological realism, diverse attempts to imagine and represent the experience of the Chimères, who appear as the apocalyptic subjects par excellence, in that through them each creative work seeks to expose and unveil underlying truths relating to history, politics, and economics, the perennial factors that create over and again the apocalyptic reality in which they exist.

The first part of chapter 4, "Religion, Nature, and the Apocalypse," considers the role of certain religious groups in Haiti in propagating apocalyptic thinking. Specifically, the chapter engages with Vodou theology and argues that this religion is distinctly non-apocalyptic in that it accentuates rebirth and regeneration rather than apocalyptic endings. Drawing on Chancy and Leslie Desmangles, the chapter shows that Vodou followers believe that death is not an ending but a stage that leads to new birth, and as such the idea of the apocalypse is largely foreign to the religion. By contrast, the apocalypse is a crucial element in the various Protestant evangelical religions that are increasingly establishing themselves in Haitian religious life. In this regard there are important connections between contemporary Haiti and what Hoefer terms the "southern apocalyptic imaginary," which ascribes, he says, catastrophic consequences to "violations of the boundaries of the race, class, gender, family, community, region, and nation" (4). Importantly, however, this apocalyptic imaginary is also a "reservoir of hope" that promises deliverance from injustice and worldly suffering (ibid.). As such, the evangelical apocalyptic imaginary has important temporal aspects in that it explores the unveiling of the future in the present, and the encroachment of a new order into a chaotic historical situation (5). The chapter analyzes the evangelical presence in Haitian culture and society by drawing on the recent work of Elizabeth McAlister and other sociologists of religion, such as Laënnec Hurbon. This strain in religious thought is read in terms of a pretext to disaster, which anticipates, prepares for, and to some extent wishes catastrophe to come in order to end a social, economic, and political situation that is disastrous, but which is not total disaster, and as such maintains people on the brink of disaster without ever having the release of finally falling into the abyss. In short, I argue that the expectation and fear of imminent disaster are to some extent harder to bear than the experience of disaster itself, and that the discourse of some of these evangelical groups reflects this psychological, social, and cultural reality.

The second part of chapter 4 considers the relationship between Haiti's apocalypse and the natural environment, arguing that the two are intimately connected, and that without a reversal in the nation's long ecological decline, apocalyptic understandings of Haiti's past, present, and future will persist. Notoriously deforested and prone to natural disasters, the Haitian environment has long been an ideal milieu for the propagation of millenarian ideas on the fate of humankind in the world. The chapter engages with the long history of European characterization of the tropics as "danger zones," of associating exotic landscapes with a malevolent nature. This was related to what David Arnold terms a discourse of *tropicality,* one of the most striking elements of which was the invention of the sense of *otherness* that Europeans associated with the tropical environments. In Arnold's terms, tropicality is "a Western way of defining something culturally and politically alien, as well as environmentally distinctive, from Europe and other parts of the temperate zone"(6). As the chapter further argues, the very concept of natural disasters is part of a broader historical and cultural "geography of risk" that sets apart large parts of the world as dangerous for Europeans (Bankoff 27). Importantly, as Bankoff states, it also serves to justify Western interference and intervention in places such as Haiti, "for *our* and *their* benefit" (27, Bankoff's emphasis). Also, the proliferation and greater global visibility of natural disasters in the twenty-first-century tropics has refigured places such as Haiti as danger zones, diseased and impoverished, and always on the edge of an apocalyptic collapse.

The chapter ends with close analyses of two works published in 2009 that in fact evoke and celebrate something of a return to nature. Dany Laferrière's *L'énigme du retour* and Lyonel Trouillot's *Yanvalou pour Charlie* are remarkable in that they ultimately re-situate their protagonists from the apocalyptic city, and in Laferrière's case the isolation of exile, to the country, in which can still be found a different reality, and a potential source of regeneration, both for the individuals and for the nation as a whole. In both cases, the authors are known as writers of the city, but in these works they reengage with the Haitian hinterland and find in nature a source of comfort and inspiration, a potentially healing balm not only for their own grieving characters, but also for their battered and bruised nation. In reconsidering nature in this way, these two novels echo the interest in early Haitian and broader Latin American and Caribbean writing in nature as part of the "foundational narratives" of emerging nations (Anderson 18). They also in effect write against the wider historical discourse about tropical environments, which has since colonial times presented nature as a source of danger (for the European) and an explanation for issues of poverty and disease. The chapter ultimately argues that to blame, fatalistically, or in apocalyptic terms, the environment for social and economic problems in effect obscures the many and complex detrimental effects of European interventions in the Caribbean.

This book's conclusion begins by situating the apocalyptic narratives studied in relation to David Scott's argument that in the broader contemporary Caribbean, where a sense of imminent, positive historical change appears diminished, "time has suddenly become more discernible, more conspicuous, more at odds, more palpably *in question*" (*Omens* 12, Scott's emphasis). Time is therefore the immediate preoccupation of the conclusion, which also considers the relationship between the 2010 earthquake and the various apocalyptic texts, figures, political movements, and religions discussed in the preceding chapters. Specifically, it reflects on the prophetic qualities of apocalyptic discourse. I reconsider certain prophetic phrases contained in the pre-earthquake works, and relate them to the play *Mélovivi*, by Frankétienne, in whose work the apocalyptic has long been a key aesthetic and philosophical principle. The play, set following an earthquake, and in rehearsals on January 11, the day before the 2010 earthquake, is now considered by the playwright to be a "visionary" work. What, this book ultimately asks, is the relationship between apocalyptic art and the future, and can art influence time to come?

In his book on post-earthquake Haiti, Jonathan Katz questions his motivations for writing the work, and wonders "whether the world really needs another American's personal account of living in Haiti, a country whose people are more than capable of speaking but struggle to be heard" (4). In fact, his book succeeds as it engages with Haiti from an "inside" perspective, and positions itself largely within Haiti, looking outward so that Haitian issues and points of view are privileged. In a different but complementary sense, the present book engages primarily with Haitian reality and with some of its artists, authors, and filmmakers, critical voices who are indeed, to use Katz's terms, "more than capable of speaking." Arguably, too, Haiti's creative voices "struggle to be heard" on the outside, especially perhaps in the Anglophone world, where there has been a great proliferation of works on Haiti, and many of the authors of these works have, quite naturally perhaps, become the principal interlocutors for English speakers interested in Haiti.[18] This is partly a linguistic issue: most Haitian authors write in French, and translations of their works are not always freely available. When they are translated, it is often with a considerable time lapse, which leaves Anglophone readers somewhat out of synch with Haitian culture and thought, which evolve dynamically, much as the political and social spheres change rapidly. There is also, more importantly, an inevitable sense of non-Haitians (myself included) being to some degree out of step with Haitian intellectuals, and their particular perspectives on national history, society, and culture. In many cases, Haitian intellectuals offer interpretations of Haiti that are quite different from those of non-Haitian commentators.[19] Moreover, Haitian authors write primarily in the context of a rich intellectual tradition that generally supersedes broader critical frameworks, such as postcolonialism. This book's principal focus is on Haitian intellectuals, and the ways in which their works engage with, complement, or contradict one another. It also offers a response to the question posed by Amy Wilentz, when she writes of a contemporary "silence" in Haiti, which she says will not be broken through Western intermediaries such as herself, "but in some new Haitian way invented by Haitians like the Haitian Revolution, in some new Haitian way that you and I cannot predict" (289). I would argue that the arts and literature in particular are characteristically "Haitian ways" that have not remained silent, even following the earthquake. Indeed, the opposite is true: there has been a remarkable burst of creative activity since 2010, and even before then, Haitian literature had been enjoying something of a golden era, with prizewinning works by, among others, Dany Laferrière, Lyonel Trouillot, Evelyne Trouillot, and Yanick Lahens. Such remarkable creativity in effect demonstrates how disaster can "dynamize . . . culture," and how natural disasters are often "agents of cultural formation as much as physical events" (Anderson 8).

Even in the most richly interdisciplinary anthropological or historical studies of recent and contemporary Haiti, creative writing and the arts more broadly are rarely engaged with in a sustained way. For example, Erica Caple James's excellent work on trauma and violence in Haiti is elaborately interdisciplinary in its use of "theology, medical and psychiatric anthropology, law and political science, human rights and humanitarian studies, and studies of race, gender, and religion" (18). It does not however extend its interests to the arts, or to literature in particular, some attention to which would no doubt have further enriched the understanding of the workings of trauma and violence, given that these are such prominent themes in contemporary writing. Literature, and especially poetry, have long had a particular social and political significance in Haiti and the broader Caribbean, in part because, as Myriam J. A. Chancy argues, "the Caribbean novel has traditionally served the purpose of filling the gaps of official history" (*Sugar* x). The importance of literature in Haiti is suggested when Laurent Dubois—one of the few Haitianist historians to draw extensively on creative writing—notes how during the occupation U.S. officials found it "odd and amusing that before the start of meetings, Haitian cabinet ministers might engage in erudite discussions about recent surrealist poetry and similarly unexpected subjects" (285). Also, many Haitian leaders have been intellectuals, most notoriously François Duvalier himself, who once asked a group of army officers, "Do you know why I have succeeded where other intellectuals, like Firmin and Bobo, failed?" His answer underscores the crucial relationship between writing and power: "I was the first to have a pen in one hand and a gun in the other" (qtd. in ibid. 330). Michel-Rolph Trouillot further suggests the importance of "culture" more generally in Haiti, in his argument that "'nation' has everything to do with culture, for culture and history are its sole constant referents. Claims of nationhood always imply a reference to some past and to the cultural present eventuating from that past" (*State against Nation* 24). The most prominent element of the "cultural present" in Haiti since the revolution has arguably been literature, and as such an understanding of the development of Haitian writing is vital to any understanding of the broader nation.[20] Jana Evans Braziel makes a similar point when she writes that despite Haiti's high illiteracy rate, "literature is vital to Haitian national survival," in that "it launches pointed critiques . . . and textual attacks against injustice—national and international, political and economic" (*Ghosts* 32). Braziel pays particular attention to Haitian diasporic literature, which she judges to be "crucial for rethinking (and revaluing) Haiti in the Americas . . . and rethinking the Americas as an imperialist zone" (ibid.). Valerie Kaussen is similarly convinced about the importance of Haitian literature, and argues that it is now "more relevant than ever, reminding us of the historical underpinnings of contemporary globalization and calling into question the global relationships of power to which we are all subject and for which we are all responsible" (*Migrant Revolutions* 21).

In contrast to Braziel's (and Kaussen's) primary interest in diasporic literature, this book engages with works produced both inside and outside Haiti, one effect of which is to suggest that the critical context in which to best discuss Haitian culture is one that extends from Haiti to the diaspora and that puts Haitian intellectuals at home and abroad in constant, if irregular and unpredictable, dialogue with one another. I am consequently less interested in, and less convinced of the primary importance of the "larger extraterritorial forces" to which Braziel attributes much of the blame for Haiti's ills (*Ghosts* xii). The workings of international relations are an important background to the works I discuss, but I believe that the critical and intellectual foreground in which they are best understood is that which they create in and between themselves, by their singular contributions to long-standing debates on issues of, for example, nationhood, politics, history, love, sexuality, gender, exile, social class, language, and identity. In effect, the works themselves provide the proper contextualization for one another, in that they come out of largely the same historical and cultural reality. Close reading is the most effective way of understanding that reality and the ways in which individual works relate to one another. As such, the book pays close attention to the specific contexts and the specific language(s) of texts, in a way that echoes Spivak's advocacy of the principles of close reading in engaging with works of the "Global South," and her insistence on the importance of the "critical intimacy of literary learning," the attainment of which is perhaps this book's primary aim (104–5n2).

Cultures of Disaster

While this book insists on the primary importance of reading closely diverse examples of Haitian writing, it also makes implicit and explicit connections to disaster studies, an emerging interdisciplinary field that engages with the cultural and political implications of disasters. The most significant and direct connection between the Haitian examples this book examines and disaster studies lies in the universal importance of literature. As one of the leading figures in disaster studies, Mark D. Anderson, writes, following independence many Latin American nations looked to the United States and Europe for models of development, but lacked the governmental and academic institutions for mediating unexpected events such as disasters. "In lieu of technical specialization, literature became a key space in which notions of risk and vulnerability were formulated and debated" (17). As such, literary works became the sites in which disasters were theorized, in a way that allowed Latin American societies to stand back from disaster and "assume a more critical stance toward highly traumatic experience" (17–18). In short, literature in Latin America and in Haiti constitutes, in Anderson's terms, "a powerful means of persuasion" (18).

Anderson's statement that "nothing shakes one's worldview more than the experience of a natural disaster" could be directly applied to contemporary Haiti (1). Disaster is "conceived of as a rupture or inversion of the normal order of things; natural disaster denotes that moment of disjuncture when nature topples what we see as the natural order of human dominance" (ibid.). For instance, an earthquake uproots the metaphorical solidity of the land and the notions of identity that are often attached to it, "sweeping the ground from beneath our feet and reducing to rubble our literal and conceptual edifices" (ibid.). Disaster studies insists that the relative effects of disasters depend not only on forces of nature but also on the economic, social, and cultural conditions in which human communities exist.[21] Disasters have "no inherent meaning discernable by humans outside that which we assign them," and as such they call for interpretations, which are largely determined by the culture of the human communities that bear witness to them (3). These meanings are inherently unstable, and change according to place and time. In places like Haiti, so prone to natural disasters, meanings not only change but perhaps also disintegrate completely over time, to the extent that they lose all meaning, or at least become virtually impossible to decode in any coherent way.

That said, since colonial times and particularly the eighteenth century, during which there were frequent earthquakes and other natural events, there has been in Saint-Domingue and Haiti something of a "culture of disaster," one where natural disasters are not only physical events, but also "agents of cultural formation." In effect, cultures of disaster come into being when "frequently occurring natural hazards are integrated into the schema of daily life" (8). In exploring the theme of the apocalypse in Haiti, this book suggests that Haiti's culture of disaster has long had distinctly apocalyptic overtones. As Anderson argues, natural disasters involve "human interaction with the environment and as such must be mediated through culture" (1). In Haiti, as the present book shows, literature in particular has often been a prime site in registering and memorializing natural and other disasters. Literature, and indeed literacy, are also related to forms of power in that "culture is never apolitical; rather politics represents the process by which cultural trends are formalized and institutionalized as political power" (2).

Disasters also cast into sharp relief humans' relationship with nature, particularly if one holds that human subjectivity is formed in and through nature, and that the earliest human cultures were created as a means of mediating and drawing meaning from the relationship with nature. For many early Western thinkers, politics and social organization were understood in terms of a dialectical relationship between nature and human culture. In his book *Political Nature* John M. Meyer investigates this relationship in Western thinkers such as Aristotle and Hobbes, arguing that both were fundamentally interested in the "nature of motion" (58). For Aristotle in particular nature followed a teleological movement, and motion and change in nature were indications "of something striving to fulfill its natural potential or to find its natural place" (ibid.). In Western religious thought, too, nature has often been understood in teleological terms. Dante wrote of a world understood as time and nature, and which "embodies an ultimate and eschatological goal" (Altizer 119). That goal is derived from the will of God, who has by means of nature or the creation "established an end for the whole human race" (ibid.). Beginnings are thus related to endings, and the fate of humans is intimately connected to that of nature. When nature is recast as a "fallen" phenomenon, as it is for instance in the poetry of William Blake, its endings take on distinctly apocalyptic qualities—for Blake, the American and French Revolutions were events that marked the coming of a "truly new world, an apocalyptic world, for this advent is inseparable from the end of all previous history" (ibid. 185). Thus, apocalyptic political events are in some complex ways related to nature, and to human culture's changing, volatile conceptions of time and history. Humanity, or at least Western humanity, has long inscribed into readings of nature notions of time, teleology, and eschatology that reflect distinctly ontological concerns, and that underscore Anderson's point that "nature has neither collective agency as subject nor fixed meaning as object outside of the dualistic relationship with human culture" (4).

Interpretations of contemporary disasters tend to consider less the philosophical implications of catastrophe than their material, social, and political causes and effects. As Gregory Button writes, whether disasters are labeled natural or unnatural, they "highlight the asymmetrical distribution of power and foreground the struggle of the state, corporations, and human agency for the redistribution of power" (16). Thus notions of power and control are of fundamental importance to contemporary studies of disaster—who controls information, and thereby has the power to produce the meaning of a particular event? These meanings are often inflected by issues of social class or gender, such as in Susanna Hoffman's reading of forms of disaster narrative that present catastrophes as assaults on Mother Nature's inherently nurturing qualities. Metaphors of ravaged, abused nature are part of a broader narrative that presents disaster as one stage in a cyclical movement toward rebirth and regeneration (133). In many cases it is the male and the masculine element that intervenes, and that saves feminized nature through its technological interventions. Indeed, such a narrative is inscribed deeply into Haitian literature's most widely read work, Jacques Roumain's classic 1944 peasant novel, *Gouverneurs de la rosée*. In this work, the natural disaster is a drought, which turns the land to dust, which in turn has clear connotations of death and sterility. The male hero figure Manuel returns to this scene of disaster and in order to reverse it evokes his essential (and racial) connection to the land: "That is me: that land there, and I have it in my blood. Look at my color: it is as if the color of the land itself has run into us. This land belongs to the black man, and each time that they have tried to take it from us, we have weeded out injustice with our machetes" (79).

As in Hoffman's reading of Mother Nature's nurturing functions in disaster narratives, Manuel frames the deforestation that has led to the long drought around a narrative of a mistreated, feminized land: "the land is like a good woman, if you mistreat it, it will revolt: I saw that you have deforested the hills. The land is naked and without protection" (43). And, much as in Hoffman's readings, it is the male, technological interventions—the discovery of a spring and the channeling of its waters to the barren land—that saves the land and Mother Nature, or indeed Mother Haiti. Roumain was certainly not the first Haitian writer to figure nature and the feminized land as guarantors of authenticity, or as, in

Dash's words, "the source of a national ethos" (*The Other America* 48). From the earliest articulations of Haitian nationalism in the nineteenth century, nature was presented as a marker of authenticity, and as the long disaster of deforestation in particular took hold, nature became as in Roumain's novel associated with images of abused womanhood, a feminine figure to be saved and redeemed by masculine interventions.

Hoffman's conception of the feminized land is however complicated in Haiti and other Caribbean sites through the dimension of race. When Manuel says, as he does above, that he has the land in his blood, that the color of the land is that of his skin, he evokes a racial element that reinforces the masculinism that Hoffman critiques. In saying that "this land belongs to the black man" (79), Manuel indicates clearly the doubled and exclusive sense of ownership of land and nature, and hints at the color and class conflicts that have long shaped relations to and representations of the land in Haiti. Many of Haiti's political struggles have turned around notions of the land and a troubled or incomplete sense of belonging. As the Haitian sociologist Laënnec Hurbon says, it was the desire to truly inhabit the land that compelled the slave armies to drive the French colonizers from the land, the dream of "becoming master of the land that had been in the beginning constituted as a place of exile" (qtd. in Chéry 132). Thus one senses in Haiti and elsewhere in the Caribbean something of the close and complex imbrication of natural disasters with other, historical and social catastrophes.

In a similar way, issues of mass urbanization, of central importance to disaster studies, are reflected in and rendered even more complex in the case of Haiti. The urban theorist Mike Davis writes of the ways in which mass urbanization transgresses notions of environmental common sense, so that what he calls the social construction of natural disaster is largely obscured by a system of thinking that "simultaneously imposes false expectations on the environment and then explains the inevitable disappointments as proof of a malign and hostile nature" (5). Davis also writes of a "planet of slums," of how since the 1970s slum growth has outpaced urbanization, and how in many cities of the Global South there has been in the same period a "rapid urbanization of poverty" (*Planet of Slums* 17, 156). Drawing on a diverse set of urban sites, Davis speaks of slum dwellers as "pioneer settlers of swamps, floodplains, volcano slopes, unstable hillsides, rubbish mountains, chemical dumps, railroad sidings, and desert fringes," and of how such areas are "poverty's niche in the ecology of the city, and very poor people have little choice but to live with disaster" (122). In this sense, Haiti's slum dwellers are part of a global population of the displaced and dispossessed, living with and through endless disaster.

Slums, Davis writes in a phrase that seems particularly applicable to Haiti, "begin with bad geology" (ibid.). The bad geology that led to the 2010 earthquake lies in the Enriquillo fault system—the 2010 event is considered to be a re-rupture of the source zone of the major earthquake of 1701, and may indicate a new period of seismic activity along the Enriquillo fault system (Bakun et al. 28). Slums also begin with bad economics: in Haiti's case the mass urbanization of the 1980s that was the result of neoliberal agricultural measures that created, in Mark Schuller's terms, a "'reserve army' of unemployed, the lumpen-proletariat, justifying low-wage industrial jobs as beneficial to this desperate and vulnerable population," which led in turn to Haiti's food crisis, most notably the "riots" of April 2008 (*Killing with Kindness* 163). In fact, mass urbanization dates back at least to the U.S. occupation of 1915–34 and the subsequent "hyperconcentration" around Port-au-Prince, the intensity and scale of which are indicated in the 2010 population figure of 3 million, in a city built for 250,000, and in the population density in the slums: the shantytown called Jalousie in the Pétionville hills houses 43,475 people per square kilometer, and 80 percent of the city's population lives on 20 percent of the territory (Etienne 28).

The economics of mass urbanization and the high concentration of impoverished people in sites unsuitable for human dwellings increase human vulnerability to natural hazards and create the conditions for what Anderson calls the "megadisasters" of recent years, of which the Haitian earthquake is a foremost example (6). In Anderson's terms, disaster is something of a floating signifier, but is always a "conceptual negative" with no inherent meaning apart from its "opposition to socially defined normality" (6). Disaster is moreover related to loss, psychological or material, the absence of hope, self-esteem, or love, as much as that of food, employment, housing, or education. Disaster in fact calls into question the very notion of "normality" that Anderson writes of as the conceptual counterpoint to catastrophe, and as he says at one point, to live constantly in an "underdeveloped" place is also to be in a "permanent state of disaster" (6). That said, Anderson is careful not to imply that Latin American cultures are "traumatized by a state of permanent or unending catastrophe" (15).

One might say, in contrast to Anderson's latter statement, that Haiti does indeed exist in something of a state of permanent catastrophe. Such a perspective is expressed by Laënnec Hurbon, who writes of a contemporary experience of relentless disaster in Haiti that implicitly calls into question the existence of any notion of "normality" as a counterpoint to disaster. Hurbon speaks of a condition of "permanent catastrophe" in Haiti.[22] The frequent, apparently incessant occurrence of disasters in Haiti—from the floods in Gonaïves in 2004 to the 2010 earthquake to the cholera epidemic to Hurricanes Sandy and Isaac in 2012—in effect destroys any notion of non-catastrophic normality so that the population "risks taking as natural every calamity" (9).

There are important political dimensions to this condition of permanent disaster in Haiti and no doubt elsewhere, for as Hurbon argues disasters are "godsends" for politicians in that they give those in power a source of legitimacy, which otherwise they would not have (9).[23] Moreover, Hurbon says, governments have a "desire for disasters," as catastrophes can be blamed for lack of economic or social progress (9). As Hurbon argues, the causes of permanent disaster are as much political as environmental, and the various signs of environmental degradation—deforestation, pollution, etc.—can be read as "the expression of the failure of the Haitian State" (10).[24]

One important effect of living in permanent catastrophe is that the memory of even the most deadly events fades quickly and merges into a general sense of ongoing disaster, without beginning or end. Writing in 2012, Hurbon describes feeling already that nothing happened on January 12, 2010, and that a "leap has been skillfully made beyond that date" (8). Hurbon indicates that the government is not interested in a public memorial for the 2010 earthquake, and as such the disaster is not considered past, but part of the catastrophic present (9). The population exists, Hurbon says, "without a perceptible future" and "in the condition of being superfluous (floating between life and death)" (10). This in turn has serious consequences for ideas of and plans for reconstruction, for living with and in permanent catastrophe implies, even requires, the forgetting of any time in which disaster was not a daily reality, and virtually erases any sense of what was there before that should now be reconstructed.[25]

In the absence of state memorialization, there exists still a quite natural need to remember, commemorate, and testify to the experience of natural disaster. Catastrophic experience is at once individual and collective, intimate and public, contemporary and historical, and as such narratives of disasters are composite in nature and form, and involve, in Anderson's terms, a "process of dialogue and negotiation" with "existing local traditions as well as broader national and globalized frameworks of knowledge" (6). Haitian disaster narratives may be distinctive in this and other regards, in that disaster theory, at least in Anderson's version of it, identifies a prominent political function of such narratives. The processes of narrating disaster involve, Anderson says, the mobilization and renegotiation of social and political power relations, and imply always a "political posture" that serves to legitimize or delegitimize competing political discourses (7). This process leads finally to a consensus among competing accounts, a single version that "achieves canonical status" and is the basis for political action (7). The language of time used here—beginnings, processes, endings—suggests a teleological, or dialectical movement that results in synthesis. It also suggests an ability to "move beyond" the disaster, again in a forward-looking, teleological way. Given Hurbon's idea that Haiti exists in a state of permanent catastrophe, such a sense of moving beyond, and of an identifiable past, present, and future is considerably more difficult to envisage. Also, the political import and effect of Haitian disaster narratives is considerably compromised by the weakness of the Haitian state apparatus.

The limitations of the Haitian state were perhaps no more apparent than following the 2010 earthquake. Patrick Sylvain has written of the failure of a particular Haitian politician, President René Préval, to articulate the state vision of how Haiti should respond to the disaster (87). Sylvain critiques the "executive silence" that followed the earthquake, most notably that of Préval himself, whose silence is judged to be unethical in a time of disaster (90). There is, Sylvain says, nothing new in the state's silence and inaction: "The landscape of indifference is so deeply rooted in the nation's history that silence by Haitian executives has created a political culture of ineptitude and passivity" (91). This long history of state indifference and impotence in effect undermines the capacity of disaster narratives to function, as they do in Anderson's critique, as the basis for political action. Instead the virtual absence of a coherent state discourse reinforces the sense of living in permanent disaster, an unending end time that is in turn the fundamental condition of the diverse apocalyptic narratives that are discussed in the following chapters.

1 The Duvaliers and Apocalyptic Memory

Noirisme was a form of political and cultural ideology that grew out of indigenism, which in turn was a reaction to the American occupation of 1915–34.[1] During the occupation, Haitian intellectual culture was reenergized in diverse and often contradictory ways, constructing a discourse of resistance that would finally imprison the nation in a rigid idea of cultural and racial authenticity that served also as the ideological justification for the worst excesses of the Duvalier regime.

In 1919, Jean Price-Mars's *La Vocation de l'élite* had evoked the concept of the "national spirit" (*l'âme nationale*) and had warned of the dangers of "fragmentation" if the Haitian people did not "instinctively feel the need to create a national consciousness from the close solidarity of its various social strata" (qtd. in Dash, *Literature and Ideology* 67). Indigenism was held together by a shared desire to resist the United States, but when the Americans withdrew in 1934 and the question of national reconstitution became all the more pressing, the differences between the various factions became more polarized.

The departure of the Americans laid bare the differences between the Marxist and Africanist factions in indigenism. The Marxists' tendency was to look outward, to place Haiti, as intellectuals such as Louis-Joseph Janvier and Anténor Firmin had hoped in the nineteenth century, in the vanguard of progressive nations. In contrast, the Africanist Griot movement in post-occupation Haiti, and chiefly figures such as Carl Brouard, Lorimer Denis, and François Duvalier, tended to look inward, and to further elaborate the theories of race and culture that had begun in the earlier investigations into "the Haitian soul."[2]

The Griots' racial ideology implied a sliding scale of authenticity: the true Haitian soul was black, and the fairer the skin, the less Haitian one was. To the indigenists, the rediscovery of Africanity and popular culture had been a creative and open-ended act, but the Griots were strategically reductive, and systematically closed down the meanings associated with blackness and Haitian authenticity. Africanity and racial authenticity became the tenets of the political ideology of the rising black middle class, who saw in this ideology "the rationale for a black cultural dictatorship" (ibid. 101).

Noirisme's many cultural forms included newly formed folkloric choirs and urban ensembles such as the group Jazz des Jeunes, which was formed in the early 1940s, and considered to be the first popular dance band to have incorporated the *noiriste* ideology of the Griots. Their music, known as Vodou Jazz, drew on traditional folkloric rhythms, Vodou songs, and also hybrid Haitian-Cuban styles, and was received enthusiastically by the pro-*noiriste* press for its expression of the "true soul" of Haiti (Averill 58–62).

The Griots believed that Marxism had no relevance to Haitian reality. For Denis and Duvalier, "the ultimate hope" was to conserve "our spiritual structure that can guarantee our originality and assure the continuity of our Race."[3] Elaborating a "black legend" of Haitian history, the Griots promoted a turn to indigenist ideals in education, religion, and culture. Noirisme was fundamentally antiliberal, and promoted an authoritarian and exclusive state, which would be realized in the presidency of François Duvalier (1957–71). As Price-Mars, the great idol of the Griots, had cautioned, the social divisions created by the movement undermined indigenism's aim of national unity. And, as he prophetically warned, "a politically radical black consciousness could ultimately lead to despotism" (Smith 27).

Duvalier's noirisme was in effect an apocalyptic ideology, one based on the claimed existence of absolute differences between the oppressor and the oppressed, whiteness and blackness, and the elite and the peasantry. For Duvalier, history was similarly framed around dichotomies, and the present and the future envisioned as new epochs characterized by the overturning of the previous order. "I knew," he wrote in 1966, tellingly following the apocalyptic event of Hurricane Inès, "that the period in which I took power was without precedent in national history. I knew that this period was born from the new conception of human relationships at the heart of a political, economic, and social order at the service of the masses, and that, consequently, it would be for a long time shaken by shockwaves and conflicts" (15–16). He knew this, he continues, "as the spirit of revolution preached by DUVALIER was that the ordinary Haitian man can forge and that he does forge, in the melting pot of the new humanism that is the triumph of the Duvalierist revolution, a new destiny" (16). In reality, Duvalierism resulted only in the "deterioration of social cohesion and the complete dehumanization of a people" (Chancy, *Framing Silence* 143). In addition, it "brought the manipulation and violation of cultural norms to new levels" (Caple James 57), and led to the "near annihilation of a rich culture," the creolizing way of life that had evolved during and after slavery, and which was predicated less on an understanding of cultures as absolutely different from each other than on a proto-Glissantian model of relation, contact, and unpredictable evolution (Chancy, *Framing Silence* 143).

In some senses, the stated aims of noirisme were laudable. To Duvalier, the fundamental problem in Haiti was a "moral" one, which had three basic causes: the persistence of the "colonial mentality"; the resistance to an education system based on "National History"; and the destructive actions of foreigners, who had systematically sought to "de-Haitianize the National Soul" (Denis et al. 2). In essence, this was a classic nationalist, anticolonial program designed to assert the value of the local and the indigenous in the face of the foreign and the colonial, to "empower" Haiti through its "reconciliation with its native cultural institutions and practices" (Laguerre 106). Crucially, however, unlike indigenists such as Jacques Roumain, the *noiristes* did not share the belief that "no culture was superior, either in *savoir-faire* or *savoir-vivre*" (Michel-Rolphe Trouillot, *State against Nation* 132). Instead, noirisme "claimed the power of the people and, in so doing, usurped it" (Chancy, *Framing Silence* 146). This was, in other words, a dangerously self-justified ideology driven by a sense of injustice and the perceived need to exact forms of social and historical revenge on those that it identified as the causes of the "Haitian malaise" (Denis et al. 2).

Duvalier conflated his own being with the nation, and therefore anyone who opposed him was also opposing the entire country. Following the execution in 1961 of a group of Haitian insurgents that included Jacques-Stephen Alexis he declared, "Revolutions must be total, radical, inflexible," and added "I have conquered the country. I have conquered power. I am the new Haiti. To wish to destroy me is to wish to destroy Haiti itself. It is thanks to me that it breathes, thanks to me that it even exists" (qtd. in Dubois 328). The terror he wreaked touched all sectors of society, as no one, regardless of their color, gender, social class, or age was completely safe from the threat of violent retribution. Individuals "beyond the socially accepted range for victims of state violence" were targeted; rape was used as a tool of political control; rank and status in civil society were disregarded; and violence was used against distinctly non-political groups, such as sports teams (Michel-Rolph Trouillot, *State against Nation* 148). The terror was compounded by Haiti's isolation, by the disinterest of foreign government, and indeed by the support given to Duvalier by the U.S. government. "Trapped on the western tip of the island," Chancy writes, "Haiti suffered through an apocalypse" (147).

One might also say that the Duvaliers instituted something of an apocalyptic state apparatus, a paradoxical concept in that states exist fundamentally to maintain and perpetuate themselves, but in Haiti's case the post-Duvalier state, again paradoxically, exists for and through its own destruction. Amy Wilentz suggests this when she writes of how many outsiders consider the Haitian government to be "disorganized" and cautions against being "fooled" by appearances (154). In her view the government is "organized," and has been purposefully set up "to be porous and incompetent, to allow for corruption" (ibid.). It is a mechanism, she says, "into which money is poured and then siphoned off. . . . It's an organized disorganization, an ordered disorder." Patrick Sylvain complements Wilentz's understanding of Haitian government in his analysis of "executive silence" in Haitian political history, a phenomenon that has created a "landscape of indifference [that] is so deeply rooted in the nation's history that silence by Haitian executives has created a political culture of ineptitude and passivity" (91).[4] It is telling, too, that Wilentz believes it was "the Duvaliers who perfected" the state as a dysfunctional/functional phenomenon, an entity that succeeds in effect through failure (154–55). They did so through what Arthus calls the "*macoutisation* of public administration," the removal of experienced executives and their replacement with Duvalier's own supporters, who were often unqualified for the positions (138). Michel-Rolph Trouillot offers a detailed account of the historical roots of such a system of government in Haiti, and how François Duvalier refined it into a form of totalitarianism, thereby making apocalyptic outcomes virtually inevitable. In carefully describing the evolution of the apocalyptic state, and by showing for example how the U.S. occupation "accelerated Haiti's economic, military, and political centralization" in Port-au-Prince, Trouillot reminds us that the apocalypse has material, historical causes, and that any sense of inevitability about apocalyptic outcomes is created by the ways in which Duvalier "pitted the state against the nation" in a deadening relationship that transformed the authoritarian political model of the past "into a totalitarian apparatus" (*State against Nation* 104, 17).

In this chapter, my interest lies less in recounting the apocalyptic violence of the Duvalier period than in considering the ways in which the memory of the events resurfaces in the recent present, notably in works of art. The terror inflicted on Haiti was in many senses "unimaginable" (Chancy, *Framing Silence* 145), and yet one feels too that it has to imagined, that it must be re-conjured and revisited in all its horror in order for individuals and the whole society to in some way comprehend what happened during the Duvalier period and consign it finally to memory. Trauma theory, as Kaussen writes, is particularly useful in reading postcolonial texts, as it has much in common with postcolonial theory. Both emphasize, Kaussen says, "memory and the individual experience of historical forces over 'official' histories that efface the complex effects of history on the subject" (*Migrant Revolutions* 191). Furthermore, the way in which postcolonial theory levels the difference between colonizer and colonized and its view of power as "dispersed and indeterminate instead of binary, resembles trauma theory's leveling of the difference between victims and perpetrators" (191–92). In Erica Caple James's terms, without proper strategies to address trauma, "the power of memory and the embodied legacies of acute victimization will render attempts to mitigate suffering . . . ineffective" (xxiii).[5] As Chancy argues, Caribbean authors bear a particular responsibility: "one debt to history, and another to memory" (*Sugar* xi).[6] Chancy further describes Caribbean women authors as "new archeologists of a historical site we would do well to call 'amnesia'" (xxii). More generally, one could say that if the past is never recovered or revisted by authors or others in the present it risks becoming the future, reappearing in various forms, and making the time to come an endless repetition of the past.[7]

It seems significant in these respects that some of the most vivid novelistic accounts of the Duvalier period have been published in the twenty-first century, more than thirty years after the death of François Duvalier.[8] Paradoxically, the more time passes, the more the memory takes shape and reappears more fully formed than in the past, when it was to some extent repressed, or else only reappeared in fragments. In the first part of this chapter, I consider Raoul Peck's film *L'homme sur les quais,* a work that is indeed characterized by a fragmented, faulty memory of the early Duvalier period. I show how the incomplete memory is the product of a traumatized sensibility, and how the trauma dictates not only the content of the film, but also its form, its uneven, shifting chronology, the muted lighting, and the apocalyptic mise-en-scène. Peck's film is then compared to three key literary works published in the 21st century—Edwidge Danticat's *The Dew Breaker* (2004), Kettly Mars's *Saisons sauvages* (2010), and Evelyne Trouillot's *La mémoire aux abois* (2010). These works revisit the Duvalier period and address the memory of that time in ways similar to and yet different to Peck's. Danticat's novel, for instance foregrounds questions of forgiveness and redemption, while Mars offers a vivid, unflinching account of a bourgeois family's experience of the dictatorship, and suggests that the people are to some extent complicit in their own subjugation, and Trouillot shifts the focus to Simone Duvalier, and addresses the memory of the dictatorship and the desire for revenge. Ultimately, the chapter considers the ways in which the memory of the Duvalier apocalypse is still alive, and reflects on the role that artists play in recuperating that memory.

As stated in the introduction, apocalyptic memory is the guiding critical concept in this chapter, despite and because of its apparent conceptual and temporal contradictions—most notably the paradox of having a memory of the end of time, of living in an apocalyptic future when the apocalypse seems to close down any sense of the future. To write in this way of past but unfinished apocalyptic events is to narrate apocalyptic memory—to remember endings and to live still in that sense of an ongoing ending. Narrative is thus a means of invoking the past in order to break with the sense of living endlessly in that time, and memory becomes a means of resistance, a deferred way of challenging the dictatorships and the amnesia that allows the terror of the past to haunt still the present. The works studied here function therefore in a sense anti-apocalyptically, against amnesia, and in favor of memory. To recover memory is also to unveil or uncover, in accordance with the Greek meaning of the word *apocalypsis*. Narrating memory reveals that which has in one sense been lost and forgotten, but which in another way is everywhere felt as a repressed, omnipresent memory of the apocalyptic past.

Apocalyptic Memory in *L'homme sur les quais*

The closer one is to a traumatic experience, the more difficult it seems it is to recall it in all its color, sound, and emotional impact. It seems also that the more traumatic the experience, the longer it takes to recall it. Indeed, whole lives can pass without ever arriving at the point where the individual feels able to recall and relive such an event. Released in 1993, Raoul Peck's *L'homme sur les quais* returns to events that took place thirty years previously, near the beginning of the Duvalier years. The film, Peck says, was intended to be a "document that would keep us from repeating the past," and "supposed to be a monument to a time *passed,*" but ironically, only weeks before shooting started President Aristide was overthrown by a military coup, launched by Chief of Police Michel François (Peck and Taylor 246, Peck's emphasis; Dupuy 128). It was as if real events called into question the viability of an artistic project that would seek to commit past events finally to memory. Indeed, one might say that the coup altered quite radically Peck's belief that the film could enact a final movement beyond the Duvalier era into a new epoch. For, even after three decades, the memory in the film remains potent and unsettling, so that it cannot be incorporated fully formed into the narrative, but is revealed only gradually, piece by piece. There is no final unity of memory, in that the pieces remain fragments, shards of memory that lose little of their ability to pierce the present, returning the narrator to the past that she lives constantly, haunted as she is by the apocalyptic events of the early 1960s.

The narrator is named Sarah, now an adult in her late thirties, apparently living outside of Haiti, which seems forever and uniquely fixed in her memory as the source of the trauma that shapes her life and her narrative. The film revisits her childhood, a formative time punctured by a series of related events, all of which are fundamentally linked to the coming to power of the Duvalier regime. Most importantly, her parents have been forced into exile, following a power struggle with the local macoute leader, Janvier, and the brutal rape of her uncle Sorel, an incident that Sarah recalls only in fragments.[9] Sarah and her sisters are forced to hide out for long periods in their grandmother's attic, a situation that perhaps recalls that of Anne Frank, another refugee from apocalyptic history. There is a sense that the emotional, physical, and psychological shocks inflicted on the young girl are representative of those endured by the whole society, as it finds itself in its new, apocalyptic reality.

The single rider of this apocalypse, Duvalier himself, remains unseen throughout the film, though one also senses that his every word and action seep into every home, spreading terror to all parts of the country. The film is set in a provincial town, a setting something like that of Chauvet's *Amour,* the novel par excellence of the lived experience of Duvalierism.[10] Duvalier's omnipresence is suggested as the opening credits roll and, before any images of the town are shown, a well-known speech of his is heard, in which he names all the regions of Haiti, the middle class of Port-au-Prince, the nation's intellectuals, teachers, and students, telling them that the authorities have "gone mad."

The town, by contrast, is characterized by silence and empty streets. It appears almost as a wasteland, a site not so much physically destroyed as bereft of people; and it is chiefly people and their lives that have been laid to waste. One could say that the presentation of the town is dreamlike, in the way that dreams can present not reality but a simulacrum of it, a vague yet vivid semblance of the real. Similarly, apocalyptic memory in the film shifts between moments of sharp clarity and a kind of shadowy haze that communicates the narrator's inability or unwillingness to conjure up the past in all its disturbing reality.

The theme of memory is immediately raised in the song that is sung at the very beginning and throughout the film: "Three leaves / Three roots / To throw away is to forget / To pick up is to remember." The song is at once a memory from the past and a means of accessing that memory through rhythm and repetition. More subtly, the song is heard in recorded form during one of the key scenes that inhabit Sarah's traumatized memory: when she sees the macoute Janvier with his gun to her uncle Sorel's head and her father complies with Janvier's wish to have Sorel punished for his apparent "subversive" activities. The "Trois feuilles" song plays softly in the background as this scene develops, and seems lodged in Sarah's mind as a reminder of this key, traumatic moment, which pits her in the middle of the three men and their competing claims to authority: the sensitive and kind Sorel, the somewhat weak and cowardly father, and Janvier, the ruthless brute who prevails. The conflict between the father and Janvier enacts the contemporary power struggle within the ranks of the *cagoulards,* the pro-Duvalier civil militia whose upper ranks were initially occupied by middle-class officers such as Sarah's father and which had within and outside its ranks groups of lower-class, ultraviolent militia, who became known as the macoutes (Trouillot, *State against Nation* 189–90). The memories of these struggles and their violent effects seem at once distant and immediate: as Sarah says, "It was so long ago and yet it was yesterday."

Significantly, Sarah is first presented behind a locked door, in the half-light of the attic, which contrasts with the brilliant blue of the sky outside. The attic is perhaps the key site of memory in the film, one that is at once a haven and a prison for Sarah, who is forced to spend the days there with her sisters, living in fear of being discovered by the macoutes. The attic's mise-en-scène—a photograph of the grandmother that sits in front of and obscures another photograph, mirrors that capture only parts of Sarah's body, furniture covered in dust sheets, comic books on the floor, a doll that Sarah grooms maternally, a photograph of the exiled parents, a suitcase in which Sarah stands, playing with her mother's wedding dress—evokes the main themes and characters of the narrative, and as Sarah flits restlessly from one end of the room to the next, we get a sense of her inner confusion, of her traversing already a landscape of memory and loss. "I was eight," she says, "and my world was already starting with a disaster."

The disaster that predominates in her memory is the brutal assault of her uncle by Janvier and other macoutes. She views this assault from the balcony, which she accesses by way of a barred heavy wooden door, which stands as a marker of the boundary between the interior world of the attic and the outside, with its connotations of violence and danger. The door thus marks a threshold between safety and danger, between "innocence and corruption" (Petty 206), although one could say that her innocence had already been corrupted in her exposure to the previous conflict between her father, Sorel, and Janvier. The doorway seems also to mark a temporal transition from the world of relatively benign memories contained in the half-lit attic to the glaring light of the outdoors and the assault of the uncle. The assault throws her into the present and indeed the future, for her life from this point is determined by the scene she witnesses, as her traumatized mind at once attempts to flee and forget the scene, and is forced to return to it endlessly, in incomplete fragments of memory.

The specific nature of the assault is not made clear the first time that it appears. Sarah's confusion is suggested by the reverse-angle long shot of her looking down on the scene from the distant balcony, while the assault is framed around the three key male figures: Janvier, who carries out the assault, the father François, who is powerless to stop it, and Sorel, the victim. The following scene cuts back to the half-light of the attic, and Sarah being comforted by her grandmother. Sarah shakes and sobs, her head on her grandmother's lap, facing left, a pose that reflects that of the uncle as the camera returns to him, his bloody head on the ground and turned to the left, his eyes staring lifelessly in the direction of the empty balcony. The visual cue at once suggests the close relationship between Sarah and Sorel, and the ways in which both of their futures will be shaped by this moment. For, even if the grandmother subsequently rejects Sorel and refuses to help him, and seeks to console Sarah by repeating the phrase "It is only a bad dream," for Sarah and Sorel the scene is all too real, and cannot be consigned to memory in any easy way. By extension, the "bad dream" of the Duvalier era cannot be easily forgotten by the nation as a whole; the collective unconscious will long be haunted by the memories of such incidents.

From this moment, the lives of Sarah and Sorel diverge, and yet there remains an unspoken intimacy between the two. He is nicknamed Gracieux, a mocking reference to his ungraceful walk, the result of the assault. He becomes the titular "man by the shore," an outcast, both from society and from the family of which he was previously an integral part, while she lives a separate but parallel life, her destiny tied inextricably to that of her uncle.

Sarah's future is linked closely to her uncle's, as he is a major part of her past and figures prominently in the warmest, most vivid memories she has of the period preceding the trouble. One scene in particular identifies Sorel as a devoted and cherished uncle: following a post-assault scene in which he is rejected by the grandmother, a short fragment of memory appears, which presents first the open windows of the family house and the pastel colors of party streamers. A dolly shot moves gently to focus on Sorel, his arm on the window, singing "Happy Birthday" to Sarah. As he moves away from the window, the camera takes his place and captures an indoor scene that is unique in the film in its bright colors and the warmth of the lighting, as the scene reveals itself in the multicolored balloons, the colorful dresses of the girls and their guests, and the general atmosphere of relaxed familial insouciance. Perhaps tellingly, however, the father is dressed in his militia uniform, and as he sings to Sarah his wish that she have a good year, the mother fixes him with an anxious look, the reason for which is later revealed as her concern for the fate of Sorel, the focus of Janvier's campaign against "subversives." In this scene, however, the focus is on conviviality and Sorel's particularly loving relationship with Sarah: it is he who sings solo the final line to the song, framed in the window and lit from behind by the brilliant sunshine that floods in giving him an almost saintly, enhaloed appearance.

Tellingly, too, the scene ends with a long focus on Sarah's suddenly apprehensive face, and then cuts to the faded light of the attic, with Sarah holding another of her aide-mémoire, the accordion that Sorel used to play to her. Shortly after, she peers from behind blinds in the attic down to the street, where her uncle is playing his role of the madman, asking the Syrian Assad to order him a rifle, a Winchester, "just like Jack Palance. To blast them off." Sorel seems aware that he is playing a role, in this case and in other instances that of a would-be gunslinger, a hero who would save the town and the country from the macoutes. As Sarah watches him he looks up to the window and she is holding a small plasticine model that she plays with throughout the film, and which appears to be a representation of her uncle, or else her father, the two men who have left her. Sarah's problem, but also one of her saving graces, is that she does not forget Sorel, however much her grandmother and the tense political situation encourage her to do so. Memory is related to love for Sarah: she complains to her grandmother that her exiled mother no longer loves her and her sisters, as she "has forgotten" them. To remember is to put oneself in danger, but it is also to retain a human quality and an attachment to the truth of what has happened that few others manage to hold on to.

Sorel becomes a kind of guardian angel figure, always on the lookout for Sarah, and using his peculiar status as a madman as something of a cover that allows him to protect her from Janvier and the macoutes. In one sequence, he sleeps on the street below the attic as Sarah plays above with his accordion and various other objects including her father's militia uniform that are arranged around her with candles as if it were a kind of shrine to the two men. Reaching in a drawer, she takes out her father's gun, which she handles with a mixture of care and recklessness, almost caressing it and then holding it, aimed at her own face. The connection between Sarah and Sorel is further emphasized when she drops the gun on the floor, which wakes Sorel on the street below, and leads him to look up at the light coming from the attic. Simultaneously, Janvier's jeep turns into the street, and Sorel hides in a dark corner, unsuccessfully, as the macoute spots him and stops directly below the attic. Glancing up at the light in the attic, Sorel creates a diversion by first asking for a cigarette, and then dancing rhythmically in the street, emphasizing the movement of his hips and apparently reminding Janvier of the crime he committed against Sorel. The strategy works and Janvier drives away without seeing the light in the attic.

The father is an altogether more ambiguous figure. It is important that in Sarah's memories of him he is always in uniform, another aide-mémoire for her that she caresses in the attic, as she does the gun. The two objects appear in one key scene, in which Sarah recalls her uniformed father's lesson to her on how to use the gun. As she pulls the trigger, Sarah looks away and the camera, in a series of rapid reverse shots, zooms in on both Sarah and her father, who are now apart, the effect of which is to create uncertainty over whom the gun is now aimed at. The memory closes with the father holding the gun, apparently aiming it at Sarah. It seems that this aspect of the memory is based not so much on what actually happened as on the way in which Sarah's memory has processed it. In this distorted but symbolic representation of the past event, the father becomes at once Sarah's protector and her potential assassin.

Sarah also processes the traumatic events and her thoughts on her father in her dreams. In one dream, she first sees Sorel being assaulted before hearing his voice booming, demanding to know who she is, what race she belongs to and, crucially, who her father is. Lying in bed with her doll—another human substitute and aide-mémoire—she shouts repeatedly in Creole, "Ma pa konnen" (I don't know), which suggests again the difficulty she has in reconciling the loving father she knew with the somewhat cowardly militia man he also was.

The confusion she feels about her father is most directly related to his betrayal of Sorel, who is accused by Janvier of painting anti-macoute graffiti on a wall in the town. As the "Trois feuilles" song plays on a radio, Sarah and her father come across Janvier, who is holding a gun to Sorel's head in the middle of the street. In the conversation between the two militiamen, the father pleads that proper procedure be followed, but Janvier prevails and the father is forced to hand Sorel over to the macoutes. As the father explains why he must pass Sorel over to Janvier, Sorel and Sarah sit together in the backseat of the car, symbolically side by side as the father betrays both of them. "Act like a man," the father tells Sorel, thereby referencing the key theme of competing masculinities, which confuses Sarah and by extension the entire nation so profoundly. One is left to wonder, who is a man, and what constitutes a man in such a distorted, apocalyptic reality?

For Sarah, the question is not simply related to masculinity, but to paternity, to the question of what is a father. This issue is raised when she sits by the sea with a friend whose father has been "disappeared" by the macoutes and who asks Sarah if it was true that her father was a macoute. "No," Sarah replies, "it is not true. He loved me very much." Thus are conflated and confused in Sarah's mind François's dual roles as macoute and father. Her friend seems to wonder if the two roles are compatible, while Sarah protests that they are, but nonetheless seems to be confused by what exactly a father should be and do.

Sarah's confusion over questions of masculinity and paternity is perhaps most prominent in one scene in which an image of her father appears framed in the doorway of her grandmother's shop. Her face lights up in a broad smile that however fades as the camera switches to reveal it was not the father in the doorway, but Janvier, wearing the same militia uniform. The two men are fused in her mind, and her memory of her father is being supplanted by the presence of Janvier, who seems all too willing to play a fatherly role to Sarah. This scene is also remarkable in the way it suggests that Janvier the macoute is playing a role, one that is evolving rapidly in the Duvalier era. As he walks round the store, he picks up various items before settling on a pair of dark sunglasses, which he tries on before looking at his own image in a mirror and turning to ask Sarah how he looks. Later, he tries on a red tie. In these ways, he prefigures the later uniform of the macoute, the iconic look, of which sunglasses and red neckwear were essential parts.[11] He, too, it is suggested, is playing a role, constructing an image of himself that is at once menacing and paternalistic. As he removes the glasses, his voice softens and he reassures Sarah that he is her "friend" and that he is "not so bad." Sarah says nothing to encourage Janvier, but also does not openly reject him, which seems to suggest further her confusion over the macoutes, masculinity, and paternity.

Sarah's muted attraction to Janvier is suggested in a complex scene toward the end of the film in which she goes with her aunt to the macoutes' barracks to ask for the release of the grandmother, who is being held there. Before they leave, the aunt carefully applies her makeup and puts on her earrings and one of her best dresses, taking great care with her appearance. Sarah is again caught between two adults, this time the aunt and Janvier. There is in this case the added element of class conflict and sexuality, in that the aunt in her appearance and her gestures makes clear that she is prepared to sleep with Janvier to ensure the release of her mother. Janvier seems for a time less interested in the aunt than in Sarah, whom he fixes in a long stare, and who senses what her aunt is proposing, a realization that leads her to break free of her aunt and run toward Janvier. For several moments, Sarah is caught between the two, and indeed seems to side with Janvier as she runs to his side and is framed solely with him, while she calls her aunt "méchante," meaning cruel or mean, but also wicked or bad in a moral sense.

It is perhaps telling that immediately following this scene in which sex is presented as a marker of class and color conflict the full horror of Sorel's own rape is finally revealed. This time the shots are handheld close-ups that capture the ugliness of the incident. François sweats and pleads with Janvier to cease his torture of Sorel, who asks what he has done to merit the punishment. To Janvier, Sorel is a "subversive" and a "piece of meat" that he brutally sodomizes with a wooden pole. At the same time we hear again Sarah's scream, the full reason for her horror now apparent. François reacts physically not to the punishment, but to Sarah's scream, which also unnerves Janvier. As François is beaten, Sorel's head falls to the left and his eyes close, as if this moment marks the end of him and the beginning of his alter ego, Gracieux. The use of sexual violence in effect demonstrates Erica Caple James's point that, in times of political upheaval, "rape, including gang rape, and even forced incest were among the forms of torture used strategically to damage and control not only individuals but also families and larger communities" (39). Indeed, in the film the rape has such a three-sided effect: the individual is broken and adopts an alter ego in order to survive; the family disowns him and is itself split; and the sense of community dissipates as trust is diminished and individuals retreat into the private sphere. The film moreover shows that Duvalierist sexual violence was not only the product of "historical, global structural inequalities between the sexes," and that men were also at risk of such acts (40). Peck is sensitive to the ways in which Duvalierism "transgressed cultural taboos to exploit, control, and destroy individual and collective bodies," and how the "violation of sex, gender, and kinship norms was intrinsic to the Duvalierist apparatus" (57). As such, Peck implies that sexuality is a form of power and control, in a way that echoes Foucault's insistence that "In a specific type of discourse on sex, in a specific form of extortion of truth, appearing historically and in specific places," the observer requires to understand primarily "what were the immediate, the most local power relations at work" (97).[12]

In the film it is the man who apparently challenges the power relations most openly (through anti-macoute graffiti) who falls victim to sexual violence, and who exemplifies Caple James's idea that Duvalierist violence "targeted not just the material body but also the cultural and psychological foundations of identity" (57). It is also paradoxically the broken, psychologically traumatized man, Sorel, who is the one who remains the most human, in that he acts in large part selflessly, dedicated to saving Sarah. He also refuses to forget that there was a different reality before the Duvalierist disaster. "Do you remember me?" he asks Sarah in one moving scene, at the end of which she gently kisses him on the cheek in an act of vindication and recognition. Although Sorel withdraws in a sense from society, becoming an outcast and a figure of ridicule, he also remains paradoxically the most community-minded and the one who embodies an ideal of society that Duvalierism has all but destroyed. He is also the only one who questions the apocalyptic present that the rest of society has fallen into, largely without protest. As the rest of the community celebrates a mass commemorating Duvalier's "Haitianization" of the Catholic Church, Sorel is on the deserted street, drinking and offering his own fragmented critique of Duvalier. "Who invented the macoutes?" he asks himself, as if struck by a moment of clarity. "And what about Duvalier?" Throwing his rum bottle against the wall, he walks down the middle of the street, his arms raised as if he were Jack Palance carrying his Winchester.

Sarah herself takes to carrying her father's pistol following the scene at the macoute barracks, deliberately tying it with a belt under her dress before she goes out with her friend to the beach. As Janvier's jeep draws up behind them, we see Sorel running furiously toward the beach. Janvier grabs Sarah's friend and is about to rape her as Sarah runs back to the scene and pulls the pistol out, aiming it at Janvier's head as he kneels, in an image that recalls at once the shooting lesson her father gave her and Janvier's initial subjugation of Sorel. Sarah pulls the trigger, but the weapon is not loaded and as Janvier reaches to grab her we hear a gunshot offscreen and Janvier falls dead. As Sarah leads her friend away from the scene, the camera pans right to reveal Sorel on his knees, holding a pistol and sobbing uncontrollably. The camera does not stop to focus on him however, but continues to pan right to focus on the sea. The final implication is that Sorel's life is all but over, and the future for Sarah and for many others will involve journeys far beyond Haiti's shores. The broad shot of the sea also seems to suggest something of the abyss that the country was falling into in this early Duvalier period. As the film ends, the emphasis is once again on memory, as Sarah narrates that many years after the events she still wakes at night in a sweat, and hears again her grandmother's voice insisting that it was all just a bad dream. It seems that the memory retains its haunting quality largely because the present has not changed; in the absence of substantial social and political improvements, the past will continue to inhabit the present, and the Duvalierist apocalypse will continue to play itself out.

Saisons sauvages and the *Gwo Nèg*

Although in *L'homme sur les quais* Sorel in a sense prevails, his tears at the end of the film suggest that he knows that in killing Janvier he has sealed his own fate, and that there is no real sense of vindication in murdering the macoute. In contrast to Sorel, who is a nuanced, individualized character, Janvier is more of a caricature, an archetype of the macoute figure, and one senses that in Duvalier's Haiti he would soon be replaced by another like him. While the film explores Sarah's particular attachment to Sorel, in truth she vacillates between the modes of masculinity suggested by Sorel, her father, and Janvier. Her attitude toward Janvier in particular is ambivalent, and seems to indicate a broader, national attraction to the *gwo nèg*, the strongman figure that has become a kind of cult, which "operates on the local, national, and diasporic levels," and which "suffuses all levels of Haitian culture" (Braziel, *Artists* 1). The status of the *gwo nèg* is not just a matter of political authority; it also "derives to some extent from his performance abilities as a man-of-words. More than that, it is his everyday style and charisma, his personal power, that attracts followers" (McAlister, *Rara!* 142–43).

The particular attractions of the *gwo nèg* are further invoked in Kettly Mars's *Saisons sauvages,* a work published in 2010, and which constitutes a prime example of contemporary Haitian literature's mature and daring rethinking of the history of the dictatorship. Where Peck's film is tentative in its approach to memory, and only gradually reveals the apocalyptic horror that haunts its narrator, Mars's novel is bold in its full evocation of the same, early Duvalier period. In particular, in its treatment of the Duvalier apocalypse, Mars's novel is at once a critique of the dictatorship and a provocative statement on the allure of power, the entanglement of sex and politics, and the people's complicity in their own subjugation. In this sense, Mars's work seems to validate the paradoxical idea that the more time passes, the less difficult it is to recall the past in all its color, sound, and emotional impact. In terms of her own career, too, this work is in some senses a natural development of previous novels such as *L'Heure hybride* (2005) and *Fado* (2008), both of which explore sexuality, specifically bisexuality and prostitution, and the ways in which sexual identity is closely intertwined with notions of social class and politics.[13] In framing similar interests in regard to the Duvalier period, *Saisons sauvages* makes a powerful statement on the dictatorship, and the sexual aspects of class conflict.[14]

In an important sense, Mars's novel is a contemporary reworking of Marie Vieux Chauvet's classic 1968 trilogy, *Amour, Colère, Folie,* in its re-visitation of the Duvalier era, and its development of the themes of politics, race, color, class, and sex, which are central to the first work of Chauvet's trilogy in particular. Mars's work is the story of a middle-class mulatto woman, Nirvah Leroy, whose husband, Daniel, is arrested by the Duvalierist authorities for engaging in left-wing political activity. Nirvah visits the secretary of state for public security, Raoul Vincent, to ask for news of her husband, but in order to ensure her family's survival, she becomes the minister's lover, a situation that is humiliating and demeaning but also affords her a certain prestige in the society ruled by the Duvalier dictatorship. It is the ambivalent position of the woman that Mars explores in a novel that revisits the unhealed wounds of dictatorship and the ever-relevant themes memorably evoked by Chauvet and which have to a certain degree set the thematic agenda for subsequent generations of Haitian authors, both male and female.

The particular situation of women under the apocalyptic dictatorship is introduced in the opening chapter, in which the narrator, Nirvah, presents herself waiting to be received by the minister. Already kept waiting for two hours, she immediately appears as powerless, at the mercy of the minister and by implication the dictatorship. "Since the minute I stepped into this building," she says, "my time, my well-being, my life depend on the whims of the Secretary of State" (9). She is also excluded from the political activity of her husband; just before leaving her home to come to the office, she discovered Daniel's secret diary that detailed his thoughts and plans to oppose the dictatorship. Unlike her politically engaged husband, she does not "have the time to think," and is driven less by political conviction than practical considerations, chiefly the protection of her family (11). At the same time, she is not completely unaware politically, is conscious of the "mentality of the formerly colonized that still hinders us," and unlike Daniel doubts that the solution to this lies in communism (100).

Vincent, the secretary of state is presented as a cold, barely human individual, a Duvalierist apocalyptic figure. His office is air-conditioned to the point that he exists in a perpetual "glacial ambiance"; the palms of his hand are "icy and dry," and his handshake "soulless" (12). Crucially, Nirvah remarks that he is dark-skinned, a feature that in this context differentiates him from her, and signifies a social gap between the two that both are highly aware of. Nirvah is particularly sensitive to issues of color and class. She remarks that Vincent's driver is a "grimaud," a light-skinned man, and she is generally highly sensitive to visual appearances, especially because her own color and physical appearance, so long signs of prestige and status, now mark her out as vulnerable, an object infused with political and social meaning. Indeed, it is the visual and the unspoken elements of her communication with Vincent that are most significant. By way of excuse for making her wait, Vincent says that he had been called away by the president, but she realizes that her waiting signifies something quite different, fundamental to their relationship. "He doesn't fool me," she says. "This deliberate and calculated wait defines clearly the situation. He has me at his mercy. His power can save me or destroy me. I am in the worst situation that a citizen of this country can find themselves in" (13). Verbal and visual communications are distorted in this relationship so that words, tone of voice, and looks tend to signify something like the opposite of their apparent meanings. The softness in his voice denotes not kindness but cruelty, and does not reassure her, but "scares" her (14), while his smile is "predatory" (16). Immediately, too, her body becomes a site of contestation and conflict. At first sight of him, Nirvah feels a "pressing need to urinate," a feeling that only intensifies as she sits in the cold office, faced in a sense with her destiny (12). As the pain grows she struggles to not let it show, and to not have to ask him to use his personal toilet, for to do so would be to remind him that she has "a body, urinary organs, a vulva" and leave her "vulnerable and denuded" (15). In a sense though, her efforts are futile as her body has already been established as the stakes in this social and color conflict—for him, it is the spoils of war; for her, as for the aunt in *L'homme sur les quais,* it is a means of negotiation and survival. As she says later, the only "weapons" she has in this battle are her skin, her body, and her sex (108). As she leaves his office, and feels his gaze "burning" her nape, her shoulder blades, her buttocks, even her ankles, she is in no doubt about this; the predatory "wild glimmer" that she discerned in the way he looks at her marks her out as his prey (17–18). That she is no longer in control of her own body is signaled as she returns home from the meeting and feels "powerless" to stop the flow of urine that comes as she reaches her front door (19).

It is only when the narration switches to third-person mode that a fuller sense of Nirvah's effect on Vincent emerges. Tellingly, Vincent is the only major figure in the novel not to speak directly in first-person narrative. His perspective is communicated indirectly through a third-person narrator and narrative techniques such as free indirect discourse. It is as if the author hesitates to humanize Vincent completely or feels otherwise unable or unwilling to communicate his voice directly. An hour after her departure, Vincent feels still the "electricity" that she emitted and feels "mentally drained" (20). He had thought himself "battle-hardened to the combats of the flesh," but believes Nirvah to be "a woman like no other," a woman for whom a man "damns himself" (20–21). Again, it is the unspoken elements that mean the most to him. Behind her "innocent look" he senses a "secret world of class, caste, whispers, discreet laughter. A haughty and inaccessible world. A hypocritical and corrupted world" (21). Beneath her skin lies the key that offers him "journeys in forbidden territory" (21). She had come to him, he realizes, because of the changes in political power. Duvalier's *noiriste* regime marks the ascendancy of the black classes, and she is aware that "supremacy has changed color and sides" (21). This newly gained power has become for him a "drug" that he is free to indulge in, and Nirvah's presence in his office is to him the ultimate confirmation of his near absolute power (22). For she signifies to him much more than sexuality: she symbolizes "a divided nation, a history badly shared, wellbeing and privileges for an insolent small number and a heritage of contempt for a majority of men and women" (22). Nirvah embodies at once everything that he hates the most, and everything that he most desires; and he would give anything to possess her (22–23). This confusion of hatred and desire is the legacy of history and is a powerful combination that makes the body of the mulatto woman the vehicle through which history's unresolved conflicts are played out and revenge exacted.

The history of color and class conflict in Haiti skews politics and ideology in quite particular ways. Specifically, it is the educated bourgeoisie that leads the left-wing challenge to the lower-class-led administration, which develops an extreme right-wing ideology that one might describe as "black fascism."[15] Nirvah's husband, Daniel, epitomizes the light-skinned Marxist radical who finds himself struggling against the lower classes, and as such without support outside of his own small group of bourgeois intellectuals. His voice is communicated directly through the pages of his journal, which begins in October 1962, and details the continued rise of François Duvalier, himself a petit-bourgeois intellectual, in whom the majority of the people foresaw a progressive leader, but who turns out to be a "master in the art of dissimulation" (24). Daniel's means of resistance is through a clandestine network of small cells that he coordinates, but which is rendered largely ineffective by the weaknesses of the Haitian left, many of whose members have left the movement to take up posts in the regime (26). The left is further weakened by its social composition: he realizes that the revolution can never succeed with the sole support of a "handful of intellectuals and journalists" (100). His politics are naturally anti-American, and he critiques the role of the United States in undermining the Haitian left and in perpetuating the "tacit pact" with Duvalier (26). He records, as Peck does in *L'homme sur les quais,* the daily changes in behavior that make the apocalyptic dictatorship possible, the evolving "threshold of tolerance that adapts itself to our descent into Hell" (96). Although he knows he faces "certain death," he refuses exile, for he realizes that he could not escape Duvalier even overseas, that wherever he goes his "conscience would go" with him (96). Faced with the weaknesses in the Haitian left and Duvalier's ever tightening grip on Haitian life, Daniel's vision of Haiti's future is "apocalyptic" (27). He resembles his wife in the sense of helplessness that he expresses: like her, he is powerless to resist a dictatorship bent on realizing the apocalyptic future that is his and his country's destiny.

As Daniel's case shows, thought and expression are repressed in virtually every domain, so that, as with Nirvah's meeting with Vincent, everyday communication is rarely direct and is effected through visual signs and words that often mean the opposite of what they apparently say. For this reason, dreams become important—again, as they do in Peck's film—as means of exploring and expressing the thoughts of those caught in the repressive situation. Nirvah in particular experiences dreams in which she confronts her new reality and her feelings vis-à-vis Vincent. One dream pictures her in Vincent's office, forced to cover herself in bird feces, and ending up on his bed. Apart from the expected feeling of repulsion, she expresses a sense of relief at finding him, feels she is "saved," before Vincent and his "glorious erection" (30). Finding herself naked, she revels in the mixture of repulsion and sensuality, remarking, "What pleasure! What happiness!" and feeling that she is like a "cat in heat" whose orgasm lasts five minutes (30–31). Vincent seems to awaken in her elements that Daniel writes of in his diary. Daniel writes that she is a "carnal woman," who was a virgin when they married and in whom he finds still an "unsatisfied curiosity, the intuition of more sublime wonders" (50). This theme of repressed sexuality intertwined with hypermasculinity and blackness constitutes a further echo not only of Peck's film, but also of Chauvet's *Amour,* particularly the repressed attraction that the narrator Claire feels for the macoute Calédu, and which is expressed in dreams. As in *Amour* the dreams raise some troubling questions concerning sexuality, power, and the way that raw, violent power appears to attract the bourgeois women on a certain level. It also complicates further the relationship between Nirvah and Vincent, and suggests that she is in some way complicit in the abuse that she will be subjected to. As she reflects later, there exists between the two a "strange complicity" (86). Just as troubling is the muted suggestion that the relationship has historical resonances; specifically that it echoes a master-slave bond, which manifests itself in the present and perhaps throughout Haitian history in social relationships that replicate the cruelties of slavery. The past reappears in the unfettered brutality of Vincent and the certain masochism of Nirvah, who almost needs to suffer to continue to exist. There is also a sense of martyrdom or of willful suffering in her submitting to Vincent; as long as Daniel suffers, she says, she will "remain completely" with her own misfortune (110). But her martyrdom is judged to be false by her daughter Marie, who later writes of her mother's and Vincent's lovemaking, something that Marie says she is not concerned about, as long as Nirvah does not "play the little martyr afterwards" (160).

The stakes involved in Nirvah's relationship with Vincent are indirectly presented during a discussion she has with her neighbor Solange, a lower-class prostitute and *manbo,* or Vodou priestess. The contemporary dismantling of traditional class relations is shown in the way Solange has recently moved to the middle-class neighborhood and makes no apologies for being there. "It is true I am not quite your typical resident," she says, "but things have changed these days, the country belongs to everyone" (42). The two women and their two worlds, which previously would not have crossed in everyday life, are now closely intertwined, much to the dismay and shock of Nirvah, who wonders what she is doing in the company of a woman "who hangs out with macoutes" (45). In another sense, though, the two women are not so far apart socially, in that Nirvah comes from a family that lost its standing due to bankruptcy and the suicide of her father. As such, Nirvah has identified with a class of which she bears only the "external attributes," and is a "hybrid being, bourgeois when she wants, one of the people when she needs to be" (49). To some extent, the Nirvah-Vincent relationship seems to echo that of François Duvalier and his wife, Simone, a light-skinned woman whose social status was precarious before she met Duvalier.[16] In the novel, the two women are able to shift between two social worlds to a certain extent, and their lives come to reflect one another in unexpected ways. Solange has "taken the asson"; that is, she has become a Vodou priestess, which is why the macoutes come to her, looking to buy "pwen," objects seen as being charged with magical powers (45). She has become a manbo because she was called to do so by Déméplè, her *lwa,* or god. To Nirvah, the god's name has connotations of a person of "unpredictable nature, with a bad character" (45). Tellingly, the god came to Solange in a dream when she was in a desperate state, and ordered her to kneel before his "enormous sex" (46). She refused, but the god pursued her relentlessly in her dreams until she finally agreed to be his servant (47). Solange's experience in effect stands as a warning and a prophecy for Nirvah, who has herself been visited in dreams by her own all-powerful male figure, and whose own future well-being will depend on her submission to him. Nirvah's confused feelings toward Vincent are expressed when she returns home more than a week after her visit to his office to find him waiting for her, and she reflects that seeing him again was something she had been "hoping and fearing at the same time" (55). The prospect of seeing him again quickens her heartbeat so that she feels ill (56). Revealingly, too, when she goes to check on her children, she finds them watching a cartoon in which Betty Boop is lost in a forest and about to "get herself devoured by the monstrous head of Louis Armstrong, rolling two enormous eyeballs . . . while singing an agonizing blues" (57). It is as if her unconscious is preparing her for her own similar fate; the connection between the Armstrong cartoon figure and Vincent is strongly indicated in the subsequent description of the minister's eyes as "even more protruding" than she remembered them (58). What is interesting too is the use of the verb form "to get herself devoured" [se faire dévorer], which suggests that she is not completely helpless and in some way gives herself over to her fate. For his part, the visit to the home is like an excursion into forbidden territory, which gives him a feeling of "total power" (63). Vincent is aware that the destiny of Daniel Leroy and his family depends on him, and compares the family to his own, whose upward social mobility cannot hide the relatively vulgar tastes of his wife (64). He appreciates by contrast the easy bourgeois sophistication of the Leroy family, while at the same time holding in contempt Daniel, whom he judges to be a weak mulatto intellectual "without ambition," the worst kind of mulatto, less concerned with money than with writing subversive articles and engaging in philosophical debates (65). Vincent is in this sense starkly different from Daniel, and in possessing Nirvah he will be a "brute, a cynic," for he feels that she will only give in to him "by force" (66).

His force is not solely a physical phenomenon; it is also shown in the way that he orders the paving of the street, the dust from which had previously covered everything, enveloping Nirvah and her home in a gray powder. The black asphalt of the paved street seems to stand as a symbol for his *noiriste* power, which, as Nirvah understands, serves the "impulses, instincts, and lust" of the regime (71). The paving of the road is a manifestation of this power, and creates in her a sense of foreboding as her near future "amasses like the black clouds of a storm" (71). At the same time, Vincent realizes that there is a danger in his obsession with the Leroys, and that they could finally cost him his power and money. The "madness" that is taking hold of him makes him vulnerable to his many political enemies (79). There is something in his character of the classical tragic figure whose ascendancy is reversed by the fatal flaw, who is aware of the flaw, but who follows it and to some extent wishes his downfall to come. In this sense, he is like Daniel, who is "the author of his own misfortune," and Nirvah, who also is in some way complicit in her own tragedy (83). The three seem to share the belief that the Duvalierist era can end only in an apocalyptic denouement.

The play of power between Vincent and Nirvah is thus not completely one-sided, and Vincent's ascendancy, far from curing him of his color and class complexes, seems only to accentuate them. The power that Nirvah possesses is demonstrated when Vincent first touches her. As he draws closer to her he collapses unexpectedly at her feet and falls into a kind of fit, his body convulsing, his mouth foaming. For all that she is repulsed by his presence, she feels compelled to help him and brings him out of the fit by throwing water on him (89–90). While she sees the episode as a case of epilepsy, he attributes it to a "mystical" cause; touching Nirvah's skin has opened up to him "the world of the dead and that of the living" (91). He judges her to be protected by a force, a spirit, and wonders which spirit she serves, while reflecting that he has neglected his own spiritual protectors, which has made him expose his weakness to Nirvah (92). Without her intervention, he would have died, and to him this act seals between them a "pact of life and death," the consequences of which are to tie her fate ever more closely to his (93).

Vincent tightens the bond between them deliberately, through a series of gifts and favors that also function as traps. Following the road paving, he sends fine jewelry, of which Nirvah is initially suspicious, but which she wears one night at the cinema, gripped by a "sudden impulse," which she suspects is a way of getting used to "this other side of myself, to this woman who was about to open her home and her body" to Vincent (115). The third gift-trap Vincent sends is an air conditioner, a means of preparing her home for his presence and ensuring the frigid temperatures in which he feels most at ease. The generator to Nirvah seems like a living being, "with blood, nerves, and fangs" (123). As she realizes, it is a further manifestation of the trap that is "closing in" on her (123). And as she gets used to this other woman that she is to become, she learns to speak against herself, to "say the opposite of what I am thinking" (127). Again, she anticipates this transformation with a mixed set of emotions, as she awaits his next visit, "fearing" and "hoping for" it at the same time (129).

There seems to be a subtle political analogy that is developed through Vincent's entrapment of Nirvah. Most apparently, the forced-desired relationship suggests some of the historical complexities of class and color relations in Haiti. More precisely, Vincent takes possession of Nirvah just as Duvalier is perfecting his complete control of Haiti, destroying all opposition, and naming himself president for life. The two acts seem closely related; the invasion of Nirvah's private space and her body is synchronous with the omnipresence of the macoutes, who themselves "infiltrate" every area of Haitian life. Vincent's statement to her that he will not harm her "as long as you do not make me do so" is a loaded promise that echoes the broader tactic of confusing offers of protection with threats of violent retribution (134). Nirvah seems to be aware of the close relationship between the two projects when she remarks that there is no hope, that "the roots of dictatorship sink deeper every day into the land of Haiti," while at the same time Vincent is about to "achieve his deepest fantasy, to dominate and possess a mulatto woman" (135).

When he does inevitably begin to enact these fantasies with her, the experience is for him like a spiritual event, the culmination of which was the moment he perceived Nirvah's "broken body . . . give in despite herself to the sting of pleasure" (138). The experience for Nirvah is however quite different, at least initially. Her only impulse is to wash herself, to cleanse herself of "that pleasure taken by force from my body" (141). To do so, she turns to Solange, who prepares a bath for her, placing leaves over her body and chanting a song, which has an unexpected effect on Nirvah. She has her own spiritual experience, a feeling that it is no longer Solange that is touching her but her *lwa* Déméplè, Dantòr the black virgin, Fréda the white virgin, and "the good Lord" with all the saints and angels. The bath is for her a "deliverance," almost a new birth, one that is marked by grief—her tears for Daniel and for all that she has gone through, and has yet to face (144). Crucially, at this point she burns Daniel's journal, an act that signifies not only the end of his story for her, but also a farewell to the life they had before, when everything was "clear, predictable, and wonderful" (145). Covering her head in the ashes from the journal, she undergoes an improvised mourning ritual after which she declares herself to be "a widow" (146). As Nirvah's daughter Marie remarks, her mother no longer appears like a living person, but is "a phantom" with no substance, who wanders aimlessly around the home (158). Again, Nirvah's personal suffering is related to that of the broader country. Just as she is ravaged and left to mourn her past, so the nation is assaulted by natural forces, Hurricane Flora, which strikes with an unimaginable power, leaving Port-au-Prince "raped" and "writhing for hours like a woman giving birth." Much like Nirvah's rebirth however, all that the city gave birth to during the storm were "cadavers and desolation," a new apocalyptic time of death and fear, during which "a wind of madness blew across the country" (152).

Nirvah's rebirth leads to a reconsideration of her relationship with Vincent, and a pragmatic acceptance of the advantages she has gained. No longer the "sweet little Nirvah" who lived happily in the shadows of Daniel Leroy, she accepts freely the new privileges and material pleasures she has, guided only by her "survival instinct" (164). Later, she discovers in her "submission" to Vincent a level of sexual pleasure that she had never before known. "Raoul taught me to be a woman," she says, "to seek out the satisfaction of my flesh . . . to the point of falling into the unknown" (189). She moreover comes to think that her husband is to blame for her family's situation, in that Daniel was so obsessed with political causes that he did not think of how his activities would make the family vulnerable (163–64). Having burned his journal and subsequently removed from her room all visual reminders of Daniel, Nirvah understands that such forgetting is not only crucial to her own personal survival, but is also for the government a "tactic for doing away with its opponents" (168). She also comes to reconsider Vincent, and sees in him a cultured side, an avid reader and a keen Hellenist, with a passion for Greek antiquity (170). In this period, she believes that "everything is going for the best" and that she has found the "infinite sweetness of days" (171).

Nirvah's perhaps willfully naive understanding of her situation is however contradicted by Marie, whose first-person narrative reveals the ways in which Vincent's presence is corrupting the family, destroying it from the inside. Specifically, Vincent has been sleeping with Marie since she was fifteen, unknown to Nirvah. Marie resents her mother for her acceptance of the "macoute peace," according to which if you do not provoke the macoutes with strikes or other political activities, your chances of being hurt are slim (174). Somewhat like her mother, however, Marie has adapted to Vincent's presence and physical demands, learning to "like what he did to me" (175). She allows the relationship to continue "as if to make herself suffer"; it is as if everyone in this situation must suffer in some way (252). And yet, Marie does not forget her father, and feels that they have all "betrayed" him, that "in our bodies, our thoughts, our acts, even the house forgets him a little more each day" (176). Again therefore, amnesia is vital to the survival of individuals and the regime, as they in a sense sleepwalk into their future, leaving behind any memories and any sense of the past that might disturb the illusion of well-being in the present.

In effect, each of Vincent's acts is motivated by his desire for revenge. The conquest of Nirvah is driven by social and historical factors that make the possession of a mulatto woman a sign of his power and prestige, while the abuse of Marie is to some extent an act of vengeance directed at the bourgeois intellectual Daniel, a reminder of the father's inability to protect his children in his own home. When Vincent inevitably moves next to abuse Nirvah's son Nicolas, it is presented as an act rooted in Vincent's own earliest sexual experiences. As an adolescent, Vincent had been introduced by a well-meaning uncle to a respected acquaintance with the aim of supporting the promising student, whose future chances were dimmed by his poverty (179). The acquaintance however took the young Vincent to a "secret homosexual club," in which he was subjected to the worst abuse from "brutes and perverts" (179). Vincent has already exacted revenge on the club members, killing all of them. He retains however homosexual urges that are presented as the consequences of his being abused, and of which he hides "the shameful memory like a stigmata" (180). These urges are tied up with Vincent's passion for ancient Greece, and are reawakened when Nicolas asks him for help with translating a Greek text. In doing so, Nicolas takes Vincent back to "a time of fears and wonders, discoveries and pain" (181). In Vincent's mind Nicolas will be Eromenos to his Erastes, and he will teach the adolescent about "life, politics, pleasure," as in the "noble tradition of the Greek aristocracy" (182). Although it is stated that he is not motivated by the "spirit of vengeance" there does remain a sense that Vincent is at least recuperating his own experience and perpetuating it, making another suffer as he did (183).

Just as he brings chaos and abuse to the family, so Vincent spreads disorder and death around the country. Dispatched to the southwest to quell an invasion led by bourgeois militants, he leads a force of macoutes and peasants that quashes the revolt and exacts revenge on the families of the militants. The peasants are forced to participate in the slaughter for fear of being accused by the macoutes of complicity in the revolt. Deprived of their lands, property deeds, and women by the macoutes, the peasants find themselves "defenders of a cause that is fatal to them but which excites in their heads a perverted patriotism. They are defending the territory[,] . . . the fatherland" (198). The dictatorship thus distorts the notion of patriotism, and makes of itself the defender of the country, while at the same time destroying the nation from the inside—the very modus operandi of the apocalyptic state. The paradox for Vincent and other ministers is however that the more they impose their power through the sole use of violence, the more they fundamentally weaken their own positions, and the more they are themselves subject to plots and counterplots, the "silent dangers" that for Vincent are hidden in the corridors of the National Palace (205).

One of the most powerful weapons used by both the state and Vincent is the imposition of silence, the fear of speaking out on national or personal issues. When Nirvah finally breaks her own silence and asks Vincent outright about the fate of Daniel and the rumors of his abuse of her children, her fear "disappears," the "masks slip," and the illusions that held their relationship together fall away (216). After Vincent confesses to the abuse of her children and accuses her of hypocrisy, Nirvah reflects that he is a "master in the art of confusion," and that he "no longer knows the meaning of the word truth" (218–19). His imposition of silence and fear allows illusions and distortions to take the place of reality, to the extent that he and the state seem to lose all notion of the truth.

One consequence of this culture of silence and fear is that the political elite exists in a constant state of suspicion, and the more elevated the position one holds the more serious the threats are from rival politicians. Duvalier's government is riddled with mistrust, plot, and counterplot. It is also not immune to older rivalries, specifically the color and class antagonisms that are the apparently permanent legacy of colonialism. As one of Duvalier's most senior officials, Vincent is subject to jealousy, and susceptible to the plotting of his rivals in the government. His actions in repressing the revolt in the southwest attract the ire of Maxime Douville, the secretary of state for finances and economic affairs, who lost several distant relatives in Vincent's purge of the families of the invaders. Douville's anger is directed solely at Vincent, the "principal executor of the dictatorship's dirty work" (224). Douville's resentment is heightened by his knowledge of Vincent's involvement with the Leroy family. "All the same, these blacks," Douville reflects, "their humanity is only legitimized by the presence of a light-skinned woman in their bed" (224). Douville's plan is to control tightly Vincent's finances, to expose the financial regularities he has incurred in assuring Nirvah's favors. Also, he has persuaded key ministers to vote for the release of Daniel Leroy, while Vincent, caught up in his dealings with the other Leroys, has neglected to lobby the other ministers to keep Leroy in prison. This has fatally weakened Vincent's political position, and as the votes are cast for Leroy's release, he realizes that it is "the beginning of the end" for him (226). The deadly machine that he helped create now turns against him, ready to crush him (251).

Similarly, when Nirvah's home is raided soon after by macoutes, she knows that Vincent no longer commands fear and that "the winds have changed" (237). Faced with this change in her circumstances, her pragmatism and her instincts for survival come once again to the fore as she is gripped by the "need to live, to save my life and that of my children" (238). She also accepts finally that Daniel will not leave prison alive, and that Vincent will fall soon. Again in pragmatic mode, she sells the jewelry given to her by Vincent and other possessions to raise the funds required to leave the country (241). She is however assailed by the memories and consequences of Vincent's intrusions into her family, as Marie almost dies from aborting Vincent's child. Echoing once more Chauvet's trilogy, she moves gradually through the novel from *amour* to *colère* to *folie*. Finding that her mind is functioning "outside of" her head, she wonders whether "one can sink consciously into madness" (270). Torn between the past, the present, and the future Nirvah feels that she is at once herself "and several other women at the same time" (256).

This uncertainty surrounding identity and character extends to Vincent, who sacrifices his own safety by accepting a bribe that he knows will lead to his own downfall but that will allow Nirvah and her children to leave the country. Just as it is difficult to judge Nirvah—is she a pragmatic survivor or naive and hypocritical?—Vincent is a multifaceted character whose morals are to some extent determined by the situations that he finds himself in. At the height of his power, he is egocentric, self-serving, and abusive, while when his power fades he appears more humble and human, prepared to sacrifice himself for the others' safety. The effect of this fluidity of character is to suggest that individuals' decisions are determined less by their essential, unchanging values than the realities, demands, and opportunities of their circumstances.

This idea is reinforced as Nirvah prepares to leave Haiti with her family. For Nirvah, the departure offers the opportunity to put behind them the "hostile years," and to forget Haiti, Port-au-Prince, the macoutes, and "all that is wrong in our country, which no longer wants us" (282). They will discover, she says, "other suns" and a "new dawn" (282), phrases that recall Jacques-Stephen Alexis's classic novel *Compère Général Soleil* (1955), which ends with its Haitian exiles returning from persecution and slaughter in the Dominican Republic and rediscovering an idea of Haiti's glorious past. The central character in Alexis's novel regrets his time in exile and realizes that "the great truth" for him is that "the sun of Haiti shows us what we need to do" (349). Mars's novel by contrast more or less reverses this idea and suggests that Haiti is no longer the nurturing motherland of which Alexis wrote. Tellingly, when she tries to leave Haiti she does so not by the light of Alexis's Haitian sun, but under cover of the night, with an "enormous moon" (284) guiding her through the darkness, which for the first time "reassures" her (287). The "new dawn" and "other suns" that Nirvah foresees are situated elsewhere, and Haiti appears finally as almost uninhabitable, a place to flee rather than a viable home. She has "no regrets" about leaving her country, and implicitly critiques nationalist authors such as Alexis when she says that notions of nostalgia, Haïti chérie, and other romantic ideals of "exiled poets" seem to her "ridiculously lyrical" as she seeks to leave Haiti (289). The final ironic twist is that her flight into exile is intercepted at the border, as her route is blocked by two jeeps "the color of night," and volleys of automatic rifle fire that, significantly, come out of "the dust," the all-enveloping stifling force that Vincent had temporarily removed from her life but which now reappears as he himself has been arrested, and Nirvah's own dream of escape ends in a deadly scene that only reaffirms the power of the dictatorship (295).

Unlike many Latin American literary traditions, Haitian literature has arguably not produced a great dictator novel.[17] Indeed, the best-known novel of the Duvalier dictatorship is probably Graham Greene's *The Comedians* (1966). When they have addressed the Duvalier years, Haitian authors have tended to do so allegorically, as in René Depestre's *Le mât de cocagne* (1979) and Frankétienne's *Ultravocal* (1972) or by other indirect means, such as Chauvet's setting her trilogy in 1939. Time and readers will decide whether Mars's *Saisons sauvages* constitutes a great dictator novel, but it is certainly a bold attempt to revisit that most traumatic period in Haitian history. Duvalier himself has a shadowy presence in the novel, which focuses more on subsidiary figures such as Vincent in its exploration of the effects of the dictatorship on everyday life, notably the way that it invades the private sphere. While it deals with the past, one feels too that Mars is exploring these issues because they are still relevant to contemporary Haiti. Reading this novel after the earthquake and following the events of early 2011, it seems to have moreover a prescient quality and to act as a warning for the future. The book is a reminder of some of the horrors that the nation has experienced just as one of the phantoms of the past in the form of Jean-Claude Duvalier was about to return to Haiti, himself a ghostly throwback to one of the nation's most troubling *saisons sauvages*. Finally, Mars's work confirms that fiction is a highly potent means of revisiting the apocalyptic past, bringing it to life and working against the kind of forgetting that allows dictatorship and tyranny to exist.

Reconciliation and Redemption

One of the fundamental problems in addressing the memory of the Duvalier period is that there has been no sustained official attempt to address the human rights abuses that were a primary feature of the regime. While Jean-Bertrand Aristide set up a National Truth and Justice Commission in the mid-1990s to investigate the human rights violations that took place during Raoul Cedras's military regime (1991–94), there has been to date no similar initiative to investigate the Duvalier era.[18] Given that more than 5,500 people provided testimonies to the Aristide commission, which identified 8,667 victims and 18,629 violations of human rights, one can only imagine what those figures would be in relation to the twenty-nine-year Duvalier era.[19] Perhaps the sheer scale of human rights abuses by the Duvaliers and the fact that virtually no family was left unaffected by those abuses would make the work of such a commission almost impossible to undertake and execute. Perhaps, too, there is no real political will to set up a commission on the Duvalier years, based on a feeling that revisiting the past in this way would create more problems politically and socially than it would resolve. And yet, in cases such as Guatemala and South Africa, such commissions have had a degree of success, and have helped considerably in the recuperation of traumatic memory, by recognizing the existence of abuse and validating the experiences of the abused.[20] The aims, generally speaking, of truth commissions may include "to reach out to victims, to document and corroborate cases for reparations, to come to firm and irrefutable conclusions on controversial cases and patterns of abuse, to engage the country in a process of national healing, to contribute to justice" (Hayner 82).

In the absence of such a commission on the Duvalier era, Haitian arts and especially literature take on important memorial and testimonial functions. Novels in particular, such as Mars's *Saisons sauvages,* become means of testifying to individual and general suffering, and of keeping memories alive and thereby validating experiences that would otherwise never be spoken about and consigned to the recesses of memory in the form of unresolved trauma. This seems to be because literature is "interested in the complex relation between knowing and not knowing" (Caruth 3), between a memory that is real, but which is often denied and lived as untrue in order for the traumatized subject to survive in the present. Crucially, too, in Haitian literature, works of fiction at times become forums in which themes of forgiveness, redemption, and reconciliation are addressed in ways that rarely happen in public and political discourse. In this section, I will analyze two further novels that address the legacy and the memory of the Duvalier era, that foreground in particular the themes of redemption and reconciliation, and that as such begin to suggest a means of ending the apocalyptic cycle of history. As such, these works may be read as anti-apocalyptic in their suggestion that the recuperation and narration of apocalyptic memory is perhaps the most effective means of moving beyond trauma; that is, through recognizing and representing the apocalyptic past, authors seek to reduce the capacity of that past to determine the narrative of the present and the future.

In this regard, such works of fiction may be compared to the *testimonio* or the *crónica,* genres developed throughout Latin America since the nineteenth century as means of bearing witness to contemporary social events. The *crónica* is described as a "brief hybrid essay combining personal observation with social documentary" (Anderson 146). As Anderson writes, the *crónica* is characterized by its "social focus, its concision, and its blending of literary tropes and symbolism with journalistic techniques and reporting" (164). As a hybrid form, the *crónica* often incorporates documentary and testimonial modes. According to the critic April Shemak, there has been a trend in Caribbean fictions to "represent subaltern voices by mimicking *testimonio,* a genre that arose out of Caribbean and Central American social and political movements as a way to foreground the voices of the oppressed" (Shemak 83). One of the conventions of these fictional *testimonios* is the narrator who serves as "an eyewitness to acts of brutal oppression" (84). Often, as Shemak says, fictional *testimonios* represent actual historical events, "but challenge existing histories through their representations" (ibid.). While the Haitian works of fiction discussed below certainly have such testimonial functions, their political impact is probably less significant than that of some of the prominent Latin American examples. The *crónica,* for instance, was developed as a "tool for negotiation between individuals or collectivities and the state," and in the months following the Mexican earthquake of 1985, for example, intellectuals "played a key role in bringing the popular movements' demands to the negotiating table" (Anderson 163). In Haiti, however, there is little sense of testimonies and chronicles having any salutary political effect; indeed in the case of Haitian fictional writing on the Duvalier period, there is often a temporal distance that renders the testimonial aspects more as acts of memory than direct engagements with contemporary political reality. Bearing witness is thus often a deferred act, the testimony a means of commemorating events from the past whose effects resonate still in the present.

Judgment and Redemption in *The Dew Breaker*

Published in 2004, Edwidge Danticat's *The Dew Breaker* has in common with her previous two novels a concern with exile and alienation, which are associated in each case with "a broken sense of the past, of connection, and indeed of personal identity" (Gallagher 147). In her third novel, Danticat extends her common preoccupation with loss and trauma to include a father figure, the eponymous character through whom the author explores a "whole new set of ethical dilemmas linked not just to the moral issues of silence, guilt, complicity, witness, and redemption, but also to the more political question of justice and the matter of responsibility toward the 'third party'" (ibid.). In other words, this is a text that is at once a work of fiction and that functions to some extent in the way a truth commission might, in its re-visitation of the Duvalier period and its consideration of the possibility of personal and societal redemption.[21] Importantly, too, as Braziel points out, although the book focuses on the violence of the Duvalier era, the work "cast[s] stormy and foreboding shadows over the present [and] indicts the present political terror or state violence" (*Ghosts* 220).

The father is presented from the beginning as an enigma: "My father is gone," writes his narrator daughter Ka in the book's first line. The unnamed father has absconded from the Florida hotel they were staying in, as they traveled from their home in Brooklyn to deliver a statue Ka has made for a Haitian actress. Ka's fascination with her father is suggested immediately in her statement that the only subject of her sculptures to date is her father (4). She seems particularly interested in his physical appearance and the ways in which it either reveals or conceals his past. His age and modest stature—he is sixty-five, five feet eight inches, one hundred and eighty pounds, with thinning, graying hair—suggests a benign, grandfatherly figure, while the scar on his face he gained he says during a year in prison in Haiti and the dentures he wears as a result of falling out of bed during a nightmare are physical markers of a more troubled past (4–5). These physical signs of the violent past indicate indirectly that the original Greek meaning of the word *trauma* was of course "wound," an injury inflicted on the body (Caruth 3). As such, the father's physical signs of trauma are visual reminders of the past, of the ways in which physical and psychological trauma are closely related, and that the latter, however less immediately imperceptible, is often as ineradicable as any physical scar.

It is telling that, in the absence of her father, she checks the statue to "make sure it was still whole" (6–7). Also, the wood she had used to make the statue was "naturally flawed," and there are a few cracks in the finished work that remind the artist of her father's own scars (7). She is however worried about the imperfections and wonders if they would appear "amateurish and unintentional, like a mistake," and if the wood would come apart with "simple movements or with age" (6). "Would the client be satisfied?" she asks herself (7), in a self-conscious way that seems to be an indirect commentary on behalf of the author on her own novel, a work characterized by a fragmented structure that "enacts the brokenness of the lives portrayed and performs the concealment, displacement, and disconnection that the book also configures thematically" (Gallagher 148). Thus, through the statue and the figure of the sculptor Danticat reflects indirectly on her own art and her situation as a writer, anxious about her work and how it will be received by its readers.

Once the work is out of the artist's hands, however, her control over its potential meanings slips, and others are liable to appropriate the work and impose on it their own interpretations. This is the case with the sculpture, which the father takes with him when he leaves the hotel, and which he leaves in an artificial lake, near a highway (15). His reasons for doing so are complex, and related to his need for redemption. In explaining why he left the statue in the lake, he first reminds Ka of why he gave her that particular name, after the ancient Egyptian concept of the "double of the body," the body's companion through life and the afterlife (17). The father compares the concept of ka to the Haitian notion of the *ti bon anj,* the good angel that guides the soul. When his daughter was born, he says, he looked at her face and thought "here is my ka, my good angel" (17). When he first saw the statue, he "wanted to be buried with it," and to take it with him into the other world (17). The statue is thus to him an extension of the daughter, in that both represent to him potential means of salvation, guides through life and the afterlife.

The father is preoccupied with the notion of judgment: if the heart of the dead person is heavy, he says, "then the person cannot enter the other world" (19). Recalling the imperfect statues that he would take her to see at the Brooklyn museum and how she would pay more attention to what was missing than what was there, the father says to her that he is like one of those statues, flawed and incomplete (20). "I don't deserve a statue," he says to her, before announcing the reason behind his behavior (20). "You see, Ka," he says, "your father was the hunter, he was not the prey" (20). He was not the prisoner, he reveals, but the captor, and the scar on his face was inflicted by one of his prisoners, whom he shot and killed, "like I killed many people" (21–22). The revelation does not however lead easily to forgiveness or redemption: Ka wishes she could give to him what he had been seeking in telling her his secret, but as she reflects, he "must have already understood that confessions do not lighten living hearts" (33).

Indeed, the confession leads only to more questions, not so much on the specific past activities of the father, but on the role of Ka's mother, Anne, in the father's story. The father's revelation prompts Ka to question in her mind if the father's past explains her mother's piousness and if the mother herself was implicated in the Duvalierist violence. "Was she huntress or prey?" Ka asks of her mother. "A thirty-year-plus disciple of my father's coercive persuasion?" (22). Another image of her mother appears to her, one of her as a young woman taking her father in her arms, and Ka wonders at what point did her mother decide she loved him and "When did she know that she was supposed to have despised him?" (23). Immediately, therefore, the emphasis is placed less on the past, violent acts than on their implications for those around the father, chiefly the mother and the daughter. In the mother's case, the questions raised relate primarily to how one can live with and love someone whose violent past one is aware of, while for Ka, her dilemma is that of someone who has already loved her father but who finds out much later of his violent past and attempts to come to terms with that knowledge. The father, by contrast, is relatively fixed (in imperfection, like his statue), his being largely determined by his past actions, and the only thing that can change for him is his relationship to his family. What good, the novel seems to ask, does it do to know such a past, and who benefits from that knowledge?

These questions are all the more complicated in that they are raised far from the site of the father's crimes. In Brooklyn, the family members are able to fashion lives that seem to some extent cut off not only from Haiti the place, but also from Haiti the memory, the past time whose repercussions they are apparently protected from in the United States. In another way, however, the physical separation only accentuates the memories, and neither the mother nor the father can truly find redemption or salvation in the new place. Grief and trauma follow them like traveling companions; in the mother's case, every time she passes a cemetery in New York she is reminded of her brother, who drowned at sea in Haiti. The brother's body was never recovered, and she imagines him now walking the earth "looking for his grave" (71). In this case, and in that of the father and his victims, a violent death seems to condemn the dead to forever haunt the living, their incomplete deaths mirroring the fragmented lives of the killers, their accomplices, and those who mourn.

Also, contemporary events in Haiti serve as pervasive reminders of the past, for instance the case of Emmanuel Constant, the leader of the notorious Front for the Advancement and Progress of Haiti, which was accused of mass murder, rape, and torture in the 1990s. Constant's image hangs around the streets of Brooklyn in flyers that state that he is a man wanted "for crimes against the Haitian people" (78). The family had never spoken about the posters, but Anne feels a strong desire to pull them down, as despite the time that has passed since her own husband's crimes, she fears that she could find one day posters with his image pasted on the lampposts (80). Constant's very name seems to suggest the unchanging nature of Haitian politics, and the way in which the past reappears in new guises, the effect of which for Anne is that she lives her life "like a pendulum between forgiveness and regret," oscillating between the present and the past (86).

More directly, the past inhabits their present in the shape of Dany, one of the Haitian immigrants who share the room under the Dew Breaker's barbershop. In a community that is at times preoccupied with recognition and dissimulation, the face of the torturer remains unmistakable, so that when Dany meets the Dew Breaker for the first time, he recognizes the older man as the one who had killed his parents and waved a gun at him outside his family home many years previously in Haiti (105).[22] The Dew Breaker's choice of trade is an interesting one, in that it involves contact with bodies, cutting, and the latent capacity to maim. It also calls to mind notorious barber-murderers such as Sweeney Todd, and phonetically is not so far removed from the word *barbaric*. It is perhaps these connotations that make Dany's heart "race" every time he sits for a haircut: he sweats and shakes as the barber shaves him, in a scene that plays out in commuted form the torturer-victim relationship that relates them to their shared pasts (106). Waiting for an opportunity to avenge the Dew Breaker's victims, Dany enters one night the older man's bedroom and stands before the sleeping barber, contemplating whether he should kill him (107). He loses the desire to kill however, not out of pity or forgiveness, but in the realization that nothing he could do would ever explain "why one single person had been given the power to destroy his entire life" (107). Dany moreover sees still in the Dew Breaker the capacity to kill, and even when he returns to Haiti shortly after, he cannot free himself of the feeling that "after all these years the barber might finally make good on his promise to shoot him, just as he had his parents" (108). Indeed, the Dew Breaker's latent capacity for violence is suggested when he reacts angrily to Ka's mockery of him, grabbing her wrist, "crushing the bone, almost splitting it apart," in an act that suggests the continued presence of the anger and self-doubt that motivated his previous barbarism (20).

The novel however places the emphasis less on the Dew Breaker's acts of violence than on their multiple, damaging effects. Also, the direct victims of the violence are less (or differently) haunted by the events than their children, those whose lives have been shaped by the apocalyptic past and who inherit its trauma without wholly understanding its causes. Thus, by the time that the novel details in the final chapter one of the Dew Breaker's specific crimes, we have already seen their effects, which creates the sense that we are reading history backward, and that the violence stands as a sort of original sin that taints forever the experience of both victim and torturer, and indeed ties their fates together inextricably. The story of the victim cannot be understood without that of the torturer, and in the closing section that missing story is finally related.

The particular victim is a preacher whose radio sermons evoke biblical stories of resistance to tyrants and who refers to Duvalier as "our beast" (186).[23] The narrative of this murder simultaneously reveals some of the Dew Breaker's own personal history, which serves to explain some of his motivations, and to complicate the victim-torturer binary relation. The son of landowning peasants who had their lands stolen by army officials shortly after Duvalier came to power, his father had subsequently "gone mad" and his mother had disappeared, perhaps eloping with a lover (191). Following his mother's departure, he joined the militia, abandoned the land, and moved to the city, where he attended a speech by Duvalier, who appeared to him as a kind of savior and possible source of redemption. Standing for hours in the heat listening to the speech, he had a kind of epiphany and imagined seeing above the palace a "flock of winged women," whom he took to be "angels, caryatids, maybe a soul for each of us standing there in the sun" (193). It appears therefore that the deeper reasons for his becoming a macoute are quite complex: struck by the initial trauma of losing both his family lands and his parents to the Duvalierists, he seeks salvation and redemption not in resistance, but in devotion to the source of his misfortune, to the figure and ideology of the ultimate torturer, Duvalier himself. Thus, positions of victimhood and torturer become complicated, enmeshed, and dependent on each other. One cannot truly become a torturer, it seems, without being first a victim—an idea that recalls the figures of Janvier and Vincent in Peck's film and Mars's novel, respectively.

In this case the torturer—who killed the preacher, but only after receiving a blow that scars his face deeply—becomes the potential prey, in that he fears the repercussions of his act, which went against the orders of the president. His face bleeding heavily, he quickly becomes a kind of victim, in need of solace and salvation, which he finds in the shape of a woman who takes care of him, treating his wound. It is Anne, the stepsister of the preacher and the Dew Breaker's future wife. "What did they do to *you*?" she asks him, which was to him the "most forgiving question he'd ever been asked" (237). The question, putting him in the position of the victim, liberates him and he says that he is free, "finally escaped" from his life, to which he no longer wants to return (237). The reasons for her waiting outside the barracks were unclear to him, but he feels that she had been there to "save him, to usher him back home and heal him" (237). For her part, she is not fully aware of what motivated her to save him, apart from the general feeling of "hollow grief" and the "penance procession" that had begun in 1957 and which was "yet to end" (238). It appears that just as the torturer needs a victim, so a savior needs a fallen, desperate person to save.[24] It seems finally significant that as he slept on the night he killed the preacher, the Dew Breaker dreamed of his childhood and working with his parents in their garden in Léogâne. The family works together in the "golden mist" of the early morning, and soon the seeds they had planted grow into trees—mango, papaya, guava, and avocado (235). His mother takes his hand and guides it toward the leaves of a mimosa pudica or "shame plant," which turn in on themselves on the first touch and then reopen naturally. The dream is complex, but seems to situate the suffering of the Dew Breaker in the connection he had with his parents and with nature, which was ruptured in the early years of Duvalierism. If his dream stands as a projection of his pain and desire, then it seems that what he wanted most deeply was some kind of reconnection with that which was taken away by Duvalier, and that all the killings he carried out were a form of revenge for all that he and his family had suffered. The truly destructive element in those acts lay in their being directed not at the ultimate source of the wrongdoing, but at those most like himself, those who were seeking redress, albeit in quite different ways, but who became trapped by the vicious, apocalyptic cycle in which one was virtually forced to become either victim or torturer, or indeed, both at the same time.

Forgiving the Mother in *La mémoire aux abois*

The relationship between victim and torturer, and the question of forgiveness are further explored in Evelyne Trouillot's *La mémoire aux abois* (2010). The title foregrounds the importance of memory and suggests that to remember is potentially a fraught, perilous act. Memory, the title suggests, is something to be kept at bay, lest it overtake completely the present and the future. In contrast to the works by Peck, Mars, and Danticat, Trouillot writes in an allegorical mode, so that Haiti is referred to as Quisqueya (the Taino name for the island of Hispaniola), and the names of the major figures of the Duvalier era are altered; for example, François Duvalier becomes Fabien Doréval. In this sense, the novel recalls René Depestre's *Le mât de cocagne* (1979), both in its treatment of history and in the allegorical mode used to remember and critique the dictatorship. In both cases, allegory seems to destabilize the concept of history as a "fixed monument," by showing it to be always the product of "discursive practice." As such, allegory allows "the possibility of transformation" of historical discourse (Suk 6).

The possibility of transformation in the understanding of history seems to be one of Trouillot's prime motivations in writing this novel. Indeed, and somewhat paradoxically, this allegorical novel is also perhaps the most historically accurate of the works on the dictatorship analyzed in this chapter. The novel is a medium through which historical facts and key, though in many cases little known, events are evoked, while the allegorical style saves it from being a straightforward narrative list of past events. The historical facts and anecdotes are communicated in the allegorical mode so that the reader is encouraged to rethink history and to consider the particular, rarely heard perspectives presented in the novel. The most striking and original feature of the author's work in this regard is the way that she focuses not on the dictator himself, but on his wife, Simone, or as she is named in the novel, Odile.[25] Immediately, this shifts attention away from the issues of masculinity and fatherhood that are centrally important to the Duvalier-related works of Peck, Mars, and Danticat, and on to questions of femininity, motherhood, and the ways in which women experienced and remember the dictatorship. Although the dictatorship is connected most directly in the popular memory to male figures—Duvalier himself, his chiefly male entourage, the mainly male macoutes, the prominently male rebels and insurgents—the novel shows that Duvalier's wife was an absolutely essential part of the regime, and that she carefully cultivated a certain image of femininity and motherhood that complemented in many ways her husband's public persona.

The novel specifically sets up a potentially antagonistic and troubling relationship between Odile, who lies dying in a Parisian hospital, and her nurse, a young Haitian-born woman whose mother was forced to leave

Haiti during the Duvalier period, and who carries the full weight of that history. The novel alternates between the nurse's first-person narration and a third-person narrator who communicates the thoughts and memories of the dictator's wife. As in Mars's *Saisons sauvages,* the perspective of the figure most closely related to the dictatorship is narrated in the third person, as if the author hesitates to adopt the voice of the oppressive figure, or as if there is finally something impenetrable and unknowable about such a figure. The novel is therefore a kind of silent dialogue between the two figures, and thus between the past and the present, between the apparent cause of the historical trauma and someone who lives with it every day.[26]

Odile seems initially to the nurse to be a figure of abjection: she writes of how she would return home after work with the odor of Odile's "decrepit flesh" on her hands and the image of her almost lifeless body in her mind (7). The visual image of the dictator's wife is something that has been with her all of her life, as one aspect of the "horrors" of the Dorévaliste period that have haunted her existence and that of her mother. "How could one forget it?" she asks (8). The nurse has inherited from her mother the history of the dictatorship years, and the broader history of the country, which was related to her by her mother in a tone "at once belligerent, sad and dignified" (12). As in Danticat's *The Dew Breaker,* the emphasis is placed largely on the generation that did not experience the dictatorship directly, but which now lives it as a legacy of history. As the nurse says, she has "lived the dictatorship through a third party," and it is "stuck to her skin" as a kind of brand, marking her and determining her existence (99). The nurse says her childhood was "contaminated" by her mother's stories of Haiti (17), and that her mother would not listen to her everyday concerns, which were "anodine" compared to the horrors that the mother had experienced (23). One of the effects of this history is that the nurse thinks of death constantly, and of her own suicide: the sidewalk below the hospital window "taunts her desire to jump" (9). As such, the novel suggests there is in the nurse a form of the "fidelity to trauma," that La Capra writes of, "a feeling that one must somehow keep faith with it" (La Capra 22). "One's bond with the dead," he writes, "especially with dead intimates, may invest trauma with value and make its reliving a painful but necessary commemoration or memorial to which one remains dedicated or at least bound" (ibid.).

Bound in this sense to the traumatic past, and exiled in Martinique at the age of four, the nurse carries Haiti with her in her "injured look," and in the way she is taunted at school through perceived associations with poverty and the boat people (22). The mother and child are forced to change their names and to speak French, which to the mother seems like an "invasion" of her independent, Creole-speaking self (25). The mother's whole existence is related to Haiti and to the terrors of the dictatorship, which she recounts endlessly to her daughter. The nurse's narrative serves to recount in some detail the everyday horrors of the dictatorship, the lived experience that is perhaps lost in much historiography of the period. For instance, the paranoia and mistrust created by the dictatorship is suggested through the memory of schoolchildren who arrived late at school and were suspected of doing so to avoid repeating the vow of allegiance to the leader and the revolution. Immediately, the late arrivals would be sure to pronounce the vow louder than the rest to avoid suspicion, not just of themselves, but of their entire family. In such a totalitarian society, parents sought to "instill fear in children to avoid any mistakes. To inculcate in them the cult of silence" (54). Also, in a further echo of Danticat's novel, the narrator writes that many families contained victims or torturers, or both. "Monsters and heroes, good and evil," she writes, "were sometimes found together in the same family" (109).

At times, the two narratives relate the same events, albeit from starkly different perspectives. For instance, following the attempted kidnapping of the dictator's son, he issued an order for all school students to be held in their schools, and stated that if the son were hurt, the other children would all be killed. In Odile's narrative this act is presented as a necessary show of strength to an "ignorant people" (23). By contrast, the nurse's version, inherited from the mother, expresses the horror of parents and children alike, and remains in the narrator's memory as one of the many "anxieties" that constitute her mother's "heritage" (28). The form that this heritage takes in the present is anger, an emotion that the nurse holds on to, for fear that it might change into sadness and leave her "with no weapon to fight despair" (50).

For all that time and history separate them, the nurse and Odile have much in common, not least the anger that both hold as a heritage from the past, and the fact that Odile was herself a nurse before meeting her future husband. For both, silence is a refuge that allows (or forces) them to live in memory, cut off from the here and now. For her part, Odile remains in silence in the hospital, and takes refuge in remembrance, a process on which she must impose some "order," so that her thoughts do not "fray" or escape her control (9). She must not, for example, think of the view of the sea she had from the palace windows, or of the sunsets and the bustle of the city. For her "peace of mind," she feels compelled to revisit her own history, which begins not with the dead dictator, but with her four children, and her idea of herself as a "loving and devoted mother" (14). Thus, the emphasis is put on her maternal aspects rather than her role as the dictator's spouse. This goes against her popular perception in Haiti, where she was not generally considered to be a caring mother, no doubt due to the "austere face" she wore as part of her public image as First Lady, a "mask" that "supplanted all the others" (14).

One of these other, lesser-known "masks" is that related to her own childhood, in which she was abandoned by her mother and sent to live in an orphanage. In contrast to the other girls in the orphanage, she would never speak of her mother, maintaining toward her a "resolute indifference" (18). Her desire for order is related to the way in which she began to structure her life in the orphanage, to how in the absence of parental love, she "ordered her life while waiting to leave that clean and sterile prison" (19). The only advantages she inherited from the "sordid story" of her mother's liaison with a prominent intellectual were her light skin and her "face with the aristocratic contours" that would attract her future husband and allow her to always look imposing and haughty in photographs (19).

The further legacy of her childhood is a feeling of injustice, which validates in her mind the revenge that she seeks in adulthood. "Beyond all other humanitarian or affective consideration," the narrator writes, Odile was inhabited by "the determination to avenge herself for the disappointments of life, and the need to succeed" (30). Her marriage to the future president and her position as First Lady are essentially acts of revenge and vindication that she feels justified enjoying "in compensation for all those uncertain mornings, all the looks of disdain, all the denials signaled by a simple gesture" (56). The narrative of her life as First Lady presents her as a close confidante and advisor to her husband, someone implicated fully in the affairs and workings of the president, with whom she shared "the ecstasy of power" (130). As the novel shows, the story of the dictator's wife is of prime importance in understanding the dictatorship and the motivations of the first couple, specifically the righteous anger that was their historical legacy, and which apparently justified in their eyes the long authoritarian regime. At the same time, however, the dying Odile is liberated to some extent from the principal roles she played, as mother and spouse. She no longer wants to be "a simple appendix" to the dead dictator, "as if she could not exist independently. As if her own story had no importance in the greater scheme of things" (100).

Odile's life has a cyclical quality, in that she finds herself at the end of it as she was at its beginning: alone. Her solitude and her approaching death render her life's "illusions and lies" useless, like masks that need to be shed (46–47). Similarly, her memories become increasingly fragmented, "playing tricks" on her when she tries to recall her last Christmas with her children (148). Tellingly, the only memory that comes to her at that time is of herself alone in the orphanage, a period of loneliness that along with her isolation in the hospital bed serves to frame her life. All her other memories "seem vain," without meaning (149).

The thought of exacting revenge on Odile is never far from the nurse's mind. The older woman's face symbolizes to the nurse "the sum of all the horrors of a regime that left its mark on my country of origin" (76). With the tables turned to some extent, she is excited by the thought of avenging and "honoring the memory" of her father, mother, and uncle (56). Revenge appears to her as a chance to renew her life, to "make a decisive break with my past," she says, "to assume it and to move beyond it" (56–57). The prospect of revenge seems to liberate and rejuvenate her, and she feels young for the first time (62). She feels a sense of duty, that in killing Odile she would be avenging not only herself and her mother, but all the "mutilated destinies" of those who lived through the dictatorship (113).

The more the nurse thinks about killing Odile, the more she feels liberated. The "thought of action" begins to deliver her from her nightmares; and speculation on the best method to carry out the killing replaces hatred and anger (132). It also seems to free her to some extent from the past that she has inherited: her "dives into the past" become less "destructive," she says (132). She thinks first of poisoning Odile, then of asphyxiation (145).

However, as the two narratives reflect more on loss and death—the nurse mourns silently her mother, while Odile thinks of her husband's death and her own impending demise—there is a kind of rapprochement between the two. The sight of Christmas lights outside, contrasted with the deathly atmosphere of the hospital, seems to further encourage this coming together. "More than ever," the nurse writes at this point, "the immobile form on the bed seems to call to me" (151). As she approaches the bed, she silently summons Odile, demanding that she look in her face, answer her questions, and "confront justice and her memory" (152). The two women share suddenly a "lucid look," and Odile's hand touches the nurse's arm, which makes the younger woman recoil and make for the exit (152). As she is doing so, she hears Odile calling her name—Marie-Ange—which marks the first time that her name is pronounced in the novel. The name itself is loaded with connotations of motherhood, perfect femininity, and the possibility of redemption.

Indeed, Marie-Ange becomes the focus of the dying Odile's attention, and the older woman seeks in her a kind of salvation. "Was it the ultimate need to be if not loved at least understood that made her follow Marie-Ange's footsteps?" the narrator asks (154). Odile recognizes that Marie-Ange is also from Quisqueya, and given that she was also a nurse in her younger days and that she sees in Marie-Ange a sense of pride and haughtiness, one senses too that the older woman sees in the young woman a reflection of herself, distorted by time and history (155). For her part, Marie-Ange questions why she is showing goodwill and kindness to a woman who contributed to so many deaths and destroyed so many families, including her own. "I must not forget that," she writes. However, the largely unspoken bond between the two develops, and Odile holds Marie-Ange's wrist, the dying woman's face suddenly alive and animated, as she makes every effort to say to the nurse "Merci" (163). The bond is apparently sealed when Odile is saved from death by the intervention of Marie-Ange, when it would have been possible for the nurse to simply let the older woman die (181). Questioning her reasons for saving Odile, Marie-Ange thinks of her mother, and realizes that she could never have left the woman to die, for "There are already so many deaths around me" (182).

While these scenes seem to create a bond between the two women, the effect of this relationship is to finally begin to free Marie-Ange from the history that Odile represents. Her interactions with Odile lead Marie-Ange to a state of mind in which she is able to begin to address and apparently move beyond the nightmares of the past. "I think," she says, "that it is time for me to say farewell to my phantoms" (169), the most notable of which is the murder of her own father (172). For the first time, too, she is able to contemplate the future in terms other than as an endless repetition of the past. "I want to live," she says, "Without this oppressive weight that has been handed down to me" (180). She will build for herself, she says, "multiple and generous spaces, intimate and complicit, where sufferings and joy cohabit, where memories and possibilities will find their place" (175). It is not therefore finally through revenge that Marie-Ange finds her own salvation. Rather, it is in resisting the urge to avenge the dead that she allows herself to live, freeing herself from the past and thereby creating a sense of a life to come that will not be wholly determined by the past. Beyond the story of personal redemption, the novel stands as a powerful and relevant parable of the importance of forbearance in addressing the unfinished past in Haiti. In this sense, the novel recalls Roumain's *Gouverneurs de la rosée,* with the important difference that there is no new martyr in Trouillot's work. Life and the living will not be saved through death, and a single unnecessary death, the author seems to suggest, is a tragedy that multiplies itself immeasurably over time, tying forever the fates of the killer and the killed.

2 Utopian Ends

Aristide and the Apocalypse

THERE IS in Haiti and elsewhere a curious relationship between utopian discourse and apocalyptic outcomes. One might argue that many of the apocalyptic wars of the twentieth century were driven and justified by utopian discourses—Marxism, fascism, religions, and various forms of nationalism. The fall of the Berlin Wall seemed to announce the start of the "happy '90s," and gave rise to Francis Fukuyama's utopian idea of the "end of history," the belief that "liberal democracy had, in principle, won out, that the advent of a global liberal community was hovering around the corner, and that the obstacles to this Hollywood-style ending were merely empirical and contingent" (Žižek, *First as Tragedy* 3). For Žižek, the outcomes of Fukuyama's utopia were, first, September 11, then the global economic collapse of 2008. "Fukuyama's utopia of the 1990s had to die twice," Žižek writes, "since the collapse of the liberal-democratic political utopia on 9/11 did not affect the economic utopia of global market capitalism" (5). Perhaps within what Žižek calls "the utopian core of the capitalist ideology" (ibid.) there is an apocalyptic element that is not some rogue by-product of capitalism, but its inevitable and essential principle. Thus, one might talk, as Naomi Klein has done, of "disaster capitalism," an economic system that thrives on catastrophe, and which makes utopia and dystopia virtually one and the same thing.[1]

One could also say that Haitian noirisme was utopian in its vision of racial and cultural purity, and that its apocalyptic consequences are in some way related to its essential utopianism. In many ways the counter-narratives to noirisme, the Marxian novels of Jacques Roumain and Jacques-Stephen Alexis offer nevertheless "utopian fantasies" of the "restoration of an archaic lost paradise cleansed of the complexities of Haiti's national past" (Kaussen, *Migrant Revolutions* 122).[2] More recently, one year after the departure of Jean-Claude Duvalier, a new Constitution was passed in Haiti, one that Wilentz describes as "a liberal, utopian document that is today more honored in the breach" (75). One need cite only a single paragraph of the 1987 constitution to discern its utopian character, and to gauge the distance between its vision of Haiti and the reality that has since ensued. On behalf of the Haitian people it proclaimed "national unity, through eliminating all discrimination between the populations of the towns and countryside, by the acceptance of the community of languages and culture and by the recognition of the right to progress, to information, to education, to health, to work and leisure for all citizens." The 1987 constitution offers perhaps the most striking example in recent Haitian history of a utopian vision preceding an apocalyptic outcome.

Liberation theology is another utopian discourse that has shaped recent Haitian history, with apocalyptic results. In the broadest terms, liberation theology considers Christian faith to be inextricably associated with a concern for the world's poorest people, and Christians to have a solemn duty to protest against and rectify poverty. In his seminal work, *A Theology of Liberation: History, Politics, Salvation* (1971), Gustavo Gutiérrez identifies three main aspects of liberation. The first of these is political and social in nature, and involves the eradication of poverty and social injustice. The second is the liberation of the poor and all oppressed groups from "oppressive structures which hinder persons from living with dignity and assuming their own destiny." The third dimension is spiritual, and is related to liberation from selfishness and sin, and a renewed bond with God and other people (n.p.). In sum, Gutiérrez proposes a "new kind of society (characterized by justice), a new kind of human being (characterized by other-directedness), and a new kind of Christian disciple (for whom justice is a requirement of faith)" (*Essential Writings* 3). In both its theological and pastoral dimensions, liberation theology "articulated an overtly utopian project" (Moylan and Baccolini 203). Unlike many Christian discourses, liberation theology "does not attack Utopia as a heretical turn away from the narrative trajectory of redemption and salvation" (Moylan and Baccolini 203). Instead, liberation theologians judged the collective, revolutionary movement toward freedom and justice and its opposition to contemporary forms of capitalism to be part of the broader promise and purpose of Christianity. Crucially, liberation theology proposed an eschatological vision of humanity transformed and saved in history, and a form of material and spiritual salvation for the living, especially the world's poorest, who themselves were to be transformed from voiceless subjects into key agents at the "leading edge of spiritual and political work in the world" (Moylan 203).

It is not difficult to see the attraction of liberation theology to Jean-Bertrand Aristide: it is to him "the Christian impulse that does not separate belief from action, that exasperates conservatives, and annoys so many people on the left who dream of realizing the happiness of others . . . without the others" (*Dignity* 103). In addition to its general promise of political and social advancement of the poor, liberation theology offered a new conception of the relationship between politics and religion in Haiti. In particular, it suggested a way out of the impasse that elite Haitian intellectuals such as Roumain and Alexis had presented in their work: the apparent irreconcilability of progressive politics and religion. The idea that social progress and religious belief are inherently irreconcilable is perhaps most memorably expressed in Alexis's *Les arbres musiciens,* in the following phrase: "The loas will die only when electricity comes to the countryside, when light chases darkness from the shacks, . . . when people know how to read and write" (270). In general terms, liberation theology may be considered to be "consistent with, or an extension of, the attempts of earlier Haitian writer-activists to break through class divisions and establish bonds of solidarity" with the masses (Edmondson 113). A key difference, however, is that unlike Roumain, Alexis, and the great majority of Haitian intellectuals, Aristide did not come from the elite, and that consequently, unlike many bourgeois intellectuals, there is little anxiety in his writings about connecting with and speaking for the masses. Indeed, there is often an easy and fluid movement in his writing between the first person singular and plural voices. Aristide speaks at once for himself and the people; and the people, it is suggested, express themselves through him. "Through education and community action," he writes of the people, "we have grown up confronting reality with the word of God" (*Dignity* 88).

Progress, to Aristide, is "the progress of humanity" in general, and there is no force, he says, superior to humankind. In this, and in his statement that change "is the responsibility of women and men to take control of their future; it is never the simple waiting of a people who are resigned," he echoes to some extent Roumain and Alexis's insistence on the primary importance of human existence and action (*Autobiography* 121). It is the individual's duty to resist, to "not accept the law of silence." "This is the way," he says, "chosen by the majority in the Haitian church, priests and laypersons, so many others." Through the voice of those who speak up "God continues to take human form in order to denounce injustice" (*Dignity* 88). Just as his individual voice slips easily into the collective mode, so there is a fluid relationship between the divine and the human. Aristide does not see Jesus as a divine being, but as someone who was "fully human" (*Autobiography* 121). It was through the human dimension, he says, that the divine in Jesus was revealed. Aristide writes, "He was so human that he was God: I share that theological vision" (ibid.). One implication of this vision is that any human can become divine, through their acts and by being "fully human," that is, being fully engaged with the social and political reality around them. The danger in such a vision would appear to be of progressively disengaging with the human through becoming divine. That is, following Aristide's logic, the more one does (or thinks one does) as a human, the more one risks thinking of oneself as divine, and therefore distinct from other humans. The risk, in short, is of becoming deluded about one's own mission, power, and importance. Aristide seems somewhat aware of this risk when he writes that he is "not a Messiah," and that in his time, "there is no Messiah other then the people" (120). If he refuses the title of Messiah, he nonetheless accepts the lesser role of prophet. "If I am a prophet[,] . . . if I have any talent as a visionary," he writes, "I owe it to those who have marched at my side" (121). It is in effect this supposed easy slippage between the human and the divine that fundamentally weakened Aristide: a justified prophet for some may be a dangerous tyrant to others. Similarly, the prophesied utopian future may easily slide into a new apocalypse.

One of Aristide's most trenchant critics, Alex Dupuy, has identified the prophetic aspect of liberation theology as its "guiding principle" (80). He moreover situates Aristide's version of liberation theology within a "populist current," which views the poor, the exploited, and the excluded as the sole agents of social change, and contrasts it with the more "classist" version that posits the working class as the primary vehicle for change. Whereas the classist model foresees a working-class-led socialist society as its ultimate objective, the populist model is more ambiguous, and "opens itself up to a compromise" on the form of the new social order that will deliver justice to the poor (81). As Dupuy argues, Aristide not only adopted the populist version of liberation theology, "but also tended to emphasize its prophetic side in his writings" (ibid.). Aristide's largely successful confrontations with the Church hierarchy and the military—he survived three assassination attempts by the government of General Namphy—only reinforced his prophetic qualities, and to the poor he became a savior figure who could stand up to the macoutes and "guided by the hand of God rid the country of the Duvalierist scourge that had terrorized and devastated the entire society" (83).

When Aristide decided to stand for president in 1990, he considered his candidacy essentially as a "messianic mission," and for Dupuy, therein resides the reasons for Aristide's subsequent "undemocratic, paternalistic, and authoritarian political practice" (85). A leader who believes he is charged by God with a sacred mission risks becoming a demagogue, abandoning democratic practices in the name of and for the putative benefit of the people. Crucially, too, once Aristide had installed himself as an "idol," the political and social program to a large extent became secondary to the "cult of the chief," and the mobilization of the people revolved "around the persona of Aristide the popular leader, the chief who possessed a superhuman power and was able to substitute himself for the popular organizations" (Moïse and Ollivier 154; Hurbon, "La désymbolisation du pouvoir" 52; René 136). According to Dupuy, it was Aristide's authoritarian tendency, bolstered by his belief that he was acting with and for the people and God that would prove "disastrous" for him in both his presidencies (90).

Indeed, in many ways, the Aristide presidencies were as disastrous as those of the Duvaliers, whom he had decried in apocalyptic terms, calling to Jean-Claude Duvalier in 1986 to "Get out, Satan!" (qtd. in Dubois 357). As Amy Wilentz writes, Aristide's critics believed his "plan" for the nation amounted to the following apocalyptic credo: "To save this country, you first had to destroy it," which, Wilentz says, "had also been the agenda of the revolutionaries in the era of slavery" (49). In effect, Aristide did not end the Haitian apocalypse; rather, he brought it back under the guise of prophecy and divinely sanctioned authoritarianism. Contemporary documents published by activists in Haiti and abroad in late 2003 and early 2004 are almost unanimous in their denunciation of Aristide. "Why must Aristide Leave?" asks a February 16, 2004, article written by the Canadian group Concertation pour Haiti. The article cites a long list of the government's failings, principally its reliance on "terror and corruption." "Like Duvalier in the past with his tontons macoutes," the article says, "Aristide has set up his own militia, armed to the teeth, who can carry out with impunity all forms of retribution and crimes, as long as they serve the political interests of the government."[3] The article thus alludes to perhaps the most grotesque and tragic manifestations of Aristide's new apocalypse: the so-called Chimères, the violent gangs hired from the capital's slums to bolster the government, and repress the opposition. The Chimères however had no ideological commitments, and were used by opposition groups as well as the government. As Fatton writes, the militarization of the Chimères "transformed them into armed gangs with increasingly independent interests and leaders [and became] a power unto themselves" (*Haiti's Predatory Republic* 148). In many ways, the Chimères replaced the macoutes as an apocalyptic army of the dispossessed, wreaking havoc on the country and reenacting to some degree the Duvalier disaster. If anything, the Chimères, as autonomous groups with only loose political affiliations were even more lawless than the macoutes, who at least had command structures and were ultimately accountable to the head of state (Dupuy 156). The activities of the Chimères in effect only reinforced the sense that Aristide's Haiti had fallen into a new abyss, and that his presidency had been "disastrous on all fronts—political, economic, and social" (ibid. 168).[4]

For all that Aristide has been largely discredited by most Haitian commentators, his reputation is stronger on the outside, notably among several prominent North American and European academics, whose views on the former president contrast sharply with those of most Haitian observers.[5] However flawed some of these external views may be, they cannot be simply dismissed as a harmless fantasy. This is because their singular view of Haitian history and politics is becoming increasingly influential, at least in the English-speaking world. The relatively simplified idea of Haiti as a helpless victim of external forces, used as a vehicle to further a critique of Western neoliberalism, stands in contrast to the perspective of many prominent Haitian intellectuals who, while not denying the significance of external factors, tend to look inward and to Haitian history and society in order to present a far more nuanced and complex understanding of the causes of Haiti's various problems. Divergent uses of Haitian history exemplify these differences: for many non-Haitian commentators, the country's revolutionary history remains a source of potential inspiration and salvation, while many prominent Haitian authors judge that same history and its manipulation by various political leaders to be fundamental causes of Haiti's contemporary problems. It seems self-evident that it is chiefly through an open and even-handed engagement with Haitian culture and thought from before and after the earthquake that outsiders can begin to comprehend the country. There is a pressing need for a properly balanced understanding of Haitian history, politics, culture, and society among scholars, students, and the general public outside of Haiti. Arguably the most effective way of engaging with Haiti is through its literature, which is one of the most longstanding and sophisticated of all literary traditions in the Americas, and has long chronicled the nation's history, politics, and society. Arguing that the Haitian arts offer some of the most penetrating critiques of the Aristide period, the rest of this chapter engages with three key works: Lyonel Trouillot's *Rue des pas perdus* (1996), Gary Victor's *A l'angle des rues parallèles* (2000), and Raoul Peck's film *Moloch Tropical* (2009), all of which offer distinctly apocalyptic visions of Aristide's Haiti. It is perhaps no coincidence that the theme of the apocalypse should reappear so prominently around the turn of the millennium, in that such a moment seems to incite simultaneously the fear and hope for the end of a historical period and for deliverance into a new time in which the people would be finally freed from the phantoms of the past. This is apocalyptic writing without the eschatological promise of a new age to come. All that is foreseen is the continuation of a cycle that stretches back to colonial times, which stand as the initial apocalyptic moment, a historical shock so violent that it continues to disrupt the present, rendering impossible any sense of history (as in many religious versions of the apocalypse) as a linear progression from one age to the next. What we see in Trouillot's and Victor's novels and Peck's film of the Aristide era is a people and a nation caught in a self-perpetuating cycle that confuses and confounds any straightforward understanding of ethics and morality.

Madness and Prophecy in *Rue des pas perdus*

One prominent feature of many Christian apocalyptic narratives is the final encounter of the wicked and the righteous. According to such a narrative, the former would be judged by God and sent into eternal torment, while the latter would achieve vindication, resurrection, and glorification. The sub-narrative is that the good shall prevail, and that they can finally be distinguished from the wicked. One of the fascinating elements in Haitian apocalyptic literature is that there is often little distinction made between the good and the evil; opposing political forces are often presented as being fundamentally alike, so that there is little sense of natural or divine justice imposing itself at the end of the conflict. Rather, these confrontations are worldly affairs, governed by a different set of rules in which the most violent, the most wicked, often prevail.

A key novel in the recent coming to prominence of the apocalyptic theme in Haitian literature is Lyonel Trouillot's *Rue des pas perdus* (*Street of Lost Footsteps*). Published just two years before the end of the millennium, the novel is set around one night of apocalyptic violence in Port-au-Prince in which the supporters of an Aristide-like figure, the Prophet, are pitted against those of the Duvalier-like dictator Deceased

Forever-Immortal. The specific characters living with the novel's contorted sense of ethical and moral understanding are principally the three narrators: an aging madam, a taxi driver, and a post office employee. The novel is at once about one night and the whole of Haitian history; one of the fascinating and in some ways felicitous effects of circular history is that one lives every day with and to some extent in the past, and that one can sense and know the past intimately as it returns and manifests itself in the present.

The Madam

Such is the case with the madam, whose narrative is addressed to an unidentified man referred to only as "monsieur," and who seems to be a foreign journalist, come to Haiti to "sniff the heady smell of the massacres" (79). Her narrative stretches back to the beginnings of Haitian history, which announced itself, she says, "with a great gust of wind," and a "whirl of lazy legends" (1). History has become a "corset, a stifling cell, a great searing fire, an apocalyptic calypso", a narrative encapsulated and perpetuated in what she calls the "folkloric-tropical-negritudinal rubbish" that has constituted elite Haitian intellectual culture (ibid.). Haiti is not a country, she insists, but an "epic failure factory," the site of an environmental apocalypse that has reduced its mountains "to dust," and its people to a state of impoverished despair, in which they wait for a miraculous deliverance, "in the hope of insane epiphanies" (ibid.).

Within the broader movement of repetitive history, there are smaller, related cycles, and the specific one that the madam is interested in began, she says, one April day on the state funeral of the president, who is not named, but one takes to be François Duvalier, who was buried on April 21, 1971. "Yes," she says, "it all began with this April wind that made us believe the days of dictatorship were over" (2). Poets were already writing of a new era, while people, "righteous brethren," embraced on the streets just like they did in 1934 at the end of another historical cycle, the American occupation (ibid.). This cycle is itself unfinished, as the madam writes of the contemporary presence of U.S. soldiers on Haitian soil and the effect it has had on her mother, who no longer talks about 1934, has "lost her memory," and sits now frozen in time, something, she suggests, like the country itself (ibid.). The narrator is careful however not to suggest an idea of Haitian exceptionalism, in that she says that in Haiti there is "no more or less wind here than anywhere else, no more or less lowdown dishonesty than anywhere else," only poverty and destitution that allow "stale metaphors" to perpetuate in what she calls the "endless masturbation of speechifying prelates and bureaucrats," the heirs of the dictator who re-enact in an endless loop the nation's "most morbid rituals" (3).

The madam also evokes a sense of Haitian history before the dictatorships. History in her version of it is marked by a gradual decline, prices going up and poverty increasing, "decade after decade of deprivation under our belts," she says (5). Her memory stretches back to the pre-Duvalier time, when village girls would go back and forth to the spring for their water, images of "childish poverty" that would adorn postcards that tourists would send round the world (ibid.). Now, she says, the water is almost gone, as are the villages, replaced by towns and highways (ibid.). She has been running her brothel for twenty years, employing girls who are tired of carrying pails, which weigh on their memory "like massive shackles" (6). The madam's own memory is faulty, her sense of time "scrambled" in her mind, and appearing to her like one "long night" that stretches out and encompasses images and smells of "charred flesh" and "bodies, metals, mud, fire, plastic, and death mingled in a harsh, moist odor of filth, amalgam, and heartbreak" (ibid.).

Haiti is to the madam "twenty-seven thousand square kilometers of hatred and desolation," a place where "hatred grows faster than trees" (10). In her time running the brothel, she has seen hatred "swell in the girls' weariness, in the clients' eyes, right here in the house of pleasure" (ibid.). Hatred has a near physical presence: "You can almost touch it," she says. "A flabby thing, a chancre, a venomous spider's web" (ibid.). Hatred intensifies and is passed on through the desire for revenge, "payback time," as she calls it (11). Some people, she says, "live only to kill, to get their turn at killing, to repay death with death" (ibid.). In the absence of hope for social and personal advancement, people are left with a "vast rage" that manifests itself in the general desire to inflict pain. In the contemporary context, the supporters of the Aristide-like figure, the Prophet, blame the intellectuals, "the stuffed shirts of academia who warble with their heads in a bag about theories, applications, love and brotherhood, all those old fogies of humanism," and more broadly the bourgeoisie against whom the Prophet's supporters wage an apocalyptic war. "With the word of the Prophet," they say, "we'll plunge them into the darkness where we've been cowering while they sang and danced in their luxurious belvederes" (12).

Having seen many tyrants and their supporters come and go, the madam is skeptical about the apocalyptic discourse of the Prophet's supporters. She notes perceptively that "only a new prophecy can decree the death of the old one," or indeed that only a prophet can replace a prophet

(48). She questions in particular the idea that such a confrontation was destined to happen, presaged in "premonitory dreams," or otherwise inevitable. "You'll find some," she says, who will claim that prior to the event, "every abyss, every hell, every tidal wave of the apocalypse roared out of the catacombs of the universe," and that the confrontation was the fated result of a "divined promise" (15). In contrast, the madam seeks meaning in the dead, those tortured and brutalized on the streets, and wonders what they would say of the violence (ibid.). The most fearful aspect of the slaughter was that she knew many of those carrying it out, and yet on the night of the violence she could recognize none of them, nor did she know any longer whom or where she was (17).

The madam also fears that her girls might become involved in the violence. She finds a list of names in one of their rooms and scolds the girl, telling her not to "set foot here again with that filth" (22). The paper is essentially a hit list, a series of names identified as some of the worst culprits among the ranks of the Dictator's militia. Their crimes include political killings, arson, rape, and pedophilia, and the list recommends for each the death penalty. One of the interesting aspects of the list is that it describes the criminals' social and educational backgrounds, and that while most of them were either poorly educated orphans or born of incestuous unions, others were well educated professionals who had gained positions in government. There is therefore a curious alliance between the poorest and most desperate and some of the educated elite, those with nothing to lose and those with most to gain from the violence that unites them.

The madam's own social position is quite singular, in that her profession brings her into contact with all classes in society. She is in a sense detached from the political and social conflicts, and seems more concerned with the human consequences of violence. She is particularly sensitive to the means of death and the processes of burial, the ways that bodies are dumped by "stinking streams" or at the foot of barren mountains. To die like that is she says "to be deported, killed, flushed away," and forgotten, though neither she nor her girls forget any killing they have seen or any other act of violence they have witnessed. Such deaths inevitably affect the living, who live in their own worlds, cut off from one another. "For quite some time," she says, "no one has been living companionably with anyone," before asking rhetorically "how can you live with someone when you no longer know what life is" (33).

The madam is afflicted with poor eyesight; as she watches the night go up in flames, she remarks that her eyes "don't work well anymore," which seems like a physical manifestation of her growing inability to comprehend what she sees happening in the country. She no longer has the capacity to comprehend the events; and to make some sense of them, she frequently has recourse to her memory, the bank of recollections that to some extent comforts her, but also makes the current situation seem all the more desperate by contrasting it to a previously less violent, less maddening time. The degradation of individual lives is mirrored in the damage done to the natural environment. The madam writes of a previous pastoral time, of maize and flamboyant trees on the great plain of Yaguana, and contrasts it with the apocalyptic landscape of the present: the "bluish ridge of the parched massifs, hell on earth, the scrapings of the four horizons" (56). Her life and those of her girls are, she says, "beached ships, memories of abandoned villages," and they have "nothing left but the grime on the pictures in our heads" (39). All that they have, she says, are these pictures of the past, made grubby by viewing them through the eyes of the present, a moment characterized by the worst imaginable acts: in one case, the Prophet's men force a father to sleep with his daughter, and throw her baby out of the window (ibid.). Her wish is to "remake the world" by erasing the memory of that night of "triumphant hatreds," to "cheat with history," she says, and to tell it stories that could bring out its "good side" (68), though she, like the other narrators, knows that this is impossible and that the night will stand as a landmark in her life and in the history of the nation.

It is that national history that she takes to task in the latter parts of her narration. Specifically, she identifies poverty as the force that shapes everyone's existence in the country, in the present and in history. "So allow me," she says, striking a more overtly political note, "to spit on the flags and parades, on your titles and your slogans" (94). Her protest is made "in the name of bread," which becomes her own slogan and the ethical imperative behind her denunciation of Haitian political history and those who "from prophet to prophet, from dictator to dictator" offer nothing but "orgies of apocalypse," nights such as the one she recalls in horror, half-sight, and half-memory, and which constitute the apocalyptic history that has blighted her life and subjected the entire nation to the kinds of traumas that repeat themselves in time, the one acting as a prophecy for the next (95).

The Postal Worker

The unnamed post office worker describes himself as a "lazy revolutionary," and is in love with a female colleague called Laurence, who appears distant and cold, a "well-regulated machine" to whom "every male gaze was an assault, a defilement" (7). He thinks self consciously of their romance as a mundane affair, the story of which would attract a "middle brow . . . feeble-minded reader," set as it is in a "sultry setting," with "conventional sexuality" and "low-key romanticism" (ibid.). This affair nevertheless retains connotations of romantic love, while those of this narrator's friend André, a member of the "Prophet's high command," are determined by his militancy (14). André never said he loved someone, only that they were "in the struggle together" (ibid.). The narrator is André's only "infidel" friend, the only one that wasn't part of the movement (ibid.). It is André who warns the narrator not to go out on the night of the apocalyptic showdown between the supporters of the Prophet and those of the Dictator (13).

The narrator does however go out on the night of the confrontation, walking to the Turgeau area, which "swarmed," he says, "with those tragicomic symbols of ignorance and success, the mansions of the nouveaux-riches" (17). The homes, he says, "provoke the poor," who covet them due to their sharing the same tastes as the nouveaux-riches (ibid.). Indeed, it is not only the homes that are coveted, but Laurence herself, as she had discovered one time she walked into a poor neighborhood and was followed by some boys who shouted to her "Here's one! Here's one! Soon we'll get our revenge, and you high-class girls, we'll go after you first!" (54). While Laurence is unaware of the reasons for such animosity, the narrator realizes that what the boys want is to "pay back hatred with hatred," to exact a form of social and historical revenge in which the body of the bourgeois woman becomes one of the most prized spoils of war, and which echoes similar episodes in Chauvet's trilogy and Mars's *Saisons sauvages* (ibid.).

On the night of the atrocities, the narrator takes Laurence to the home of his friend Gérard, an intellectual who had been in prison during the reign of the Dictator and who had subsequently spent time in exile (26). Gérard's experiences seem to have made him something of an apocalyptic prophet, a "myth merchant" (27) as the narrator describes him, one who sees the coming night of violence as being predestined, "written on the palms of children's hands, in the bluish arc of half-moons" (26). To the narrator, Gérard is an "oracle of decadence," caught up in various mystical systems of thought that amount, he says, to "Oedipal negritude. . . . Sorcery. . . . Prophetic ravings" (27). One feels however that it is the narrator's rationalism that is out of touch with and ill-tuned to reality. Gérard senses that the narrator does not believe his predictions, but in effect his prophecy that "the forces of evil have come together to massacre one another and many innocents will perish" is realized in full the very samc night (ibid.).

The night becomes something of an apocalyptic big bang moment: a specific time that explodes into violence and hatred and that does not end that night. Rather, its blasts of destructive energy flash into the future, condemning it to relive time after time the events of that one night, which acts in this way as a prophecy of an apocalyptic time to come. It is Gérard, the one who "hated all forms of violence," who relays the stories of the night's events, the tales "in which the horror was real and the narrative fantastic" (41). In this sense the stories constitute a kind of inverted magical realism: the events are real, but when put into words they appear unreal, horrifically fantastic. Writing and words seem in this sense to be insufficient means of communicating the events—stories of men being loaded into trucks, stuffed inside large sacks with stones and thrown into the sea; of houses being surrounded, set alight, and the fleeing inhabitants being shot down (ibid.). The words seem to flatten the stories and to domesticate them in some way. The problem is perhaps that the events inevitably become narratives, stories, tales of past events told in the past tense as if they were over, while in truth their effects are still being felt in the present. As the madam notes when she is unable to console one of her girls on the night of the violence, the "young whore did not cling to her murmuring Mama, because it wasn't a novel" (49). This suggests that the night and its effects are almost impossible to retell in fiction, and the people who lived through it cannot be reduced to the characters of a novel, their traumas neatly contained in the pages of a book.

The night has significant effects on the love affair between the narrator and Laurence, and by implication, on the experiences of lovers across the country. "The death racing through the streets," he says, "drew us together as much as it threatened us" (35). The night draws them closer not in love but in fear and terror; their lives from this point "would include horrors whose tenacity would overwhelm our joys" (ibid.). As Gérard relays news of the violence, their way of holding hands "already smacked of calculation," and they become not so much lovers as each other's "insurance policy" (ibid.). The night dared them, "defied us," he says, "to keep our affections alive," but the night's horrors lead them to retreat into silence, and to feel that they had already "grown old" (37). The most difficult thing for them is to contemplate the day after; there is a kind of comfort in living "in transit" during the apocalyptic night, but the future is something they fear, and the morning becomes a dreaded "confrontation" (43).

For all that they accept the truth of Gérard's reports, there is still to them something "unreal" about them, as they are not themselves involved in the events (53). They learn of the violence in the relative safety of Gérard's home, looking out on a starry, breezy night to his garden, in "an atmosphere of tranquility" that is rendered false by the night's terrors (ibid.). The "sole reality" of that night, he says, was the terror they heard of secondhand, and which from now on would be "the great reference point" in their lives (ibid.). Indeed, the main points of reference in their lives have been set by "similar horrors," other political events that mark out not only time but also fix individual identity, to the extent that the narrator asks rhetorically "Who'd ever had time to become a real person!" (53–54).

Somewhat paradoxically, the night also brings a sense of liberation. When Gérard retires to bed, the two lovers feel unexpectedly free and at ease with one another. The narrator begins to think that he would write the novel he had been planning and that Laurence would create the kindergarten she had hoped to manage (60). This fleeting sense of happiness and well-being brings them into a "void," that exists "outside of history," a moment in which their identity and being are for once not determined by the outside, but by an apparently truer idea of themselves and what they might be and achieve were it not for the external events that punctuate their lives, intruding on their intimacy and dragging them into history, of which they are at most times prisoners (ibid.). Crucially, too, they are brought into a closer relationship with nature, as "the scent of a garden" comes through an open door, emphasizing the feeling that they are freed temporarily from history and that history in some ways works against nature, nullifying it and making it invisible and inaccessible to the senses (61).

Nature in a sense invades the house, as the room is gradually filled with the fragrance of the garden (75). Thus cocooned to some extent from the violence and returned to a more satisfying sense of themselves, the couple made love. The act was, he says, "A small defiance," a "private revolt" and a challenge to death (82). His memory of that part of the evening is however incomplete. All that he remembers, he says is that before or after he held her feet in her hands, which made him feel that he were walking along a path, "Toward a childhood happier than mine had been. Without jackboots. Without curfews. Without rumors of murder. Of disappearances. Toward a more lifelike life" (83). His reverie was however interrupted by the end of the night, the invasion of the sunlight and mechanical sounds from outside into the room, whose only defense, he says, was its "delicate garden fragrance" (ibid.).

His memory falters further when he announces that they did not in fact make love (92). He later changes his mind again and states that they did make love (100). "How could we have made love," he asks himself, "when we were perhaps already dead, uncertain of our own existence, even incapable of imagining the point of existence?" (92). All that he is sure of is that the bedroom did have the fragrance of a garden (ibid.). Indeed, as they emerge onto the post-apocalyptic scene of the streets, on which passersby talk of rapes, murders, and revenge, the garden fragrance "clung mysteriously" to them, and stays with them even as they reach their respective homes (101). The freshness of the garden is something, he says, that he "wished to keep forever" (102). But even this certainty is called into question as he offers another version of the morning's events, in which the scent of the garden fades quickly, and completely by the time he gets home, so that as he confesses, he does not know "which ending is real" (ibid.). The confusion is created by the post-apocalyptic scene of the morning after, the effect of the barrage of sights, sounds, and smells that becomes the common history of that night, and which clouds his memory of the intimate encounter he had with Laurence. As he notes, however, even on such a night, other stories can be made, and should be recorded too, for "no human story is beneath notice" (ibid.).

The Taxi Driver

The three narrators seems to live discrete, separate lives, which is one aspect of the apocalyptic society that the novel presents. Community is anathema to the apocalypse, which in this context thrives on communal breakdown and the consequent impulse to live in one's own interior world. The novel also suggests, however, that such a closed-off existence is untenable, and that individual trajectories will inevitably cross, creating bonds of interdependency and common destinies.

This is first suggested when the postal worker and Laurence take a taxi to go to visit the narrator's friend, Gérard. As such, the third narrator, the taxi driver Ducarmel Désiré, is introduced. Indeed, the taxi driver is the character that holds together the three narrative strands, in that he had a relationship in the past with a girl who would go on to work in the madam's brothel (98). As he reflects, on the night of the terror, the couple were his last fare and, like them, he finds on the street where he dropped them, Rue Sapotille, a kind of haven, a "cool smell" and a sense of isolation that he rarely finds in other parts of the city (64). His narrative is addressed to an unnamed "kid," whom he is teaching how to drive, having lost one of his legs on the night of violence. Désiré came to live in the city from the country when people with his surname were being arrested, as one with that name was suspected of sleeping with an army corporal's girlfriend (20). Through his narrative, the city is presented as a labyrinthine, almost infernal place, with an apocalyptic cast of passengers that includes "murderers[,] . . . old women, children, false prophets, fake beggars, people shamming illness, schoolgirls . . . , servants of the Gospel eager to read you the Bible while you were driving" (ibid.). At the same time, he says, people were spying on one another, ready to inform the authorities of any perceived misdemeanor (ibid.). One particular passenger sticks in his memory: a "weird guy" who carried a pile of old papers, "stars, crescent moons, the points of the compass, maps of the city" (ibid.). The man was looking for "Rue Morte, Dead Street," which he calculated to be in the center of the city, "at the intersection of the cardinal points" (21). The man says he lives on the Street of Lost Footsteps, which he describes as a "zone of utter oblivion, where they burn dreams, memories," and where exists "the perpetual motion of our dead ends" (21).

Literally living and working on the streets, the taxi driver has an intimate connection with the city, and offers his own commentaries on what he calls "the events." He sees people going hungry and judges that is what "makes your murderers" (30). He was caught on the streets as the violence took hold, the soldiers taking control of every corner, and no route remaining safe, as he drove around in a kind of panic, feeling the "soft thump" of bodies as he drove over them (31). The more he tried to escape, the more he heard the voice of the madman coming from behind him, telling him that he has found the Street of Lost Footsteps, and that "basic rate, standard rate, all roads lead to death" (ibid.).

The city streets become an apocalyptic maze with no way out, as soldiers shoot at the taxi and the driver and the madman are forced to abandon it. To escape the bullets, they jump into the Ravine des Innocents, a "huge hole, like a shadow in the shadows" that is half liquid, half solid, a kind of apocalyptic soup that gushes into the driver's mouth. The sludge is "something still alive," he says. "Like a tangle of lizards that had been smashed but not killed" (45). His feet bump into solid objects, chairs, metal drums, pieces of cars, while the upper layer is made up of a "rhythmic flow" of old magazines, dish towels, underwear, "the whole stagnant mess of the Ravine des Innocents" (ibid.). He dives twice to pull the madman to the surface, before realizing that his companion would not surface again, that he would drown there with his papers and maps (46). In diving to help the madman, he damages his own leg, which starts to fester, and is finally left behind in the ravine. Forced to remain in the sludge, the driver becomes "one" with it, with the unnamed creatures that touch him and enter his mouth, and with the other bodies that float in it (50). The smell of the Ravine stays with him permanently, and in a sense, he says, he will "never get out of there" (51).

The driver seems less concerned about his lost leg than with retrieving his car, the Toyota whose loss feels to him "like when a relative is sick and you don't know if he'll live or die" (72). After he comes out of the ravine, his one great wish is to find the car again, and it appears that this is his way of living through the violence that he witnesses—unlike the other two narrators—at firsthand. That is, he seems to focus on the car as a means of forgetting the violence; the car is an object closely related to his own security and identity, and without it he feels lost and vulnerable, again, even more so than after losing his leg.

Because he is on the streets after the violence, his narration inevitably communicates a more direct idea of the events, their horror, and their actors. As he looks for his car, he seeks the help of a young boy, called Létoilé by his mother as she believed him to have second sight (97). The boy is unable to find the Toyota, and moreover uses his name to scare soldiers, who refuse to shoot him when they hear his name. The boy is a supporter of the Prophet. "We haven't got much hope, but him, he talks to us," the boy says of the Prophet (ibid.). Through the boy's own false "gift," there is a comment made on the nature of prophecy and the susceptibility of the people to false prophets. In the scenarios the boy presents of his encounters with frightened soldiers, he comes to realize that all he has to say is that he has second sight and that "people get scared to death" (ibid.). The broader implication is that any politician need only present himself as a prophet and that they will immediately command respect from a populace rendered frightened and vulnerable by poverty and despair.

For the taxi driver, as for the other two narrators, the night of horror has a prophetic quality, in that it remains inescapable in their memories and determines to a large extent their existences, their sense of themselves and of the country they live in. He wakes up each morning with the smell of the Ravine des Innocents in his face (106). "You'd think I'd never gotten out of there," he says, and every night he is visited by images of shootings and the other horrors he experienced that evening (ibid.). Most significantly, he is inhabited by the memory and the words of the madman, who appears in his dreams, diving into and surfacing again from the Ravine des Innocents, dragging the taxi driver down with him into the depths of the ravine, at the bottom of which they find together "images of dictators, prophets, commandants[,] . . . a few million sick children" (108). "That's it," the narrator announces, struck by a kind of dystopian epiphany. "I've found it, the wretched, blood-stained, good old Street of Lost Footsteps" (ibid.). The ravine and its sludge in this sense appear as representations of Haitian history, an apocalyptic soup of the undead in which he, and by extension his entire nation, swim, or rather drown, in memories, some of which are their own while others are inherited, the legacies of a past that lives yet drains all life from the present.

The Magical Realist Apocalypse: *A l'angle de rues parallèles*

Another important text in the recent coming to prominence of the apocalyptic strain in Haitian writing is Gary Victor's *A l'angle des rues parallèles*. First published in March 2000, the novel sets out an apocalyptic vision of Haiti under the rule of an unnamed Lavalas president, who is controlled by the omnipotent Elu, the Elected or Chosen One, a prophetic figure driving the country toward complete political and social breakdown. Victor's close alignment of the demagogue with Jean-Bertrand Aristide constitutes one of the boldest and starkest denunciations of Aristide and Lavalas in any form, and contrasts sharply with the depiction of the Haitian leader in some of the influential Anglophone discourse discussed earlier in this chapter. In his introduction to the second edition of the novel, published in 2003, Victor talks of the impact the novel had in Haiti. Many read it, he says, as an "alarm call, a pessimistic and frightening vision on the present and future of my country" (9). He had hesitated before publishing the work as it wrote against the "sacred myths" of Haiti and presented that which to him was apparent: "institutionalized lies, social cowardice, power seized by imposters and thugs, and above all the resignation of intellectuals caught up in the defense of a so-called national ideology where Vodou is presented as a 'beneficial' feature of Haitian society" (ibid.). Encouraged by friends and supporters, Victor published the book, to an "astonishing" public reaction in Haiti (ibid.). On the one hand, certain critics judged it to be the most violent and "subversive" work in Haitian literature, while on the other, readers greeted it as a "courageous and necessary" take on a society that is "completely adrift, in complete decay," in which the remaining sane individuals find themselves subject to the tyranny of the nation's "mentally ill" leaders, who themselves are supported, Victor says, "by foreign interests" (10). In this crucial regard, Victor implicitly challenges the prevailing idea among influential Anglophone intellectuals that Aristide was solely a victim of external influences. In Victor's view, Aristide and Lavalas were the beneficiaries of foreign support, at least at this point in time. Victor further complicates received notions of Haitian political relations in insisting that while the ruling classes constitute a "morally repugnant elite," the "excluded venerate their chains," that is the poor are to some extent implicated in and responsible for their own condition (ibid.). Already, Victor suggests a far more complex idea of social and political ties in Haiti than is sometimes allowed by foreign critics, who seem at times too ready to present the poor as absolutely powerless in determining their own destinies.

Haiti itself is to Victor not so much a disaster waiting to happen, but one that is already well under way, "a vegetating catastrophe," as he says (ibid.). The chief architect of the disaster is the Chosen One, the Aristide-like figure, who is to Victor a "monster that came out of the mentally-ill world of Haiti, a creation of the darkest forces that one could imagine" (11). Given the risks involved in criticizing Haitian politicians in this way, Victor's work is a remarkably bold and uncompromising critique of a leader and an entire political and social system in complete and disastrous collapse. To Victor, writing the novel is almost a duty, as in his view "only a lucid and sincere testimony can perhaps help prevent the unthinkable, the unnamable, the inhuman" (ibid.).

Ironically, then, but also fittingly, Victor's narrator is a civil servant named Eric who loses his job due to IMF-directed "structural adjustment" and becomes a ruthless serial killer who wreaks havoc across Port-au-Prince, as the city and the country descend into absolute social breakdown. This is not however a novel of psychological realism; it is rather an allegorical work that recalls at once Beckett, the *nouveau roman,* Orwell, Frankétienne, and magical realism.

Of all contemporary Haitian novelists, Victor is perhaps the one who has experimented most extensively with magical realism. Historically, magical realism, or *réalisme merveilleux,* in Haitian writing has its roots in the 1930s, in the work of Carl Brouard, Léon Laleau, and Normil Sylvain. The most influential works in the magical realist mode came however in the 1950s, in the essays and fiction of Jacques-Stephen Alexis. For Alexis, Haitian art presented the real "with its cortege of the strange, the fantastic, the dream, the half-light, the mystery and the marvelous." The meeting of the real and the magical resulted finally in a "new, more contrasted equilibrium, a composition of harmonious contradiction, an entirely internal sense of grace born of the singular and the antithetical"

(Alexis, "Du réalisme merveilleux" 263). Alexis, like later Haitian magical realists such as René Depestre, therefore suggests that the magical and the fantastic are constituent parts of a particularly Haitian conception of reality and that their encounter with the real creates ultimately a harmonious balance.

In Victor's case, however, magical realism is less a means of celebrating Haiti's cultural singularity than a mode that suggests the radical and damaging reversal of order and reason. As his narrator reflects, "This country in which you were born, is it not the negation of all that is considered, elsewhere, as normality itself?" (110). Victor's magical realism is also born of the violent and often catastrophic clash of irreconcilable social groups, systems of belief, and economic forces, which exist apart from one another, in parallel realities, as the novel's title suggests. Victor's magical realism does not suggest a synthesis of opposing values, rather it proposes there is a radical disequilibrium on many levels that has deadly effects on the poor in particular. The magical exists in dreams, myths, and nightmares that are the products of reality and history, and which, far from harmonizing contradictions, seem only to exacerbate them. The magical is transformed by Victor into a vengeful and violent force, perhaps the only means left to the author to exact a kind of imaginary retribution on behalf of his characters on a society and a political system that appear in Victor's work to be themselves monstrous phenomena.

It is a desire for vengeance that drives the central figure Eric, the civil servant who becomes a serial killer as his private world and the society around him collapse. The trigger for the general apocalyptic collapse is the malfunctioning of mirrors, which no longer reflect, and appear "dead" and "grey like frozen ash" (17). The end of the mirrors' usefulness coincides with the apparent demise of literature, and poetry in particular: Eric's cousin Anastase writes poetry that "no one reads now," and the poet himself uses drugs and seems detached, unable to grasp the changing reality around him (15, 17). The poet's eyes are at one point fixed on the shiny metal of his pen, "as if they were tracking a reflection that did not exist" (20). The pen is thus connected to the mirror, in that they are two means of reflecting reality that no longer function; the comforting effects of the mirror, assuring individuals of their existence, and of poetry, commenting on and giving meaning to society, are no longer felt.

The breakdown of the mirror and the pen is a prelude to more general breakdowns, those of the broader society and lived reality itself. These are primarily urban phenomena, and the city itself appears as an apocalyptic site, notably the shantytown where Eric lives. The day in the city is "leprous," the neighborhood "filthy" and "stinking" (21). The scenes that Eric encounters crossing the Bois-de-Chêne ravine, the site of another slum, are particularly apocalyptic. There he sees, among other things, homeless people sleeping below rusted cars, a naked mad woman masturbating with a lit candle, an old man in military uniform sifting for gold in the sand, a bearded, naked man doing yoga exercises on some kitchen utensils, and a woman hanging by her feet from the branch of a tree, reciting Psalm 121, "I to the hills will lift mine eyes" (117). As if to emphasize the apocalyptic nature of the scene, the narrator evokes the image of a pastor in shorts and a tie announcing to a pack of dogs that the end of the world will come at the end of the month (118).

The streets are filled with crowds of the unemployed, traffic stands still in the dusty heat, as groups of political agitators gather on the crossroads for the midday protests (21). The protests have brought together the supporters of the Chosen One, calling for him to be president for life, and his opponents. The opponents are fated to lose however as, thanks to the drug money that he controls, the Chosen One also controls the police and the "popular organizations" that patrol the streets (22). Again, Victor, or at least his narrator, insists that the Aristide-like figure is supported by foreign powers, and that the people "deserved" their economic fate as they were in an "eternal 'mystical-revolutionary' trance" that had installed the Chosen One to power (ibid.). The people, Eric says, let themselves be "swallowed up" by the State, in the hope of being one day in charge of the popular gangs (23). They live moreover in a "virtual reality" that consists of a "supposedly glorious past," while to Eric the truth of history is that the mulatto classes, the "bastards of a generation of black slave women raped by white colonists" appropriated power from their European fathers (ibid.). This truth is however clouded by the false historical facts that circulate in every area of Haitian culture (ibid.). Eric further observes that the difference between rich and the poor in Haiti is solely a question of money; despite stark differences in living standards, everyone thinks alike, their minds are "programmed in the same way" (28). Together, all classes share a culture that to Eric is "medieval, reactionary[,] . . . completely incapable of entering into modernity" (99). It follows that Haiti's political leaders were "in the image" of the people: "ignorant, pleasure-seeking, looking for the slightest chance to take over the master's chair" (129).

Although Eric's gift is to be able to still see beyond the "false past" (24) to the truth, and he is aware of many of the causes of urban poverty, notably free market economics (49), he is largely apolitical, and his primary interest is to kill the government finance minister Mataro, whom Eric holds responsible for the loss of his job and his partner. His first victim is, tellingly, a foreign exchange dealer, who is shot because Eric did not have the money to take him to Mataro's residence (26). As Eric crosses town in a taxi, so the virus of defective mirrors spreads, throwing the people increasingly into a disorientating, surreal reality. The U.S. Department of State forbids all American aircraft from landing on Haitian soil, "to avoid the contagion" (34). The apocalyptic nature of the city intensifies too, as Eric remarks that the people seem unusually passive, "discouraged, tired of fighting for a hypothetical survival" (45). Perhaps, he wonders, the people hope unconsciously to "put an end to this interminable collective suicide" (ibid.).

Having stalked Mataro for several weeks, Eric knows his every daily movement, except for a few hours in the evening. Following Mataro across town, Eric discovers that the minister spends this time in the company of a male lover called Vicky, from the Dominican Republic. Vicky saves Mataro by standing in front of him, but dies himself from the bullet intended for the minister (350). The minister had been expecting such a moment, for he had dreamed recurrently of his own murder. The dream is of an apocalyptic breakdown, in which he is deaf and the words he writes appear inverted on his page (37). The dream also enacts a natural disaster, in which the mountains had collapsed and the "voracious" sea had advanced to the cathedral and "devoured" the shantytowns (38). The National Palace had also disappeared, though its contours were now traced by the bodies of the dead (ibid.). At this point in the dream, Mataro encountered Eric, who kills him with a knife, "to save his soul" (ibid.). Having recounted the dream, Mataro asks Eric to kill him, but Eric refuses, his murderous plan complicated by his victim's desire to die.

Eric's vengeful quest is further complicated when Mataro claims that he was not responsible for the "structural adjustment" policy that led to Eric losing his job. Mataro blames the policy on Ti Nestor, the president's *bòkò,* or Vodou priest, whom Mataro claims to be "in the pay of the whites" (40). The Vodou religion is a further aspect of Haiti's national culture that Eric (and implicitly Victor) critiques. To Eric, there is nothing more "filthy" than the Vodou gods; one only has to look at the "decadent state of the country that is their empire" to see the effects of the religion (41). The political elite, Eric says, maintain their power thanks to the "mediocrity," "cowardice," and "ignorance" of the people, whose submissiveness is attributed to the power of the "dark spirits" of Vodou (52). This critique is extended when Eric is taken to a Vodou ceremony organized by Ti Nestor and attended by the president of the republic.[6]

The event seems to recall the Bois Caïman ceremony, which is widely believed to have marked the beginning of the Haitian Revolution in August 1791. In both instances, there is a black pig that is sacrificed to the "hypnotic" rhythms of the Vodou drums, and the blood of the pig is swallowed by the participants. However skeptical he is, Eric is not immune to the effects of the drums, and finds himself dancing, entranced, and feels the "pleasure that one can draw by giving one's body and soul over to the land" (55). The sight of the drunken president brings him out of his trance however, and he makes his way to the leader, gripped by a new urge. As he closes in on the president, Eric realizes that he could kill him, but chooses instead to "piss copiously" on his face, to which the president reacts by opening his arms "with an air of profound respect" (56). Eric takes great pleasure in the act; in his mind he was "pissing on the Lavalas people, the military, the tontons-macoutes, the indigenists, the intellectuals, our damned heroes of Independence, and on all the political imposters to come" (57). His act thus constitutes a profanation of many of the sacred tenets of Haitian national history and culture. In invoking the memory of Bois Caïman, and in transforming that ceremony into an absurd and grotesque travesty, Victor literally desecrates the memory of the revolution, which to him and Eric has been manipulated and exploited by nationalist politicians and intellectuals in order to blind their supporters to the realities of the degraded present. Later, too, another liquid, this time water, is used in an attempt to cleanse himself of the vestiges of history, which cling to him like dirt. As he cleans himself with fresh water, he imagines "the water of the origins" flowing from the past "to cleanse my memory of our *lwa,* our Toussaints, our Dessalines, our Pétions, our strong men, our Papa Docs, and all those still making our miserable history" (119). Tellingly, though, this process is interrupted when the water suddenly stops. The water company, Eric remarks, works to a "completely unpredictable" timetable. History is also a kind of prison, consisting of inescapable, recurring situations and events. This is emphasized when Eric is warned against leaving the country by Mataro, because there is a "veritable massacre" of fleeing Haitians taking place at the Dominican border, a situation that recalls previous tensions between Haiti and its island neighbor, most notably the 1937 massacre of Haitian workers at the border.

The main target of the book's political critique is the Chosen One, who is throughout a shadowy figure who only appears through official statements, and yet is omnipresent. To him, the mirror issue is a "sign from above," telling the people to no longer believe in the lies of the traditional elite. "The same stupidities," Eric reflects, "that these stinking politicians have been saying for two centuries" (63). To Eric, the Chosen One and Lavalas are but the latest manifestations of well-established political patterns, founded on nationalist ideas of Haitian exceptionalism, which is alluded to in the words of an unnamed old man who protests that Haitians do not need mirrors or to read for, he says, "We are not humans. We are Haitians" (113). In a classroom run by Lavalas supporters, Eric sees a photograph of the Chosen One among images of the great revolutionaries (66). "It was grotesque," he says, "but in the logic of filthy Haitian megalomania" (67). When he hears the famous proclamation of the revolutionary figure Boisrond Tonnerre—"We need the skin of a white for parchment, his skull for a writing case, his blood for ink, and a bayonet for a pen"—recited by children in the shantytown, it seems to him like an "obscenity" (ibid.). It makes him think that there may be young cannibals gathered nearby, ready to exact revolutionary revenge. The fact that he is not white gives him initially a sense of security, which fades quickly as he asks himself what difference there is between the skull of a white and that of a black, the blood of a white and that of a black. Even if he like every Haitian retains the memory of slavery, he questions the worth of having children still recite such formulations, which "stink of the most filthy and dark hatred" and which had "served only to let flow the blood of blacks and, finally, to tear open this land" (68). The stories of the revolution and Lavalas' theology of liberation are to Eric "shit that imposters of politicians, historians . . . fed to an army of imbeciles" (70).

The most extreme human products of this historical and political discourse are the *Chimères,* presented here as "wild rastas," the heavily drugged "vanguard" of Lavalas power, always ready to inflict violence on the orders of the Chosen One (69). These ultraviolent groups give themselves suitably apocalyptic names, such as "the Cannibal Army," and "the Vampire Army" (ibid.).

The general apocalyptic scenario is compounded by the presence of various Protestant religious groups, notably Jehovah's Witnesses, who have attracted thousands of converts since the mirrors stopped functioning, all of them convinced that it is a sign announcing the end of the world (77). As the general breakdown intensifies, Eric is not surprised to see a Protestant church "packed to the rafters" (99). More traditional, longstanding symbols of Haitian religion are themselves drawn into the absurd apocalyptic breakdown. In particular a diminutive statue of Saint Peter comes to life and shares to some extent Eric's vision of a city and society in a state of complete degradation (85–86). The biblical resonances are compounded when a plague of flies descends on the city, attaching itself to people, vehicles, houses, and churches (125).

The breakdown of logic and order is exemplified in the murder of Anastase, Eric's cousin the poet, who is said (by the escaped statue of Saint Peter) to have been killed at the angle of two parallel streets. His death was to some degree foreshadowed in the title of his most famous poetry volume, *A l'angle des rues parallèles* (At the angle of the parallel streets), which is of course also the title of Victor's novel. Again, Eric is virtually the only one to retain a capacity to think rationally, and on hearing the news of Anastase's murder at this site he feels assaulted by "all the madness in the world" (97). This feeling grows as all written texts in the country become inverted, their words only readable in reverse order. When Eric goes to view Anastase's body, he finds in his cousin's hand a piece of paper folded in his hand. On it is a carefully written message that, to his great despair, Eric cannot read. "How to read?" he asks, "there are not even any more mirrors" (105). Together these two phenomena related to reading and writing suggest something of a crisis for Haitian authors and readers. Eric's remark that there are no more mirrors seems to suggest the lack of literary models on which to draw in order to represent the absurd, apocalyptic reality he lives in, while his difficulty in reading suggests a similar crisis for readers. When he asks how to read the scrap of paper, he seems to position himself alongside the reader of Victor's novel and to acknowledge the difficulties of reading such a work that abandons logic and reason in such a disorientating way.

Although he is somewhat disdainful of Anastase's poetry, Eric recognizes that literature is important. He realizes also that the political authorities are against literature. For example, when he goes back to the home he shared with Anastase, he believes the poet's room had been ransacked by the police "because it was the workplace of an intellectual" (109). Literature's importance is emphasized through the message left by Anastase, which contains in cryptic form clues to understanding the distorted reality in which they live. The message is read to Eric by his companion Marjorie, one of several prostitutes in the novel, and consists of two enigmatic questions: "Did the mirrors become blind or was it we who chased away the light?" and "What is hidden by the saint's robe?" (106) The first question invites them to reflect on their implication in the affair of the mirrors and whether it is merely a symptom of a broader campaign against enlightenment, while the second seems to refer cryptically to religious figures and what lies behind surface appearances. The final sentence states, "At the angle of the parallel streets is found the solution to the mystery of the perpetual captives" (ibid.). The perpetual captives seem to be the Haitian people, while the parallel streets may relate to non-reconciled binaries in Haitian history and society: mulattoes and blacks; town and country; French and Creole; tradition and modernity. Only when these meet will they be resolved; but at the same time logic dictates that they cannot meet, just as two parallel streets cannot come together.

While the book becomes something of an absurd detective novel, poetry is also valorized through the figure of Marjorie who, she reveals, was forced to become a prostitute because the man she loved, the government minister for education, abandoned her while she was pregnant because of her passion for poetry. In vowing to avenge her, Eric becomes by default a defender of poetry and reading more generally, even though, as he says, he does not know whether or not he likes poetry (ibid.). Poetry reappears as an important means of decrypting the complex "puzzle" (127) related to the inverted mirrors and the series of increasingly apocalyptic events that the book presents: for instance, people start to walk backwards, a phenomenon welcomed by the Chosen One as an "accelerated evolution," a mutation that "scares the whites" (154). Marjorie is able to read from Anastase's collection enigmatic lines that seem to relate to the distorted reality they find themselves in: "The façade is the reverse of my chameleon skin/The day, hunted, takes refuge in the belly of the pachyderm/The footsteps of the Chosen One lead me to the ruins of the cathedral/The child on the doorstep mourns the decapitated moon" (145). Neither Marjorie nor Eric attempts to interpret the poem, and its meaning remains obscure, though the lines do seem to at once speak of the present and have a prophetic quality. The reversed façade suggests an inverted reality, while the "chameleon skin" seems to refer to changing, opaque phenomena and to value those phenomena. It may also refer to his poetry, which in a sense is his skin, a part of him that is exposed to the world but which remains necessarily obscure and difficult to define. The day, referring most obviously to light, is hunted down, tracked or on the run and hiding out in the belly of the pachyderm, which may be a reference to a pig, perhaps the one sacrificed at Bois Caïman and recalled in the profane Vodou ceremony that Eric attends. The Chosen One's path leads to the ruined cathedral, while a child mourns the decapitated moon, images that seem to suggest a vision of a current or future collapse, which takes place at night, a time of complete darkness with no moon and the ultimate result of the day hunted down and unseen. While the poetry seems to suggest that it will be political forces that bring about this apocalyptic future, it is difficult not to read these lines in the post-earthquake period as an intuitive insight that sensed a coming disaster. Poetry is therefore seen as vital in making sense of the past and the future, however obscure it is and however far removed it is from the simplistic rhetoric of nation and glorious revolution.

Given that Eric is a serial killer, there is obvious, and surreal, irony that he is the one who defends God. Later in the novel, God appears in the form of an old man dressed like a Haitian peasant, and riding a donkey whose eyes light up the road ahead (139). The Chosen One declares that he will kill God, and with God dead there will no longer be either morality or transcendence. The Chosen One will have all the power (154). "After having drunk the blood of the pig for more than two centuries," the Chosen One declares, "we will soon drink the blood of God" (155). Marjorie informs Eric that the death of God was prophesied in Anastase's poetry, and Eric rushes to the aid of God, in vain as God is shot dead (157). As an apocalyptic band of half-men, half-cows trap and kill the donkey, it is as the Chosen One predicted, the end of transcendence, that is in this case the end of a law or a morality other than or beyond that determined by the material world of Haiti (198). Transcendence is to Eric the only means for man "to raise himself fully to his proper status" (167). The death of God and the banishment of transcendent law signify the ultimate victory of the Chosen One, and the beginning of a final apocalyptic descent for the country, as the trumpet of the fifth angel of the apocalypse is heard in the city (161), "darkness and silence engulf the land" (158), and Marjorie wonders, "What will we become?" (159).

Eric's failure to save God leads him to critique Anastase and his role in the events. "Like many poets," Eric says, Anastase "had sensed the coming of the great wave, felt its vibrations" (160). But as Eric observes, readers and critics saw in his work only a masterpiece of writing and not a text that announced "nature's revenge on mankind" (ibid.). To Eric it is "mad" for critics to see writing "as an end in itself" (ibid.). As such, Eric seems less concerned with writers than with readers and critics. The appreciation of texts, he seems to say, should not be a simple matter of evaluating stylistic or aesthetic qualities in themselves. The prophecies contained in Anastase's work were largely ignored or misunderstood by readers, including Eric, who wonders if he should have "listened less indifferently" to Anastase (163). Indeed, Anastase's style, such as it is revealed in the novel, is itself apocalyptic and prophetic, full of obscure images and phrases that suggest his intuition of a coming general breakdown. By implication, Victor seems to call for the reader of his novel to think beyond the words and images and reflect on the "message," Victor's own intuition that the society is on the brink of a major disaster, the cause of which is again to him political, but the effects of which will be natural or environmental. Literature must in this sense be taken seriously, its insights considered as possible presentiments of events to come and as incitements to action to avert disaster.[7]

Victor's own prophetic intuition is most acute near the end of the novel, when he presents the apocalyptic events that follow the death of God. The plagues of flies block out the light of the sun and the earth trembles, "the asphalt of the road rose up, transformed itself into a solid wave" that crashes into a row of houses, which fall apart, to the agonized cries of the wounded and suffering (165–66). To the little Saint Peter, the earthquake coincides with the burial of the poet, an idea that to Eric is an unbearable "obscenity," and he kills the saint, apparently to assuage his own regret over his indifference to poetry. Tellingly, it is poetry that stops the disaster: the earthquake stops suddenly and Eric sees Marjorie, who now appears "haggard" and clings only to her rosary, having offered the book of poems to the earthquake. "I believe," she says in an ultimate affirmation of the importance of poetry, "that it was this that calmed the land," (166), a phrase that refers to the immediate cessation of the natural disaster, but also it appears to the potential of literature to bring meaning and peace to the land more broadly, to the people and society.[8]

In a crucial sense, the novel's magical realist form reflects the general reversal of logic and the deliberate elimination of systems of thought and being that transcend the closed world of Haitian history and nationalist politics. Eric refers to this process when he writes of how Haiti has always sought to overturn the logic of transcendence, "like a bad actor plays with masks to show himself in another light" (168). The aim of this play of masks has been not only to shelter from others, but also to "hide ourselves from ourselves" and to escape the changes that happen naturally with time (ibid.). This contortion of identity and being is reflected in the way that the novel overturns the categories of the magical and the real. In Victor's magical realism, the magical and the fantastic—in this case the nightmarish, the illogical, the monstrous—become real, while the real—order, logic, reason—appears as fantastic, alien, and foreign. In this sense, Victor's style itself is a product of the meeting of apparently irreconcilable forces, which come together at the "angle of mad parallels, the angle of false parallels" that characterize for him the evolution of Haitian history and society (ibid.). Victor in this way works against nature, but he knows that to do so is ultimately futile, for nature is unforgiving, and will always "take its revenge" (ibid.). His figure Eric is a grotesque and extreme example of the Haitian antihero figure, one who kills to save, who is apolitical and indifferent, but engaged and vengeful. Ultimately, in this crucial way, Eric and any individual is part of nature, a crucial element in the whole natural system that will react against imbalance and distorted reality violently, vengefully.

History and Allegory in *Moloch Tropical*

To conclude this chapter, I turn to Raoul Peck's 2009 film *Moloch Tropical,* surely one of the most critical and damning of all artistic reactions to Jean-Bertrand Aristide's rule. The title, content, and structure of the film refer to Alexander Sokurov's *Moloch* (1999), a biographical film that presents Adolf Hitler and his entourage at a Bavarian mountaintop retreat in 1942, just before the German defeat at Stalingrad. Sokurov's film is one of a trilogy that engages with major political figures—the other two films are *Taurus* (2001) on Lenin and *The Sun* (2005) on Hirohito—and which are concerned less with the "defining actions of twentieth-century dictators than with their shadowy inner lives." Also, Sokurov's three films tend to "humanize" their subjects, largely through "separating the man from the myth."[9] While Peck's film shares to some extent these qualities, it could be argued that his humanization of his tyrant figure, one based most directly on Jean-Bertrand Aristide, also involves a process of demonization, in which the monstrous politician eclipses the human figure almost completely.

What is also interesting in Peck's film is that Aristide is at once himself and an apparent amalgam of other Haitian despots. The setting underscores this idea, in that the film takes place not in Port-au-Prince but in the historically loaded location of the Citadelle Laferrière, Henri Christophe's fortress that is at once a magnificent edifice and a monument to the folly and paranoia of political leaders in Haiti.[10] Thus, although many of the references and events in the film relate to Aristide's second term in office, the temporal frame of the film is left deliberately open so that the present is forever inhabited by the past and conversely the past stands as a kind of prophecy for the present and the future.

Unlike *L'homme sur les quais, Moloch Tropical* eschews a realistic portrayal of a specific time in Haitian history. Instead, somewhat like literary works such Depestre's *Le mât de cocagne* and Gary Victor's *A l'angle des rues parallèles*, the film presents an allegorical Haiti, which again has the effect of evoking a recognizable time, place, and set of characters, while leaving open the various frames of reference so that the film's events resonate over different periods. In some senses, allegory functions in the film almost like Glissant's idea of the detour, in that meaning is often created through indirection and allusion rather than through direct commentary.

The Aristide-like figure seems to embody this allegorical form of representation. He is the first character that we see, lying alone in a luxury bedroom, with a copy of the Bible beside him and a large statue of the crucifixion lit up in a side room, an early allusion to the president's self perception as a messianic figure. Stitched into his bed sheets are his forename initials: JDD, Jean de Dieu, or Jean of God. The connection to Aristide is perhaps not immediately evident, largely because the actor is light-skinned, in fact not even of Haitian origin: the lead role is played by Zinedine Soualem, the French actor of North African origin. His first act upon waking is to accidentally smash a glass of water, the broken shards of which he later steps on, leaving him to hobble around the palace for the rest of the movie, a state that casts him as a somewhat absurd figure, limping through the events of the film.

These events are most directly situated at the end of 2003 and the beginning of the bicentenary year of 2004, a time period indicated by the television news images of unrest on the streets of Port-au-Prince and other contemporary images, such as those of the Abu Ghraib affair, of Saddam Hussein and George W. Bush, two other figures implicated in the film's critique of contemporary local and global politics. The news channels seem to be running constantly throughout the palace, and have the effect of establishing the contemporary moment as perhaps the primary point of interest, while the physical setting in the Citadelle indicates the other broader, densely layered historical frames of reference.

The labyrinthine passages, various doorways, and numerous mirrors placed throughout the palace suggest that this film is about the relationship between a physical place (Haiti) and its people. The physical features suggest a complex, though connected history, the various frames in which that history is judged and the elusive notion of identity, the need to consider one's reflection, which in the film is often refracted or presented through carefully positioned mirrors in such a way that they reflect one another, and identity seems to be either revealed or obscured through this play of mirrors.

For example, the president's wife is often presented alone, as in an early scene where she sits in a deep blue dress in a room in which the carpets, walls, and many other features are also in shades of blue. Before she appears in the scene, the camera pans slowly across her dressing table, which is strewn with bottles of perfume and other cosmetics, which are reflected in the mirror, as is her empty bed to the rear of the room. The mise-en-scene suggests opulence, while the predominant blue colors introduce a note of coldness and isolation. To a Haitian audience, the blue colors, including the deep blue dress, would probably frame the president's wife as a kind of Erzulie figure, a beautiful light-skinned woman cast here as an unloved cuckold, living in solitude in the palace.

The importance of image, presentation, and framing is underscored in the extended theme of the role of the media, and the anxiety of the president's entourage over the press's coverage of the president. An unfavorable newspaper headline sends the president's officials into a panic, and leads to their setting up a presidential address to the nation. The president is prepared for the address by his advisers and a makeup artist, all of whom are concerned with appearances and with presenting an enhanced image of the president, who is also later accused by his mother of whitening his skin. Lining up his camera, the cameraman tells the president that he is "too low," which suggests that he does not measure up not only physically, but also perhaps morally or intellectually. The president's speech evokes the memory of the revolution and the "black hero" Toussaint Louverture. Preaching a message of peace, economic justice, and security, he repeats to the people the dictum "he conquers twice who conquers himself in victory." He also refers to the indemnity that Haiti paid to France in the nineteenth century, and demands that France repay the money at today's rates, before ending with a declaration of his love for the people.

The play between image and reality, and between the public and private spheres, is further extended when, shortly after his message of peace and reconciliation, he launches a tirade against the press and those he terms the mulatto intellectuals who constitute his most outspoken critics and who are responsible for the unfavorable press he is receiving. "Since when do the people know what they want?" he asks, before demanding revenge on the journalist, who wrote the article under a pseudonym.

Just as the play between the public and the private is explored, so is that between the insular and the extra-insular. This further element is introduced through the presence in the country of an American film crew, made up entirely of African-American actors, which is there to make a film on Toussaint Louverture. That which putatively connects the Americans to the Haitians—the notion of a shared racial heritage—is quite quickly subsumed by the differences between the two groups, differences of history and racial politics that lead the Americans to cast Haiti as a legend of black insurrection, while the contemporary reality is of a country divided still by race and color conflicts and ruled by a despot.[11]

As the president's officials fret over the limited attendance of foreign officials at the bicentenary celebration events—one is aghast at the presence of "Arab or African" representative of France, and declares "I need whites"—in the dungeons below the journalist suspected of criticizing the president is tortured brutally. Stripped naked and beaten badly, the journalist appears like a modern-day slave, the effect of which is to confuse the sense of time and to emphasize the temporal play of mirrors and frames: the past is far from over, and the present is a distorted reflection of the past.

This sense of distortion is also suggested through the palace orchestra, which rehearses throughout the film for the bicentenary celebrations. Composed of young, working-class musicians, the orchestra struggles to play in tune, and the sound it creates is rather tuneless, the product of a disparate set of individuals, rather than a group playing in harmony with itself. One of the film's subplots concerns two young lovers, one a saxophone player and the other a palace servant, both of whom want to leave Haiti. While the latter receives money for sex from the president to fund her dream of leaving, when the former asks the female minister of culture for help, he too is powerless to refuse her demands for sexual recompense in kind. The class issue is further emphasized when the minister hears the young man's name, which indicates his humble background: "You won't go far with a name like that," she says. Later, too, the orchestra leader uses the word "peasant" as an insult to the young man, who subsequently attacks the leader. The suggestion in these cases is that the country more broadly is riven still by class and color divisions, that it is out of tune with itself and that the bombastic anthems of the past translate into the present as grating, discordant sounds.

As civil unrest mounts on the streets, the president is advised to "move quickly, and strike hard," through "unleashing" the Chimères, who are encouraged to "strike harder" against the demonstrators. Given the Dessalinian order to "coupe tet, brule kay," the heavily armed Chimères take to the streets, beating and slashing their way through the protesters.

While the Chimères seem to manifest one legacy of the revolution that is being celebrated—that of unresolved social division and intra-class violence—the tortured journalist recalls another: the slave beaten almost half to death but who refuses to yield to violence. Tied upright to an old metal mattress, he appears almost Christlike, or even a kind of zombie figure, beaten to a state between life and death. Summoned to the president's dining table, the journalist seems to function as the lost political conscience of the leader, who opens up as if in a confessional. "Power's not easy," the president confides, "You've always stayed on the right side of things," while the leader has endured three years of exile, and only returned under strict conditions imposed by the United States. "They didn't leave me much room, democratically speaking," he says. To the president's questions on the journalist's motivations, the hushed, barely audible reply is "I speak the truth." For the president however, there are many truths, revised and perhaps distorted by events and by power. "Democracy is costly," and "power is something you wield concretely," the president says, accusing the journalist of never going "beyond theory." The journalist refuses to yield, asking only for a cigarette, like a condemned man. Democracy, the president insists, "demands sacrifices," a statement that the journalist agrees with, before pronouncing that the president is "not a monster," for he lacks in "majesty or madness." "You have twisted everything," the journalist says, "destroyed everything." Once the "people's hope," the president "soiled the dream," through wanting to be a prophet, but ended up as the pitiful figure that the film represents. This is one of the most politically charged scenes in the film, and its resonance derives from the way it suggests an enduring bond between the two figures, who are cast as adversaries and yet have a shared history. The journalist remains true to his principles, but is beaten to death for them; the president's experience of political power indicates that a leader is almost fated to have his ideals compromised. One senses in this scene an almost existentialist examination of power, and an echo of Sartre's *Les mains sales* with its idea that one can never govern and still keep one's hands clean. Quite strikingly in this regard, just after speaking with the journalist the president is seen scrubbing his hands vigorously, as if to cleanse them of the metaphorical blood and dirt gathered in the business of running the country. Rather than two distinct figures, the president and the journalist appear as intimately connected beings, the one the flip side of the other. As the president says to the journalist as he is taken away before being sacrificially burned by the president's henchmen, "Whatever happens . . . we will always be brothers." Paradoxically, the journalist is at once the president's greatest adversary and his closest acquaintance. Watching the journalist die, the president grieves as if he is losing a part of himself, and utters mournfully "My friend, my brother."

Indeed, the president's folly only intensifies following the killing of the journalist. He appears broken, and his speech to mark the bicentenary is an incoherent mix of references to Haitian history and the "political terrorism" that has undermined the nation, in which he casts himself in relation to Christ, Joan of Arc, de Gaulle, Gandhi, and Martin Luther King Jr., among others. Later, by the light of a full moon, he runs naked through the hills outside the Citadelle citing to himself passages from the Bible, as virtually all of the other characters in the film abandon the palace, and by extension Haiti.

When the American government withdraws its support, the president resigns and is forced to leave Haiti, thereby underscoring one of the film's most important themes: that those in power will do virtually anything to remain in power and in Haiti, while the poor, such as the saxophonist and the maid, will do almost anything to leave the country. Indeed, the film closes rather enigmatically with the maid walking down the road from the palace. As the departing president's car passes her she is shot against the blue sky and breaks unexpectedly into a smile, looking to her right across the mountains and over the valley below, where bright rays of sunshine have broken through the clouds to create finally a scene of majesty, grandeur and serenity, all of which qualities seemed absent while the president held on to power.

Ultimately, the works studied in this chapter are crucially different from those discussed in chapter 1. The works on Duvalier are essentially anti-apocalyptic in that they are fundamentally concerned with recovering memory and ending the apocalyptic trauma that is still associated with the Duvalier period. The novels by Trouillot and Victor are by contrast written more or less as the events happen, and are in this sense forms of firsthand chronicles of the lived experience of the Aristide period. There is an immediacy in the works on Aristide that does not so much unveil the apocalyptic underpinnings of the society as communicate the confusion and terror of living in such a time of chaos and uncertainty. In terms of narrative style, the works in this chapter, though they deal with very immediate and real events, eschew narrative realism in favor of various indirect narrative forms—Peck's allegorical style, Victor's surreal, magical realism, and Trouillot's blend of narrative voices and styles. Finally, the sharing of the story in this way suggests the difficulty of apprehending from a single perspective the full horror of living in the apocalyptic present.

3 The Chimères and the Haitian Antihero

Maximilien Laroche writes of an archetypal antihero figure in Haitian writing, whose function is to transform "an individual decline into a collective deliverance." In Haitian literature, Laroche writes, "the hero makes himself a zombie amongst zombies in order to free the community. And it is by accepting his victimhood, by acknowledging it, that he denounces it, and thereby attacks the victimization to which he and his people are subject" (n.p.). Laroche's theory of the Haitian antihero addresses patterns of victimization and self-sacrifice in Haitian literature—notably in classic works of fiction by Roumain, Alexis, and others. His idea however seems to apply more broadly to national history, and to its very beginnings, in that Toussaint Louverture, Dessalines, and Christophe all died in the process of, or soon after, liberating their people. These seminal events seem in some ways to have left a deep imprint in Haitian political history and to have instigated an antiheroic pattern that manifests itself throughout subsequent history and perhaps most recently in the figure of Jean-Bertrand Aristide, who has consistently sought to frame his own political demise in relation to that of Toussaint Louverture, or else as suggested in Peck's *Moloch Tropical,* as a form of Christlike martyrdom. This chapter considers the figure of the Haitian antihero, in history, literature, and film. Building on the ideas of Maximilien Laroche, the chapter argues that the figure's classic movement from resistance to self-sacrifice is an apocalyptic one. The chapter considers recent manifestations of this antiheroic figure, notably in Lyonel Trouillot's *Bicentenaire* (2004) and Yanick Lahens's *La couleur de l'aube* (2008). The main part of the chapter considers the history and representation of the Chimères, Aristide's militia hired from the urban slums, and who appear in literary and cinematic works as apocalyptic figures, grotesque, nihilistic re-figurations of the Tontons macoutes. Representations of the Chimères in the two literary works are compared and contrasted to those in the films *Ghosts of Cité Soleil* (2006) and *Haïti, la fin des Chimères?* (2004). As such, the chapter revisits the complex question of evaluating and explaining the differences in representations of Haiti by Haitian and non-Haitian writers and filmmakers. In contrast to the various forms of narrative indirection identified in chapter 2—Peck's allegorical style and Victor's surreal magical realism—the representations of the Chimères discussed in this chapter are marked by forms of psychological realism, which amount to attempts to imagine the lived experience of the Chimères, who appear as the apocalyptic subjects par excellence, in that the creative works seek to expose through them the often obscured truths related to history, politics, and economics that create over and again the apocalyptic reality in which they exist.

Chimerical Beginnings

The very name Chimère has apocalyptic overtones, in its suggestion of a being made up of composite parts, a monster that is only part human, or indeed a ghost, a phantom that is aware that it is not fully alive, existing somewhere between life and death, existence and oblivion.[1] Perhaps fittingly, the genesis of the Chimères is difficult to trace, and tied up in the intricate history of street gangs and their political affiliations. Two of the most notorious Chimères, the brothers Winston Jean-Bart and James Petit-Frère—better known as Tupac and Billy—are said to have been alumni of Aristide's Lafanmi Selavi institute for street children (Deibert 166). The Lafanmi Selavi program was founded in the mid-1980s. Rooted in Haiti's liberation theology movement, the project centered on an orphanage for the street boys of the La Saline district. More generally, the project was conceived as "a new template of Haitian citizenship, built on a foundational ideology that would support the pillars of the new postcoup nationalism: justice, reconciliation, democracy, and poverty with dignity" (Kovats-Bernat 144–45). Guided by a philosophy of education that developed a "radically politicized child identity," Lafanmi held the unique ambition of not only feeding street children, but also of creating "citizen-children" (17, 167). The political contexts in which Lafanmi existed rendered such an aim extremely difficult to attain. The Cedras coup against Aristide led to martial law and the criminalization of democratically oriented groups, including Lafanmi Selavi. Politically motivated attacks on the orphanage intensified and even when Aristide returned to power in 1994, the macoutist violence against Lafanmi continued (169). In effect the macoutes had a long history of violent interaction with the street children, who had played a prominent role in the popular mobilization against Jean-Claude Duvalier in 1986 (166). Under constant threat of attack by political opponents, conditions at Lafanmi gradually deteriorated to a level little better than that of street living. Forcibly closed by a government paramilitary in 1999, the Lafanmi nevertheless produced successive cohorts of boys and young men for whom street violence had been a means of survival, and who allied that defensive instinct to the politicized sensibility that the educational program had fostered (122, 150).

There appears to be no evidence that all those attached to the Chimères had been through Lafanmi, but the direct link to key Chimères such as Billy and Tupac does seem to indicate that Lafanmi was an important training ground for at least some of the most prominent figures. In Deibert's account, one gets a sense of the ways in which the street children became politicized through Lafanmi and the generally held perception that Aristide sought to improve the lot of the poor. Hailing from Cité Soleil, the shantytown on the northern edge of Port-au-Prince, Billy and Tupac were orphaned through the politically motivated killings of their parents. Attending for a time Lafanmi Selavi, the orphans had become "child[ren] of Aristide" (179). "We want to try and help our people now President Aristide has been the only president who has tried to do something for poor people like us," Billy confided (180). The curious ethical foundation of such an enterprise is suggested in a speech Billy made on behalf of the gangs of Cité Soleil in January 2002. "President Titid," Billy read, "The *alfabetizasyon* [literacy] program cannot happen with war going on. *Alfa-ekonomik* cannot happen with war. No development can blossom if there is no peace in Cité Soleil. In that sense, President Titid, the only thing that can establish peace is to open another police sub-station in Cité Soleil" (181). The interesting thing here is that the gangsters' stated aim is to have stricter law enforcement through the establishment of a new police sub-station in the heart of their territory. This seems in turn to be the only means of achieving the broader objective of social improvement for their neighborhoods. The Chimères, or at least their leaders, in this sense appear as unwilling gangsters, forced into violence to achieve peace. As one gang member at the same meeting remarked, "We would give the guns up if we could," for "Who would want to live like this if they didn't have to?" (182).

Such ethical paradoxes underpin many of the literary representations of the Chimères. Morality and ethics are often malleable, not based on rigid demarcations of right and wrong, but subject to change according to context. The Chimère embodies and enacts the ethical paradoxes born of a social and political situation in which violence and the desire for social justice are often closely intertwined.

The Chimère is something of a shape-shifter, hyper-real and yet also imaginary, a product of dreams, fears, and desires who remains forever elusive and unknowable, between living and dying, a phantom of the past and of the future. These qualities are discernible in perhaps the best-known representation of the Chimères to date, Danish director Asger Leth's 2006 film *Ghosts of Cité Soleil.* Itself a curious, hybrid object, the film is a form of documentary, yet with elements of drama and reality TV that undercut its claims to represent an unmediated form of the truth. In terms of style and the presentation of the "gangster with a heart of gold" the film is close to fictional feature films like *City of God* (2002) and *Tsotsi* (2005), set respectively in the favelas of Rio de Janeiro and the shantytowns of Johannesburg (Garland 180–81).[2] It picks up on the story of Billy and Tupac, though in a way that is quite different to the more balanced, sociological treatment they receive in Deibert's book. In the film, the Chimères are paraded before the intended Western audience as its exotic other. The film has a voyeuristic element that allows the viewer to pass into the existence of the film's cast for ninety minutes, and then to leave it completely, strangely unmoved and only faintly unsettled by this representation of what it calls "the most dangerous place on earth."

The film does not undertake a serious investigation of the Chimères, or the social and political contexts in which they came into being. Rather, it begins in the chaotic moment of early 2004, "with demonstrations in the streets and rebels closing in," which, it says, led Aristide to "enlist . . . the support of armed gangs from the slum of Cité Soleil." The first human image is of Tupac, smoking in the dark. Tellingly, his first words are about the future, or rather the difficulty of imagining his time to come. "How my life gonna be?" he asks. His ability to speak freely in English seems to add to his hybrid, Chimerical quality, and to compound the sense that he and others like him are at once of this place and also do not belong.[3] Tupac's question has a rhetorical quality, as he shakes his head in response to his own question and can only answer by repeating twice, "I don't know."

As he does so, he closes his eyes, as if he is imagining his future, or as if he cannot picture it without absenting himself momentarily from the place in which he lives. As he says later, in Cité Soleil "you never live long. Always die young." The life of a Chimère only hastens one's demise, for as he says, "The more you kill, the shorter your life is." As such, Tupac presents himself from the outset, perhaps unintentionally, as an antiheroic, apocalyptic figure, existing (not living) in the present, apparently unable to conceive of the future as anything other than a void, the blackness to which he returns as he closes his eyes.

Cité Soleil is itself portrayed as an apocalyptic place, an overpopulated wasteland, its people living by open sewers in half-built shacks. The film does however tend to exoticize the place too, in that scenes of poverty are juxtaposed with clips of Vodou ceremonies.[4] Also, the film's music, composed by Wyclef Jean and consisting largely of hip-hop beats and rapped lyrics, has the effect of presenting Cité Soleil as the ultimate "hood," a gangster's domain, a paradise that is also an infernal dystopia. The Chimères themselves are cast in part as glamorous gangsters, ruling their neighborhood, driving through it in their 4×4 with their automatic weapons on display, again to a hip-hop soundtrack that connects them to the broader world, and similar figures, notably the gangster rappers of the United States. As Tupac states, "They may call me a gangster, but I am also a rapper."

True to his chimerical identity, Tupac plays many different roles: at various points, he is a benign gangster, a sensitive orphan-poet, an attentive father, or a lover. But he is also at times merciless: "I'm Tupac," he says at one point, "I'll eat you alive and no one will ever know." While in many ways he is portrayed as ultra-real and an authentic gangster, he also seems to see himself as an imitation, a false being made up of other people. Out on the streets, driving through the neighborhood, a Tupac Shakur song comes on his car stereo, and he declares to the camera, "That's the *real* Tupac." By implication, Haitian Tupac is something other than real, a kind of actor whose identity is as elusive and unknowable to the viewer as it is to himself.

Tupac's identity is also played against and to some extent determined by that of his brother, Billy. Again, there is a play of difference and sameness that seems to produce an individual's identity: like Tupac, Billy is a Chimère, but unlike Tupac, Billy appears to have a social and political conscience. While Tupac insists he is a "thugster, a gangster," Billy, he says, "wants to be president . . . of Haiti," an ambition that is ultimately as unattainable as Tupac's to become an international rap star. While Billy wants to be president, Tupac scorns and derides his country: "Fuck Haiti, man," he says. In effect, the brothers appear as two halves of a full being, their identities in some senses cut in two, dualistic parts, but also sharing the fundamental emptiness and despair that is the lot of the apocalyptic subject.

Billy has a more nuanced understanding of affairs than his brother. While Tupac seems to favor action, Billy is more reflective and appears more aware of the roles he is playing and for whom he is playing them. When the film begins to focus on him, he declares to the camera, "We are on the microphone. We must have the power," a statement that indicates his awareness of the power play that the very making of the film involves, and that those who have the ability to speak and to be heard are those who control various forms of power. At the same time, Billy's conception of his life is in many ways as apocalyptic as that of his brother. At one point, he says that he cannot stop fighting for Aristide, for to do so would be to bring about his own demise. "I stop, I die," as he puts it.

While in many senses the two brothers are allies, they are also in other ways rivals, most prominently in regard to the French aid worker Eleanor Senlis, known in the film as "Lele." The love triangle introduces an element of melodrama, the most interesting aspect of which lies in trying to decipher the motivations of each of the three. Lele appears almost as a caricature of an outsider attracted to the exotic thuggery that the brothers apparently represent. She mingles with the Chimères, safe in the knowledge that she can retire at any time from the slums to the security of her hotel. Indeed, when she first appears, she is on the balcony of her hotel, overlooking Port-au-Prince: unlike the brothers, she can pass freely in and out of the apocalyptic city, sense the frisson of danger that pervades there, without truly sharing the hopelessness that drives the Chimères into violence. In contrast to the more constrained movements of the Chimères, Lele is often filmed in motion; she has a dynamism that is apparently absent in the people she tends to.

Similarly shifting between the inside and outside is Wyclef Jean, who first appears in his New York apartment, taking a call from Tupac. The contrast between the two worlds is apparent: Wyclef is in his pristine white kitchen, while Tupac is shot as he often is in the darkness of Cité Soleil. The lighting casts Tupac's face in sharp relief and one can discern in his drawn features and in his eyes a kind of desperation as he tries to convince Wyclef of his credentials as a rapper, which for Tupac has become his only remaining route to salvation.

For many others in Cité Soleil—including Billy—it was Aristide who had been seen as the savior who would deliver the people from their misery. The film narrates the circumstances and some of the aftermath of

Aristide's departure on February 29, 2004. Among the more predictable reactions of the rebel and Chimère leaders, one man from the neighborhood addresses the camera and gives a striking, apparently impromptu speech on what Aristide's departure means to him: "From 1804 to 2004: that's two hundred years! Two hundred years of independence! Two hundred years! Did you ask me something? We are the people of Cité Soleil. We struggled hard to put Aristide in the presidency. You tell Little Bush we have three prayers in Haiti: school, food, and sleep. We don't need peace. We need militants to combat extravagant systems right here in Cité Soleil. Look at us now! I feel like killing you to take your camera!" The man's speech is significant in that it provides one of the rare occasions in which the film expresses a political and historical perspective on Haiti that does not come from the Chimères or their opponents. Perhaps most tellingly, the man does not call for peace, but for continued resistance to the forces that keep the people in poverty. As such, he seems implicitly aware that the apocalyptic world that the film presents is created and perpetuated most fundamentally by poverty and all that results from it.

The power that the gangsters have is itself chimerical, an illusion that is quickly shattered when following Aristide's departure they are forced to disarm and the internal conflicts within their ranks come to the fore. Billy and Tupac are split by a bitter argument, and the former says he would kill the latter were he not his brother. Tupac appears increasingly lost, uncertain of his place in the community, and indeed the country. His fatalistic, apocalyptic side comes to the fore once again. As their power dissolves, he says that all that is left is hatred, and that he is going to die. Facing a warrant for his arrest, he feels trapped. He quotes Wyclef's phrase that when a door closes another opens and finds it to be false, as he encounters only closed doors. Perhaps ironically, it is at this point that Tupac in particular appears most human—that is most directly connected to the fundamental human emotions that he more commonly suppresses as a Chimère. It is when he feels his life most threatened that he seems to become less ghostlike and to fully sense that he is alive, however precariously. When he hears that Billy has been arrested, he reacts as a brother commonly would, their conflict apparently forgotten. Tupac's brotherly instinct is to protect and avenge Billy, and as if struck by the full tragedy of their lives he breaks down in tears. His tears are also for his country, as he thinks of the cycle of Macoute/Chimère retribution, he states, "Haiti will never be changed." His only desire now is to get money and leave the country. Recalling his late mother as a good person who will now be "in the skies," he reflects that he will not be joining her, as his eyes seem to express his sense of hopelessness, and perhaps a degree of regret at the way he has lived his life. At this point, the film cuts back to the beginning, to Tupac's reflections on his life and his uncertainty over how it will turn out: "How my life gonna be?" he asks, and replies, "Lord knows." Or perhaps the opening shots were actually from the end, which would certainly emphasize the overwhelming sense that the film conveys of a place and an existence in which life is experienced as a form of death, and where every beginning carries with it already an intimation of an ending.

Billy reappears in the 2004 documentary by Charles Najman, *Haïti, la fin des Chimères?* More of a conventional documentary than the reality TV–style Leth film, this work is situated at the turn of the bicentenary year, and consists largely of a range of interviews with a broad spectrum of Haitian citizens, from writers and intellectuals to politicians, priests, students, and finally, Chimères. Recorded speeches by Jean-Bertrand Aristide proclaiming Haiti's glorious past and demanding reparations from France are counterposed by the more muted reflections of intellectuals such as Gary Victor, who judges 1804 to have been a victory solely for the propertied classes, and argues that "we're still slaves."

In the earlier parts of the film, the chief spokesman for the Chimères appears to be Paul Raymond, described in a contemporary newspaper article as "a top Chimère leader [who] threatened to bring back necklacing—the execution of political opponents by placing a burning tire around their necks, . . . which has not been seen here in several years."[5] In the film, Raymond is perhaps the most staunchly pro-Aristide voice, calling on France to pay reparations to Haiti and decrying protesting youths as "programmed and conditioned students."

When Billy appears in the film, he cuts a more solitary, reflective figure than he did in *Ghosts of Cité Soleil.* With Tupac absent, Billy appears quite muted and all the more uncertain of his future. His initial dream, he says, was to become a "militant revolutionary," to fight against "governments that act against the people." He was, he says, willing to die for his political beliefs. Cité Soleil, he says, "had many martyrs for Aristide's cause," and yet no improvement had been made to living conditions. He is filmed apparently taking a call from Aristide, in which he is told that the opposition will invade the palace, and that the Chimères are the president's only hope. However, Billy is unsure whether to commit himself once again to Aristide. Sitting around with some of his close associates, Billy reflects on the nature of the Chimères. He appears to resent the tag, as it is used as an insult by the opposition; indeed the name was coined by their opponents as a means of demonizing them. He is perceptive enough to see that the Chimères are not a breed apart; rather, he suggests, they are a creation of the circumstances in which they live. The criminality that characterizes them is something, he says, that "is in everyone's blood." Billy's disenchantment with the government is essentially an ethical and political matter. The great paradox in this regard is that Billy the gangster holds the government to account over its lack of ethics: "It's a government of liars," he says. He decries the Haitian police force for being involved in drug dealing, and judges that "there is no truth in justice, everything's about money." Such is his despair that he sees the only solution as being a second period of American occupation. To his associates' protests on the importance of living independently, Billy's terse and telling reply is, "But we don't live." In effect, Billy's politics and ethics appear to be fundamentally similar to those of the intellectuals and writers, most notably in the film Gary Victor, who also tends to deflate the perceived glories of Haitian history and who echoes Billy most directly in his declaration that successive governments have "denied existence to the masses." The difference lies in the perceived legitimacy of the two figures: the writer is apparently untainted by political associations, while the gangster-intellectual seems trapped by his economic circumstances and is caught in the paradox that the only way to make his plea for justice and truth is to first partake in violence. One imagines finally that were their situations reversed, Billy would be as eloquent as Victor and that Victor might act as Billy does, which seems to affirm Billy's idea that he and every individual are the products of their circumstances, the political and economic forces that impact everyday lives with the force of destiny.

Apocalyptic Brothers and Doubled Identity in *Bicentenaire*

Even in the absence of Tupac, therefore, the film seems to set up doubled relationships between radically different characters that reveal themselves to be fundamentally alike. Such tendencies appear in certain contemporary fictional representations of the Chimères. Perhaps most notable in this regard is Lyonel Trouillot's 2004 work *Bicentenaire,* which is more or less contemporaneous with the films and which presents a doubled relationship between a student called Lucien and his younger brother, a Chimère known as Little Joe.

In comparison to the films, Trouillot's presentation of the Chimère figure is less nuanced, at least at the beginning of the book. Little Joe apparently has little of the intellectual capacity of the figures presented in the films, especially Billy. The novel first presents Little Joe sucking his thumb while sleeping, his face peaceful "like childhood and fragile like it." The peace is deceptive, however, and he is further presented as a hybrid being. The fundamental rupture for Joe (and his brother) is with the countryside, their village of origin. Thus, Joe's face is that of a "displaced angel," and "doesn't quite go" with the rest of his body, which is covered in tattoos: "Guevara, Wyclef Jean, Tim Duncan, shoot to kill. . . . I want everything, peace and love." His hybrid, chimerical quality is further suggested in the stark difference between his sleeping state and his waking self: to wake is "painful, violent," as Joe assumes his bodily identity, which "signified at the same time everything and its opposite" (11). In this sense, Joe's being is multiply split, and his body is covered in contradictory signs that suggest the conflicts that determine his every paradoxical act.

Having "grown up quickly" in the shantytowns of Port-au-Prince, far from his mother, Joe suffers from an "absence of dreams," which is in turn either the cause or the effect of his drug taking (14). In one scene, he arrives in the bedroom he shares with Lucien, "his body pumped with acid" (17). Sitting down beside Lucien, Joe picks up one of his brother's books, takes thirty seconds to read the author's name (Spinoza), before, "taking his revenge," by launching the book with all his might against the wall (18). The book's fragile binding splits and the pages are scattered over both sides of the room—Lucien's side has no posters, while Joe's has cut-up photos of "Malcolm, Kadhafi, Kobe Bryant, and some porn stars" (ibid.). As if to emphasize the idea that he is exacting a form of revenge for his lack of education, he takes his pistol from his pocket, saying, "That is called a Glock, it is my college degree" (ibid.). As he spins and aims the gun like a Western gunslinger, Lucien reads in Joe's eyes what his brother apparently cannot put into words: "I have made the choice. . . . You will never be able to choose, you will spend your life hesitating between your dream of a normal life in a normal country—your least likely destiny—and the strength to rip from the tree the branch they say you can't have" (19). Life, to Joe, "is like a weapon," and his "plan for society" amounts to his use of his gun, which "can open every door" (18).

While the doubled nature of the brothers is rather crudely drawn in the early part of the book, later the dualistic division becomes somewhat blurred. Lucien, for instance, doubts whether he has made the right choice in opting for peaceful protest, and wishes he had a gun, too (23). He also seems susceptible to some of Joe's reasoning, notably the idea that "it is in the flesh that you need to create pain, it is in the flesh that the world changes" (ibid.). By contrast, Lucien's only weapon is the old grammar book that he uses to teach the disinterested children of the rich. The student moreover recognizes the "wisdom" in Joe's violence: "even in his delirium, he manages to see the truth," Lucien says to himself (44).

That truth appears to lie in the body, in actions, as opposed to the mind and words. Lucien and his band of student intellectuals are, he says, "losing the war," (23), while "words are empty. Words no longer say anything. Words have no presence and expect no reply. . . . Words are dead" (68–69). Joe's power is shown in the way he is able to exact a form of revenge on the doctor who employs Lucien as a tutor and who treats him with some contempt. Joe, by contrast, is able to exert his power over the doctor when he and his gang steal the doctor's car. With the doctor at his mercy, Joe recommends that he undertake some voluntary work, a command that exemplifies the shifting morality and ethics of the Chimère figure. More commonly, Joe is contemptuous of what he calls "do-gooders," but in this case, faced with a cynical member of the elite, his position shifts, as does apparently his morality and sense of civic mindedness. There are it seems, no moral or ethical absolutes, only a set of shifting, provisional positions that characters adopt according to their particular situations.

The book's subtle validation of the Chimère figure and his ability to evolve and survive (Lucien dies, apparently from a bullet from Joe's gun) is further effected through the mention of Joe's real name: Ezechiel. The biblical prophecies of Ezekiel are said to mirror those in the Book of Revelation. As such, they prophesy apocalyptic battles that herald the end times. Importantly, too, prophecy for the biblical Ezekiel was not just a matter of words; his life and actions were living prophecies. "I am a sign to you," he said. "As I have done, so it will be done to them; they will go into exile, into captivity" (Ezekiel 12: 6, 11). The behavior of the prophet in this sense constitutes a prophecy of the time to come. In this light, the character of Little Joe/Ezechiel embodies and enacts not only the present but also the future. By extension the Chimères more broadly constitute an apocalyptic army, a product of conflict in which, Trouillot seems to suggest, one can read not only the contradictions of the present, but also the almost fated continuation of conflict in the time that will precede the final collapse.

While the Chimères are in many senses products of Haiti's particular history, they also are part of a broader, post-plantation world that remains haunted by its past, by what Colin Dayan terms "the enchanted wreckage that was Atlantic slavery" (193). Dayan, again, talks of the "*haunt* of cruelty, the leavings of terror," and how in such a history "The dead do not die" (ibid.). Drawing on Michel-Rolph Trouillot's idea that the past is but "a position" and that "in way can we identify the past *as past*" (*Silencing the Past* 15, Trouillot's emphasis), Dayan asserts that "the codes and sanctions of slavery always resurface and find new places to inhabit" (194). As with Lyonel Trouillot's Chimère figure, the body is a kind of historical repository. In what Dayan calls "the cult of the residue," it is the body that remains, that contains in a sense its history and that is also a form of prophecy. "Throughout the Americas," Dayan writes, "the concept of personhood could be eliminated for the enslaved who were condemned to live in and through the body" (195). In what she calls the "landscape of death," nothing ever dies, "not oppression nor the disfiguring of persons placed outside the pale of human empathy." Haunting continues, she says. "Old forms of terror maintain themselves as they find new content" (ibid.).

The Apocalyptic Antihero in *La couleur de l'aube*

In her discussion of plantation slavery, Dayan speaks of resurrecting "the materials of a history too easily forgotten: the resilience, inventiveness, and wit of those who walk in rubbish, gaze from blown-out windows, and live in the shadow of merciless brutality" (199). Yanick Lahens's 2008 novel *La couleur de l'aube* undertakes a similar project in its presentation of contemporary, pre-earthquake Haiti, teetering, it seemed, on the verge of apocalyptic collapse. The novel can also to some extent be read as an example of the antiheroic, apocalyptic tradition in Haitian writing. In particular, the figure Fignolé is a recent incarnation of the antiheroic, Chimère figure, one who sets himself the task of addressing Haiti's social and political ills, and in doing so attaches his own fate to that of his country. His name seems a direct echo of Daniel Fignolé, the charismatic working-class leader who opposed François Duvalier in 1957 and was forced out of the country before the fateful election that year (Dubois 323–24).

La couleur de l'aube differs from Lahens's previous novel *Dans la maison du père* in that its principal narrators are not bourgeois figures, but women from the shantytowns. Lahens had previously experimented with this kind of narrator in her short fiction, notably in the volume *La petite corruption,* but this is her first full-length work written from the perspective of working-class women. In some senses the central narrator Angélique has much in common with the bourgeois women Lahens writes about in other works, and indeed with the women written about by Chauvet, Mars, Danticat, and others. In all cases, women seem to live constrained lives, in the shadows of "real life," burdened by duties, and suffering silently the effects of a society whose only future seems to be an impending apocalyptic breakdown.

Angélique's apocalyptic vision of society is expressed from the opening lines of the novel. She wakes before the dawn and prays in the dark for her island, which is caught she believes in a struggle between God and the Devil. Her night has been sleepless, as she lay listening to distant gunfire that she knows will inevitably come closer to her own home. "Like all the others, I wait," she says (12). She waits in other words for death, helpless to stop its advance, her only protection her prayers. Death has already come in a sense to her mother, who says that having lived for sixty years in Haiti she is now "beyond the shadows[,] . . . already dead" (22).

Angélique also waits for the return of Fignolé, her younger brother, who from the beginning of the novel is absent, his whereabouts unknown to his family. What distinguishes him is his courage, or perhaps more accurately his lack of fear; he is the one that "fear has not managed to put on his knees" (12). Never accepting "any dogma, any uniform, any doctrine," Fignolé fights "against . . . reality," against the structures and norms that the others accept and try to bypass rather than challenge directly (96).

Angélique's dutiful selflessness and stoicism contrast with her sister Joyeuse's more open, outgoing nature. While Angélique and her mother are devout believers—the former in Christianity, the latter in Vodou—Joyeuse is not religious, having chosen, she says, "the light, the wind and the fire" (18). As Joyeuse says, Angélique "wanted everything and since everything never came, she lost all on a single throw," while Joyeuse learned early that "something was making the world turn against me and those like me," and chose "to become the exact opposite of a defeated person" (141). The contrast between the two sisters is figured around the mind and the body: Joyeuse has faith only in her "lipstick, breasts, and ass," while Angélique "passes for being wise. Too wise, even" (20). The differences between the two are not however absolute, as Angélique in particular is a far more complex figure than her name suggests, in that she is "full of bad thoughts," and detests, she says, her street, her city, and her island (ibid.). Joyeuse on the other hand reads a lot (53), and is no less aware of the situation the family and their country are in, that time brings nothing but further decay, that the city is a "Babylon" (54) and that the land itself "is decomposing" beneath their feet. There is something of an echo of the sisterly relationship set up in Chauvet's *Amour* between the selfless though impassioned elder sister Claire and the sensual and apparently more frivolous younger sister, Félicité. This similarity is further suggested in Angélique's statement that as a result of living in such close proximity "love has taken on the color of our anger, has become mixed up and confused with our resentments," a phenomenon that echoes the confusion of love and hatred in Chauvet's work (21). In the absence of Fignolé, their anger is directed at Angélique's young son Gabriel and the family's restavek Ti-Louze, who are beaten furiously, while the real sources of the women's suffering remain "too far away" (30). Cruelty toward the young seems to be part of the pattern of poverty and despair. To justify her beating the children, Angélique remembers the saying "The whip has never done any harm to the little black boy or girl" (33). Similarly she justifies her cruelty to Ti-Louze by saying that if it were not for them the child would be already be dead (ibid.). "Eaten with rage" (13), the women are "cruel by default" and "nasty by obligation" (30).

The family's internal frustrations and rage are but part of a broader reality shared by all in the shantytown. In this district, everyone is engaged in "silent wars. Wars without victories. Without end and without glory" (35–36). Every day the people's defeat becomes ever more absolute, and this defeat is related to the long, national history, which is but "a big somber room, full of noise, fury and blood," the effect of which is to make the people "hate their very presence in the world, the black-humiliation of our skin"(36). Between the people, there is little sense of solidarity, only a deep mistrust that "the old people have always made us feel toward those who resemble us like two drops of water" (42).

Fignolé, again, stands apart from the community in that he apparently believes that he can alter society through political action. When Joyeuse finds a gun hidden among his papers, she wonders why he would need a weapon, and if he did need it, why he would have left it at home if he was in such danger. Crucially, she finds a note written by Fignolé that cites Mayakovsky: "the body leaps toward the bullet and the throat dreams of the razor" (37). As Joyeuse realizes, none of these objects is left by chance. Fignolé has in effect left a message to his family and it is up to them to decipher it. It appears that in leaving the gun, the one thing that could protect him, he is giving himself up to his fate, a prospect that is further communicated in the Mayakovsky quotation, which reads like an indirect suicide note.

The roots of Fignolé's activism, and of his tragic fate, lie in an incident that occurred during the latter days of the previous dictatorship, in which his uncle was "disappeared" by two brutal macoutes (96–99). Tellingly, these figures are presented as "two beasts escaped from the Apocalypse"; and it seems as if in evoking in Fignolé his spirit of revolt, they also condemn him to a similar apocalyptic fate. Fignolé's grandmother recognized at an early stage that he would have a tragic outcome, that "he will get himself eaten up, his flesh burned to the skin" (96), while Joyeuse is gripped by a feeling that "life will crush him" (158).

Fignolé is in effect a figure out of time, a throwback to the poet-revolutionaries of the pre-Duvalier years. He has learned to talk of revolution among his middle-class friends, but as Joyeuse reflects, such a figure "has no place in this island where disaster has killed the soul" (38). While Joyeuse knows that "hard and cold cruelty inhabits the heart of the defeated," Fignolé argues incessantly against this idea, pleading for revolt and revolution (41). His actions in leaving the gun and the note suggest however that his words do not coincide with his beliefs; that the more he argues for revolution, the more he attaches himself to the impossible, and the more he condemns himself to his own premature death. Implicitly, Fignolé believes that with death comes deliverance, salvation, and resolution, while Joyeuse has come to believe that there is no hell, only the "brutal paradise" that they live in (45).

While the women do not adhere to Fignolé's political vision, Angélique shares in another complementary discourse that is no less apocalyptic. A member of a Pentecostal church, she finds in the pastor's "fables and extravagant poetry" a kind of release from her everyday life, or perhaps more accurately, a discourse that mirrors and explains to some extent her existence. The pastor evokes the "angels of heaven and the demons of hell," which, something like in a Vodou ceremony, "take possession" of the faithful, or else take leave of them in an apocalyptic fury that acts at once as a release from anxiety and a reminder that they are fated to suffer and that the world they inhabit is inevitably infernal (111).

The hospital in which Angélique works is itself an apocalyptic site, where the victims of violence are taken to die. Approaching death, one boy injured in the street violence cries uncontrollably, and Angélique reflects, "The tears and the sobbing of a young man of eighteen years are more terrible than the Apocalypse" (135–36). However this is not the apocalypse as a singular moment marking an end, but a familiar and repetitive phenomenon. As Angélique says, "The Apocalypse has already taken place so many times in this room, so many times in this city, in this island" (136).

The city too is presented in apocalyptic terms, as an animal or a beast "stubborn and devouring" (71). As Angélique writes, Port-au-Prince is lived as an "outpost of despair," a "great implantation of concrete and mud on a savannah," a "torment" and a "punishment," whose "descent into hell" began more than two hundred years previously (109). After reading a long list of kidnappings, murders, and corruption cases, a radio journalist concludes that "there exists in this island an evil empire" (145). Virtually the only thing that grows is poverty. "The more you dig," Joyeuse says, "the more you find another misery greater than your own" (59). The city is a pitiless place, where to survive one must protect oneself above all. "From this city, I have learned one single lesson," Joyeuse reflects: "don't let yourself go. Do not let any sentiment soften your heart" (75). Human relationships are distorted; empathy is virtually absent. "We wear each other down to the bone," Joyeuse says (117). The landscape is at its most apocalyptic at the edge of one of the poorest quarters, where the land meets muddy, infested water in which scavenge dogs, pigs, and people, peasants who had come to the city "as if to Paradise," but who have only found "this open-air hell" (59). The city is also a battleground, split between the forces of the Party of the Dispossessed and "forces of order," which track down the insurgents street by street and cut off the heads of their victims, displaying the heads on picks, or else burn them to feed to the pigs (60).

Fignolé is a supporter of a political figure referred to in the novel as the head of the Party of the Dispossessed, a messianic figure that resembles closely Jean-Bertrand Aristide. It was on the leader's return that Fignolé joined the celebrating crowds, thinking that together they were finally ridding themselves of the "desperate pain of the lost, degraded, and downtrodden country" (48–49). The celebration turns into a spree of violent looting and when Fignolé returns with a television set, Angélique is initially angry but then to her surprise she finds that she approves of Fignolé's act, and that the repressed have a right to take what they can when the opportunity presents itself (50).

There is a sense that Fignolé's political activities are a kind of act, almost a parody of Haitian insurrection. In carrying out his acts of revolt, his setting up of burning barricades in order to "cry out his hatred for the men in uniform," Fignolé is accompanied by a young American journalist called John, and one senses that there is a tacit agreement between the two: the journalist gets his familiar stories and images of Haitian instability, while Fignolé gains publicity and notoriety by in a sense playing to the crowd (67). "I like this country," John declares to Fignolé's family. "I like poor people" (68). While Fignolé does not question such a comment, Angélique remarks ironically that before meeting John she did not know that someone could earn a living by liking poor people, "that liking the poor was a profession" (ibid.). John can never be part of the apocalyptic society, as unlike the people he writes about he "has a future" (100). Joyeuse is more openly critical of John, saying that his dreams of revolt on the streets of Seattle or New York are dead and that he tries to resuscitate them in Haiti, "the false paradise that he invented in his own mind" (70). Her own body is an important element in this false paradise, as she had been John's lover, his "little sorceress with the coal-colored hair," as he put it (78). She is aware that this relationship also involved a playing of roles that are inherited from the past, that he was the "demanding master" seeking in the "serene womb of the black woman" a place "to anchor his anxiety," while she was consequently offered a way out of the "interminable march of the defeated" (78). As Angélique remarks, such a personal transaction always has a political significance, one that habitually humiliates Haiti and its people. "The first Black Republic put its women on their knees," she writes, "for a few dollars, a meal, some pieces of chocolate" (82).

In John and in the other sympathetic foreigner, the Belgian priest Father André, Fignolé finds a degree of approval and understanding that he does not seem to get from his family. Revolution affords him a role and an identity that conforms to the outsiders' preconceived ideas of the Third World revolutionary, but which does not accord with the rest of his family's more pragmatic, less romantic approach to everyday survival. "Hounded by anxiety," Fignolé "seeks out pain to delight in it," while the others, no less afflicted with anxiety, tend by contrast to seek solace in the small everyday pleasures that come their way (69). Joyeuse's salvation, for example, lies in love, in the figure of Luckson, a man who has "not accomplished any particular exploit" (89), but whom she refers to as her "savior" (101). For Joyeuse, Fignolé's political acts are driven by illusions and fueled by his drug taking. His music, she insists, "will not bring the walls tumbling down" (70). Fignolé the antihero plays his role and follows his paradoxical destiny, ostensibly fighting for hope and freedom while believing only in a tragic, apocalyptic outcome.

The paradoxes created by Fignolé's politics complicate the question of political ethics. In short, as is true in much contemporary Haitian fiction, it is difficult to judge if he is completely on the "right side": drawn to a politics of liberation, he nevertheless ends up for a time on the same side as the armed gangs that terrorize the city and target political insurgents. These are once again the Chimères, the violent gangs in the pay of the government that as we have seen became notorious in the later part of the Aristide regime. Fignolé in fact has much in common with the Chimères, whom he later opposes as he turns against the Party of the Dispossessed. Specifically, they are all part of the apocalyptic narrative that makes the city the site of a battle to the end. The armed thugs are as much apocalyptic figures as Fignolé is. When Joyeuse gets caught in a shooting incident in the city, she comes across a Chimère figure who has just killed a high school student for shouting slogans against the Party of the Dispossessed. The killer is a boy of barely sixteen years; in rags and "made savage to the bone," he is "without past, without future, with no family, a nature laid bare, a bleeding wound" (90). In other words, he is an apocalyptic figure par excellence, a shell with no feeling apart from the urge to hurt and kill. A crucial component of the apocalyptic narrative is that the killer needs a victim, while the self-condemned victim needs a killer; the one completes and validates the other.

The Chimères' apocalyptic code—"destroy or be destroyed yourself, inflict fear or be afraid" (151)—does not however exist in the complete absence of human feeling. Angélique tells of one Chimère who went to her aunt Sylvanie to beg for her help. His emotions "make his lips tremble" and his words come rushing out of his mouth as if he "wanted to be rid of them" (151). When Sylvanie asks what he wants from her, he replies, "To be able to sleep in peace," before confessing a series of crimes, murders and rapes the memories of which haunt him, making his life an apocalyptic reality, a cycle of fear and violence that has caught up with him, creating deep emotional wounds that neither religion nor more violence can begin to heal (151–52). As Angélique reflects, the Chimère is but one part of an entire city in which the order of time and space has been forever overturned and which "continues to advance towards horror" (153).

The Chimères are in effect the products of the apocalyptic city, which "plants poisoned seeds" in the hearts of its citizens, from which the "deadly tree" grows endlessly (163). In the poorest parts, a boy of twelve is already "an old man," who has murdered and who floats in a drug-induced trance, while girls of a similar age have three lovers and assist the boys in their deadly acts (ibid.). For Angélique, the situation is beyond repair. "We cannot heal," she insists (ibid.). More tellingly, she poses herself the rhetorical question "Maybe we do not want to heal?" (ibid.).

In other words, the only end can be an apocalyptic conclusion, one that is feared but also desired as a means, perhaps the only means, of ending the insufferable present. If the Chimères represent one aspect of the apocalyptic reality in their nihilistic, unthinking violence, Fignolé is their mirror, the one who (much like Trouillot's Lucien) thinks too much and feels condemned, almost duty bound to die with his city. Following his split with the Party of the Dispossessed he is overcome by anger, and seems to ready himself for his fate, becoming "detached from the circle of the living," and wanting to "rejoin the world of the gods" (164).

Angélique also prepares herself for an impending disaster, in words that read retrospectively, following the earthquake, like a presage of impending natural disaster. Feeling that she is in "free fall," she is drawn to a "powerful force, invisible like that which controls the movement of the planets, the rotation and the revolution of the earth" (173). She feels that she is too insignificant to resist this apocalyptic movement, which she attributes to a "divine design written in the movement of the stars" (ibid.). The original French of this statement suggests even more strongly her sense of impending disaster: she writes of the stars, *des astres,* which is close to the word for disaster (*désastre*), which itself has its roots in the Old Italian *disastro,* meaning ill-starred, a quality Angélique attributes to her nation as she sees its fate written in the stars. Angélique's apocalyptic presentiments are again largely influenced by her religious beliefs. Citing a religious verse that evokes a vengeful God, she feels for the first time that "these words of the Apocalypse speak more truly than ever." "It is not yet the end," she says, "but all these events announce it. That instant when darkness will no longer give way to day. When the angel with the giant wings will blow her silver trumpets and proclaim at the top of her voice that time is no more" (ibid.). Again, read retrospectively, these words read almost like prophecies of the terrible event that would come, seemingly inevitably, and which was in effect a conclusion to the apocalyptic discourses that circulated in Haiti just before the earthquake, figured here in Fignolé's politics and Angélique's religion, two discourses that see disaster and death as the only ways out of an unbearable reality.

However shattering the announcement of Fignolé's death ultimately is to his family, it is not in itself the all-consuming disaster that Angélique felt was imminent. Instead, it marks a point of no return, a prelude to a more general disaster, particularly for Joyeuse, who plans to take revenge on the character Jean-Baptiste, who betrayed Fignolé and was instrumental in his death. She imagines herself seducing Jean-Baptiste before killing him with Fignolé's gun. It is now "too late" for thoughts of tenderness and love, she says, as "everything has already turned toward death" (208). The novel's closing image, of the "white, milky light" of the moon "continuing, impassive, to envelop the world" suggests finally that for all the disasters brought about by human acts, the natural world moves to its own rhythms, and if it brings disaster it does so in its own time. The final impression one has is of a nation on the brink, its human and social tragedy creating a presentiment of general catastrophe, which is again feared and desired at the same time, as the apocalyptic moment draws ever closer.

4 Religion, Nature, and the Apocalypse

In *Failles,* Yanick Lahens's first book published after the earthquake of 2010, the author writes of seeing her husband after he returns from town on the evening of January 12, announcing that he has seen the apocalypse. This statement makes Lahens think immediately of her use of the same word in her last novel, *La couleur de l'aube.* She had hesitated, she says, before using the word, striking it out three times before finally writing: "The Apocalypse has already taken place many times on this island" (27). The word had remained with her well after the publication of the novel, and she had asked herself if she had not gone too far in using it. It had seemed to her that the recent history of Haiti had taken on apocalyptic tones, but now, following the earthquake, the word "catches her again" in another way (27). There is a sense here almost of guilt for using the word to describe a situation that was desperate, but which in comparison to the earthquake was relatively bearable. Also, more interestingly, one gets the feeling that pronouncing such a potent word might have in some way a prophetic effect, that in writing of it one prepares the imaginary for its coming, and even that one unconsciously wishes it to come in order for the desperate social situation to finally end. One is left to wonder whether words might have that kind of power.[1]

Do language and literature have that capacity, the ability to somehow shape the future, and specifically to bring about an apocalyptic collapse? Common sense would most likely say that they do not, particularly as in this case in a nation with high illiteracy rates. One suspects also that the relatively small local readership of Haitian literature would moreover be the most rational in its thinking and be less inclined to ascribe any kind of mystical, prophetic power to novels and stories. On the other hand, however, those very same conditions of low literacy and limited readership seem to elevate the status of writing and writers so that they are at times, and especially after the earthquake, considered spokespeople for the country as a whole. Poetry in particular is something of a privileged genre, in that many past and present writers began their careers as poets. This, in turn, may have something to do with troubled times in Haiti, and indeed the broader contemporary world. In the words of Dany Laferrière, "Only poetry contains the silence necessary to express horror" (*L'art presque perdu* 209).

In a sense, for those who cannot read, "poetry" exists in religious texts and rituals. When one considers, for example, the Bible as a work of literature, perhaps one begins to gain a different perspective on the question of the power of written texts to determine everyday life in the present and the future. Specifically, again, one can question whether preaching about the apocalypse can create the psychic conditions that in some way lead to the desire for an apocalyptic event, and that as such act as a form of self-fulfilling prophecy. Indeed, Dany Laferrière suggests as much when he writes about his experience of reading the Bible, specifically the Book of Revelation, and suggests that the "living nightmares" of the Third Reich would be "impossible to understand . . . without John's Apocalypse" (ibid. 142).[2] This is the line of inquiry—whether apocalyptic biblical prophecy can have a material effect on a country's lived reality—that I will pursue in the first part of this chapter, before turning in the final section to the relationship between the Haitian natural environment and the apocalypse.

In Vodou, the apocalyptic, in the broadest sense is circumvented by a "firm belief in the regeneration of the world" (Chancy, *Framing Silence* 141). In Vodou, the "tragedies of life are remedied," and elements that might otherwise be seen as harbingers of an apocalyptic breakdown are welcomed as opportunities for the divine to manifest itself in the everyday: "Poverty becomes a means of salvation; illness, a source of divine power; and death is suddenly transformed into life itself" (Desmangles 61). Death marks not the end, but the beginning of being: "As the land and sea define each other at the shore, so life and death define each other by exclusion. . . . The point of departure is the first meeting between the quick and the dead" (Deren 24). Death is moreover part of the regenerative processes of the broader world. Humankind is constituted of the same elements that make up the natural world: "As the trees, the waters of the rivers, and the materials from which we build our houses spring from the earth, so are we extracted from the sacred womb of Mother Earth. The body is then consumed by death which returns it to the earth, its original source." Thus, the human is part of the natural environment, and is an "old acquaintance" with the cosmos, in that they share the same essential elements (Desmangles 64). Vodou in these senses puts the emphasis on cycles of life and rebirth, rather than on cataclysmic, apocalyptic events. Death is mourned, but also celebrated as the birth of a new being. Death rituals reinforce this anti-apocalyptic understanding of the end of life, in that they mark the birth of the deceased into "a new dimension of life," and more broadly move the "community toward the future" (69).

Vodou is of course a syncretic religion, and as such it has absorbed significant elements from Christianity. Notably, there is a millenarian element in the deity Ogou Feray, the god of war. In this case, the manifestations of the *lwa* in the body of the devotee re-invoke the Haitian Revolution, through the mention of the names of Boukman, Dessalines, and Christophe. A ceremony in honor of Ogou Feray is in this sense "an archetypal ritual, a reenactment of the beginnings of a nation" (152). Through such creolization, the Haitian religion disengages Christian millenarianism from its theological context and adapts it to "personal longings and national goals." Indeed, as Desmangles argues, if African religion had not come into contact with Christianity during colonial times, "it is doubtful that Vodou would have manifested such a millenarian character at all," for most African religions only developed a millenarian aspect after contact with European Christianity (152–53). In Haiti, the "millenarian dreams" taught by Catholic priests had a practical use in that Vodou believers adapted them to enact their hope for freedom and a "higher ideological, nationalistic order" through reengagement with the history and the figures that created the nation (152). As such, millenarianism in this context is less about the desire for a cataclysmic event that will bring about a societal transformation than providing a means of connecting with the past and using it to reenergize the cyclical process of history. The past lives, and if a form of millenarianism is present, it is essentially to "provide a reason for living" (153). As Chancy writes, by continually invoking of the memory of the revolution in Vodou ceremonies "Haitians defy the Western sense of the apocalyptic (implying even that they will cause the 'apocalypse' of their oppressors, at least within Haiti) and express a deep faith in the never-ending" (*Framing Silence* 143).

Protestantism

The contrast between Vodou and Christian millenarianism is most marked when one compares the Afro-Creole religion with the various Protestant denominations that continue to grow and reshape Haiti's religious life.

Protestantism was present during colonial times; and its importance has grown throughout the history of independent Haiti. The first missions were established in the nineteenth century, though it was during the U.S. occupation of 1915–34 that the numbers of Protestant missionaries working in Haiti began to increase significantly. Before the occupation, Wesleyan Methodist, Baptist, Episcopal, and African Methodist Episcopal churches had been established in the country for several decades, while Seventh-Day Adventists and Pentecostal congregations had recently been founded (Ramsey 197). Encouraged by the U.S. government, American Protestant organizations used the occupation to increase the number and influence of Protestant missions in Haiti. The Catholic Church in Haiti was particularly alarmed at the rise in missionary activity in Haiti in the 1920s and following the American troops' departure in 1934. Claims made by Protestant missionaries that Haitian Catholicism had become tainted by Vodou proved to be effective in increasing the numbers of conversions across the country (ibid. 198–99). That success has subsequently been consolidated, to the extent that around a third of the population is now Protestant (Hurbon, "Current Evolution" 122). In 1985, as he "sought to fortify Protestant support for his weakening grip on absolute power," Jean-Claude Duvalier recognized Protestantism as a state religion (Richman 113). In terms of Protestantism's apocalyptic characteristics and its cultural impacts in the post-slavery world, it is significant that southern U.S. evangelical churches have long believed in "an anthropomorphic God and Satan," and that such a belief constitutes "an interpretive scheme used to make sense of experiences of *this world* and events that occur in *human time*" (Hoefer 28). As one scholar writes, "The apocalyptic imaginary of southern religious cultures . . . maps an *otherworldly* conflict of good and evil onto the geographies of *this world*. The landscape becomes fraught with threats of sin and damnation as well as the apocalyptic possibilities of judgment, deliverance, and cataclysm" (ibid. 128). Given the significant presence of southern U.S. church missions in Haiti, one can perhaps begin to think of a regional, post-slavery, post-plantation religious imaginary that ties the Caribbean to the American South in an apocalyptic conception of time, history, and human relations.

In contrast to the ways in which Catholicism had assimilated certain elements of popular belief in Haiti, Protestant missions offered and demanded a complete break from Vodou practices and beliefs. "While many Catholics practice Vodou more or less openly," Métraux wrote in the 1950s, "the Protestants must break not only with Vodou but with all that would in any way recall it" (311). Specifically, music was closely associated with Vodou and as such was repressed by the Protestant churches. For Métraux, those who convert from Vodou to Protestantism seek a "refuge" from the anger of the spirits: "Conversion, far from being the result of a crisis of conscience, is more often than not the expression of an excessive fear of the gods" (312). In many cases, such converts become the "irreconcilable enemies" of Vodou, which Métraux suggests is due largely to the fear of lapsing back into Vodou (314). Protestantism also offers certain practical benefits, notably in establishing schools and engaging in adult education. Also, Métraux sees economic advantages in converting to Protestantism. Protestant sects typically demand lower pecuniary charges than do the Catholic and Vodou congregations. "We, the Protestants," one convert told Métraux, "do not spend much money. On Sundays, after the service, one gives what one can, and it is not much. We have no ceremonies to pay for. If one of us is sick, the whole community takes care of the expense" (316). Aside from this greater sense of economic security, certain Protestant sects, such as the Pentecostals and the Tremblers, which promote a form of worship close to that of Vodou in the trancelike state attained by worshippers, are attractive to those wishing to convert to Protestantism. "From all the evidence," Métraux writes, "the mystical ecstacy that one obtains through prayers and incantations is barely different to the trance provoked by the African gods. Certain Protestant sects, in spite of their intransigence with regard to Vodou, have tolerated and even encouraged behaviors that are Christian only in context. Psychological attitudes are often more entrenched than beliefs and rites" (317).

Therefore, for all its utilitarian aspects and its professed opposition to Vodou, Protestantism in Haiti has certain key elements in common with the creole religion. In particular, as Métraux suggests, the evangelical, Pentecostal end of the Protestant spectrum shares with Vodou a certain antirational, mystical aspect that manifests itself in rapturous forms of worship, and in what one critic calls the "will to live in a saturated world" (Melani McAlister 882). The paradox of U.S. evangelism, a tradition that is often defined by austerity yet which often manifests itself in unbridled, emotional forms of worship is laid bare by the same critic: "Many U.S. evangelicals are engaged in a not-necessarily-conscious effort to 're-enchant' their own experience, to activate sensuous, emotive intensities in the face of a sense—broadly shared by many believers—that modern evangelical life, however committed to faith in 'things unseen,' has left behind an abundant sense of the otherworldly" (882–83). McAlister finds a range of strategies that demonstrate the evangelical interest in the otherworldly: the general rise in Pentecostalism and/or "spirit-filled" charismatic practices, the turn to ritual, the increase in the belief in "healings," and crucially, "the fascination with apocalypse and 'end times' theology" (883).

In fact, millennialism is far from being a recent phenomenon in the evangelical tradition, nor indeed in Christianity more broadly. In the first and second centuries, certain Christian leaders "developed expectations of 'latter-day glory,'" which they associated with an "idealised final age of spiritual and environmental utopia" (Gribben, *Evangelical Millennialism* 2). Following Augustine, such earthly millennialism was generally condemned, though "eschatological optimism" endured and became prominent again at the end of the first millennium, and "repeatedly returned to haunt the medieval Catholic imagination" (3). In the first century of reformation, the millennial and apocalyptic beliefs that still shape evangelical discourse began to form, though it was during the nineteenth century that these beliefs solidified into the "discrete prophetic paradigms" that would come to dominate evangelical thinking (ibid.). The defining features of modern evangelical fundamentalism may be traced to the 1820s and 1830s and the development of a "distinctive prophetic paradigm" within academic and social elites allied to Trinity College, Dublin, and the University of Oxford (Gribben, "Rapture Fictions" 80). This nascent "dispensational premillennialism" was a "paradigm of cultural and ecclesiastical despair," and its adherents believed scripture indicated that "powerful forces of decay would gain influence towards the end of the age" (ibid.). Contemporary events were believed to confirm this reading of prophecy and to presage the "rapture," that is the catching-up of believers into heaven, which would be followed by the "tribulation," a seven-year period of unimaginable awfulness during which the Antichrist would rise to power. His reign of terror would be ended by the Second Coming, when Jesus Christ would inaugurate the millennium, a thousand-year period of peace, prosperity, and godliness, after which he would mount his last futile rebellion, the world would end, and life in the new heavens would finally begin (ibid.).

Perhaps the key element in this prophetic millennialism is that the end of the world is desired, and seen as the only way out of the current fallen and corrupt state of the world. Such a desire is evident throughout the subsequent history of evangelical millennialism, perhaps no more so in the Cold War era, which saw the movement establish itself as a feature of popular culture, particularly in the United States, which continues to see itself as a "redeemer nation," or a "righteous empire," ideas which "lead all too easily to a literal demonization of one's opponents" (O'Leary 189–90). In 1970 Hal Lindsey published *The Late Great Planet Earth*, the "most influential dispensational textbook of them all," and a "powerful monument to Cold War fear" that sold more than 28 million copies over twenty years (Gribben, "Rapture Fictions" 81). At once alarmist and entertaining, the book "blurred the boundaries between entertainment and interpretation, and for large sections of North American fundamentalism at least, defined the mood of evangelicalism throughout the 1970s and 1980s" (ibid. 80). During the same period, evangelical millennialism was also a major force in mainstream U.S. politics, notably for Ronald Reagan, who stated in 1971 that "the day of Armageddon isn't far off. . . . Ezekiel says that fire and brimstone will be rained upon the enemies of God's people. That must mean that they'll be destroyed by nuclear weapons" (qtd. in ibid. 79). Significantly, Reagan's famous, apocalyptic reference to the Soviet Union as the "evil empire" was contained in a speech he made to the National Association of Evangelicals. The fall of the Soviet Union however disproved the prophecy of Cold War apocalypse and raised the question of who, in the absence of the USSR, would be America's next "apocalyptic 'other'" (81).

To some extent, and notwithstanding the ongoing U.S. conflict with and demonization of many parts of the Islamic world, Haiti has come to play the role of America's apocalyptic other, clearly not as a military threat, but as a close neighbor that harbors a potent form of spirituality that poses a certain religious threat and makes Haiti a spiritual battleground for U.S. evangelicals. Notoriously, the day following the 2010 earthquake, the televangelist and former Republican Party presidential candidate Pat Robertson cast Haiti not so much as a political evil empire, as Reagan had described the Soviet Union, but as a land in the grip of evil demons. He declared on his Christian Broadcast Network show, "Something happened a long time ago in Haiti, and people might not want to talk about it, but Haitians made a pact with the devil; they said, 'we will serve you if you get us free from the prince.' True story." Robertson was referring, of course, to the Bois Caïman ceremony, where a group of slaves were said to have met for a political rally, during which they were said to have sacrificed a wild boar to their African gods, and swore to fight for freedom.

Although there is only tenuous historical evidence that it actually took place, the ceremony did, however, become a sort of founding myth of the nation. Robertson's statement, then, "demonizes the Afro-Creole religion the revolutionary Africans would have practiced, and by extension, Haiti's cherished past" (Desmangles and McAlister 72). While Robertson was reacting primarily to the earthquake, he was in effect repeating long-held U.S. evangelical ideas about Haitian religion, which themselves are related to the long-standing image of Haiti in American literature as a place that is "inexhaustively suggestive of mystery and carnality" (Dash, *Haiti and the United States* 105). The paradox here is that, as Métraux suggested in the 1950s, evangelicals and Vodou believers have more in common than the evangelicals would likely admit. Specifically, evangelicals tend to consider the Vodou spirits to be "real forces," but because they are not referred to in the Bible, the spirits are assumed by evangelicals to be evil (Desmangles and McAlister 72). Evangelicals make fundamental challenges to Haitian history and its meanings. In particular, their interpretation of Bois Caïman holds that the revolution, far from freeing the slaves, further enslaved them to Satan through the "pact with the devil" that the ceremony instigated. True freedom must now be brought about "by and in Christ" (ibid.).

The attraction of Haiti to evangelicals lies essentially in its supposedly fallen state: not only are the people in league with Satan but the nation itself is prone to disasters of all kinds, which seem to prove that it has angered God and become a kind of apocalyptic battleground. The earthquake energized evangelicalism, and Protestantism more broadly, in Haiti, in that it "brought to the surface the millennial dimensions of its theological discourse" (73). In this theological atmosphere, and given the lack of a strong political structure, Haiti is susceptible to being co-opted as a site upon which the apocalyptic fantasies of the evangelicals are played out. In such a situation,

> millenarian movements may take hold, in which a people can interpret their circumstances by invoking vivid images of a better world to come. Charismatic leaders or prophets often arise; they are regarded by their followers as shepherds whose task is to lead them into the New Jerusalem, a heavenly city where all who are saved will be liberated from evil and the fallibility of sin. Millenarian movements regard the world as evil and believe that the final end will consist of cataclysmic events ushered in by supernatural forces that will destroy the world. (73)

It is in this regard significant that the evangelical assault on Haitian history and its supposed "pact with Satan" intensified in the 1990s, following the demise of the Soviet Union and the end of the threat of, or indeed hope for, an apocalyptic showdown with the "evil empire."

It was in the post–Cold War 1990s that an "aggressive wave" of evangelical missionaries began to recast the Bois Caïman story with a new Christian narrative, in a way that considered independent Haiti to have made a pact with the devil (Elizabeth McAlister, "From Slave Revolt" 3). Satan was in effect the ruler of Haiti, and Haitians who continued to worship their Afro-Creole gods were ratifying the initial covenant with the devil (ibid. 4). Of course, the Christian demonization of Vodou dates back to colonial times, and as Ramsey reminds us, Haitian governments have themselves repressed the practice of the religion under its penal laws for over 150 years (1). What is new in the evangelical narrative of Haitian history is the intensity of the critique of Vodou, and that it is part of a transnational movement that was born out of a particular post–Cold War historical context, in which the United States has sought to reposition itself in various ways. The evangelical version of history relies on its promotion of the United States as a "righteous nation, founded by Christians as a Christian nation, and blessed to be chosen by God for a special destiny." Such a view of the United States only gains validity through contrast with fallen, sinful nations such as Haiti: as one American missionary put it in the early 1990s, Haiti is "the only nation to be dedicated to Satan" (Elizabeth McAlister, "From Slave Revolt" 7).

In considering the rise of evangelicalism in Haiti in the 1990s, it is also important to take into account the local political context. The Duvalier dictatorship had ended in 1986; a period that had in effect solidified the international opinion that Haiti was a place of "barbarity and wretchedness" (Dash, *Haiti and the United States* 105). In his 1966 travelogue *The Invisibles,* the author Francis Huxley had written of Duvalier's Haiti in terms that effectively pre-echoed the evangelicals' demonization of the nation and its religion. Haiti, he wrote, was "notorious for its Voodoo and its zombis. . . . Its poverty is disgusting, its politics horrible, its black magic a matter of fantasy" (9). The idea that Haiti was cursed by its own history also featured in popular fiction, notably in Benjamin Levin's 1972 novel *Black Triumvirate,* a work that presents the central figures of Haitian independence as "part of a trail of blood that led inexorably to Duvalierism" (Dash, *Haiti and the United States* 111). Writing in the 1990s, Michael Dash senses the possibility of a change in U.S.-Haiti relations and reflects, "As the post–Cold War United States and post-Duvalierist Haiti face each other at the end of the twentieth century, the question is whether the negative stereotypes of the past will persist and continue to shape American attitudes" (166). Subsequent events, notably the rise of evangelicalism in Haiti, would suggest that the negative stereotypes have not only persisted but have been consolidated and instrumentalized in an attempt to radically rewrite Haitian history.

By 1991, the bicentenary year of Bois Caïman, Jean-Bertrand Aristide had been elected president, and his administration sought to legitimize Vodou and to incorporate it into "development plans, civic life, and official historical memory" (Elizabeth McAlister, "From Slave Revolt" 11). Specifically, Aristide's government sponsored a commemoration of the Bois Caïman ceremony, and voted to make the site a national landmark and Boukman a national hero. When he returned to Haiti in 1994, Aristide held a conference for four hundred Vodouists at the National Palace, an event that marked the first time that the religion had been formally recognized at a state ceremony. More generally, Aristide sought to legitimize Vodou to an unprecedented degree, and to undo the demonization to which it had long been subject (ibid. 11–12).

Aristide's actions reenergized the evangelical movement in Haiti. The bicentenary of the beginning of the revolution called to mind the idea of the original pact with the devil, and this aspect of history was invoked to explain the turbulent present. That Aristide was also seeking to instigate a political program that challenged U.S. influence and which promised to bring about land redistribution no doubt encouraged the evangelicals' view of him as an anti-American, and therefore anti-Christian, threat. A further important element was the approaching millennium, and the promise it seemed to carry of millenarian religious conflict leading to the Second Coming. Indeed, the early 1990s saw the rise of a new school of thought in global evangelical missiology: the Church Growth Movement, which argued for the need to convert large numbers of souls in preparation for the Second Coming (Elizabeth McAlister, "From Slave Revolt" 15).

One important element of the movement was the concept of Spiritual Mapping, which involved reading history, ethnography, and sociology to identify the spiritual forces at work in a specific locale, and then "mapping" them so that missionaries could understand and do battle with "any demonic activity that might be working to thwart church growth and large-scale evangelization" (ibid. 16). Again, as Métraux recognized in the 1950s, the evangelical Protestants shared the Vodouists' belief that spirits were real and active agents in the human sphere. In effect, the evangelicals "work against the Enlightenment idea of rational progress and effectively re-enchant the nation with spirits and demons" (25). In the anti-rational "battle" between the two religions, evangelicals thus employ all the supernatural tools available to them as Christians: miracles, healings, prophecies, and speaking in tongues are used to counter the force of the local demons and to conquer souls for Christianity (17).

That this is an apocalyptic showdown between God and Satan, enacted on the battlefield of Haiti is emphasized by the vocabulary of warfare employed by the Spiritual Mapping evangelicals. Christian intercessors are known as "prayer warriors," who undertake "assignments" to go into battle with "territorial spirits" or launch "prophetic prayer action" on the "spiritual battlefield" (18). In one remarkable episode in 1997, a Haitian evangelical group converged on the site known as Bois Caïman, where it "staged a spiritual warfare crusade and exorcism of the land" in order to claim the site, and the event, for Jesus (19). The millennial aspects of the evangelicals' attempts to "break the curse" of Bois Caïman are laid bare in their view that their spiritual exorcism marked a "breakthrough," that Haiti had "reached a historical turning point," and that they were to be the "anointed leaders of the new era" (21).

The desired new era did not however materialize, and Haiti arrived at the new millennium and the bicentenary of independence in a new wave of political and social unrest. Aristide, moreover, continued to valorize Vodou as a legitimate element of national cultural heritage, to the chagrin of the evangelicals, who launched in 2003 a further crusade to "take Haiti back from Satan," which culminated in spectacular revival held at the national stadium (22). "This event," the American pastor proclaimed, "is to break the blood pact of the devil, and bring Haiti under the blood of Jesus Christ!" (ibid.).

While by no means all Protestants in Haiti support the evangelicals' attempts to appropriate national history, Haiti has remained on the "front lines" of the movement's declared war on Satan. This is perhaps no more true than following the 2010 earthquake, an apocalyptic event that seemed to many evangelicals to mark a definitive break with the past and to usher in the longed-for new era.[3] During a service held on Maundy Thursday, a Haitian evangelical preacher named Guibert Valcin announced that the earthquake was merely a sign of the end of times, and that Jesus was coming soon. "Everywhere you go, you need Jesus," he said. "Jesus is all the power. . . . Vodou can't take you to heaven, only God can. Jesus when he comes one day, he won't come to save the Vodouists. He will save only those who serve God" (qtd. in Desmangles and McAlister 73–74). The earthquake in effect brought to light the idea that the apocalypse is "both literary text and social movement," a rhetorical device that allies the written word to a vision of social and spiritual change (O'Leary, *Arguing the Apocalypse* 195).

The great attraction of the millenarian vision of a heavenly paradise is that it "transforms calamities into sacred events" (Desmangles and McAlister 74). It is the millenarian idea of a transformed and perfect world that drew crowds to Protestant services following the earthquake to listen to the ministers' homilies and be converted. One Baptist pastor in Port-au-Prince had more than two hundred people come to his church to be saved. "God struck the country and they have come to make peace that they be taken in rapture with the Lord in heaven," he said (qtd. in ibid.). In effect, such a vision of Haitian history *requires* calamitous, apocalyptic events in order to function in any way. Without such events, the millenarian narrative would fall apart, and human history would perhaps be seen in a more rational light as the result largely of human actions and natural events that can be explained, prepared for, and corrected so that apocalyptic collapse is no longer the self-fulfilling prophecy that fails time after time to bring about the new era. The prophesied golden era is a myth that offers freedom but which in effect enslaves believers far more effectively than the equally mythical idea of the "pact with the devil," the promotion of which cynically distorts Haitian history and entraps adherents in a form of spiritual bondage. There is only one way out, believers are told in essence, and that is through renouncing their history and pledging themselves to a vision of time and history that depends on the demise of their society. And even as their society falls and suffers unspeakable calamities, and no deliverance comes, so they must continue to suffer, and wait and hope for the end times to truly begin. To cite once again Yanick Lahens in *Failles,* "The Apocalypse has already taken place many times on this island" (27). And yet, despite such an apocalyptic history, the prophesied new era has not arrived, the end times seem unending, and nature appears to follow stubbornly its own ancient rhythms.

Nature

It is the rhythms of time and nature that underpin two of the most remarkable pre-earthquake novels, works by Dany Laferrière and Lyonel Trouillot that are haunted in their respective ways by apocalyptic history, but which ultimately find in Haitian nature means of earthly regeneration for their protagonists' battered and bruised souls. Notoriously deforested and prone to natural disasters, the Haitian environment seems to be an ideal milieu for the propagation of millenarian ideas on the fate of humankind in the world. Indeed, there is a long history of European characterization of the tropics as "danger zones," of associating exotic landscapes with a malevolent nature: places of unrelenting climate (droughts and floods), violent weather (hurricanes, typhoons), violent landscapes (earthquakes, volcanoes), dangerous wildlife, and deadly disease. As European contact with tropical regions intensified during the eighteenth century, "so too did the perception that disease, putrefactions and decay ran rampant in the moist warm air of the tropics" (Bankoff 21). In the nineteenth century, the increase in scientific knowledge on the tropics led to a "medical geography" that attributed local diseases to particular climates, vegetation, and physical topographies (ibid.). This was part of what David Arnold terms a discourse of *tropicality,* one of the most striking elements of which was the invention of the sense of *otherness* that Europeans associated with the tropical environment—plant and animal life, climate and topography, and also the indigenous people living in a specific environment. This was more than a scientific description of physical space, and was a culturally loaded, politically charged conceptualization of tropicality, as Arnold says, "A Western way of defining something culturally and politically alien, as well as environmentally distinctive, from Europe and other parts of the temperate zone" (6).

The idea of the tropical environment as a site of danger, a threat to European health was mitigated to some extent by the elaboration of germ theory and the discovery that bacteria and not climate were responsible for disease (21). Thus "cured," the tropics could be domesticated and controlled, and be rethought as safely inhabitable zones for Europeans, at least until the late twentieth century with the spread of the AIDS pandemic and the emergence of new viruses like Ebola fever, which shook the sense of Western "security" in relation to the tropical environment. The very concept of natural disasters is part of a broader historical and cultural "geography of risk" that sets apart large parts of the world as dangerous for Europeans (27). More importantly, as Bankoff states, it also serves to justify Western interference and intervention in places such as Haiti, "for *our* and *their* benefit" (ibid., Bankoff's emphasis). Perhaps even more significantly, the concept of natural disasters and the related notion of hazard provide a useful and enduring rationale for "blaming the poverty and inequitable distribution of material goods of the people living in these regions squarely on nature" (28). In addition, the proliferation and greater global visibility of natural disasters in the twenty-first-century tropics has refigured places such as Haiti as danger zones, diseased and impoverished, and living in an environment that is always on the edge of an apocalyptic collapse. In effect, much of contemporary environmentalism more broadly is "an apocalyptic form of millennialism," in that it relies on a tragic vision of impending ecological catastrophe (Landes 234). In these two Haitian novels however there is a discernible turning away from such a view of the Haitian natural environment, and an anti-apocalyptic, and perhaps also anticolonial tendency to see in nature, even in its degraded state, a source of healing and an antidote to the apocalyptic city. Written in the two years preceding the earthquake, there is in both cases a poignant irony in the authors' reconnection with the Haitian natural environment, just as nature was about to wreak unprecedented damage on the nation.

Mourning and Return in *L'énigme du retour*

Dany Laferrière's 2009 book, *L'énigme du retour* generally prioritizes issues of memory and forgetting. Laferrière's work, classified as a novel, but which has strong autobiographical elements, shares with Kettly Mars's *Saisons sauvages* an interest in the legacy of the Duvalier dictatorships and their apocalyptic consequences for society and individuals. Specifically, Laferrière left Haiti in the 1970s fearing for his life under the Jean-Claude Duvalier regime—an experience recounted in *Le cri des oiseaux fous* (2000)—while his father did the same under François Duvalier. Compared to Mars's novel, Laferrière's work is more directly concerned with the present and with the legacy of the past on the author's own life, which has been shaped by exile, an experience that he is forced to reevaluate as he returns to Haiti to mourn his father.

There is a well-known passage in Márquez's *One Hundred Years of Solitude* in which the Colonel expresses his desire to leave Macondo, and his wife, Úrsula, states, "We will stay here, because we have had a son here" (13). To the Colonel's reply—"A person does not belong to a place until someone is dead under the ground"—Úrsula responds, "If I have to die for the rest of you to stay here, then I will die" (13). This brief exchange says much about the relationship between a migrant people and place. Úrsula's initial statement suggests that being born or giving birth in a place creates a lasting tie to it, while the Colonel places the emphasis not on being born, but dying. It is for him the final moments of one's life that create an enduring bond with place, an idea Úrsula implicitly accepts in her offer to die to enable the rest of the people to stay and to feel that they belong.

Dany Laferrière's *L'énigme du retour* offers a quite different account of the relationship between an immigrant's death and his family's subsequent bond with the place of dying. When Laferrière's father dies in New York, it brings about a crisis of place and belonging for the author, a radical sense of displacement that he feels compelled to resolve not by renewing his bond with North America, but by returning to his own place of birth, Haiti, and moreover to the Haitian hinterland, the largely neglected and forgotten places of childhood in which he can properly grieve and begin to re-orientate his own confused sense of belonging.[4] As he reflects on his return to Haiti:

> One is born somewhere.
> If it works out like that
> you travel around a few countries.
> To see a bit of the world, as they say.
> Stay there a few years in some cases.
> But, at the end, you come back to the point of departure. (217)

Unlike in Márquez's novel, therefore, there is for Laferrière no easy connection between death in a foreign land and the exile's renewed feeling of identification with the place of exile. Rather, death seems to bring to light and heighten the underlying anxiety over place and belonging that had previously been an important feature of his work, largely managed by and incorporated into his notion of being a broadly "American" writer, but which now imposes itself upon him, demanding attention and some kind of resolution.

The Telephone Call

The manner of his father's death—alone in New York, estranged from his family in Haiti—no doubt intensifies Laferrière's anxiety over the consequences of living in exile. There is no chance of reconciliation or of being with his father as he dies; rather, the news comes via telephone, "cut[ting] the night in two," and also creating a chasm in his own experience. He had been unconsciously preparing himself for the moment, but when it comes his reaction betrays his sense of grief and uncertainty; he takes to the road in his car, "Without destination," he says. "Like my life from this moment on" (13). This is significant in that it suggests that it is in movement rather than stasis that he belongs. Also, driving without a destination allows him to think about and identify with his father, another restless soul, tormented by exile, and to try to imagine the solitude of a man "facing death in a hospital bed in a foreign country" (14).

The shock of the death seems to have an effect on his style, as the book marks a striking new development in his writing, a hybrid form that is sustained throughout the book and resembles that of the long prose poem, not too distant from certain passages in Aimé Césaire's *Cahier d'un retour au pays natal,* another Caribbean classic of return from exile. The death seems in a sense to act as a catalyst for Laferrière and to bring him closer to his long-stated aim to write "without style," that is without the stylistic conventions of the novel. His "cause," as he had said before, was style, "or rather the attempt to achieve the absence of all style. . . . So that the reader forgets the words to see things as they are" (*J'écris comme je vis* 44). In this work, he seems close to attaining this purified state of writing and to have pared back style to such an extent that it is the unembellished emotions and the consciousness of the narrator that are exposed and that seem to speak directly to the reader, almost without mediation. As such, the book exists on the very margins of the novelistic genre, at a kind of vanishing point that communicates the author's own subjective state on the edges of the places he calls home and in the solitary throes of grief.

Aimé Césaire's influence on the book is not only stylistic; he and his work inhabit the book and the author's thoughts throughout the text (though most prominently in the early parts) so that the work becomes a double eulogy to the father and to Césaire, who died in 2008, and was a kind of literary father to Laferrière. Césaire's line "Death expires in a white pool of silence" is cited by the author as a tribute to and commentary on the father's death, as Laferrière wonders what Césaire could have known about exile and death at barely twenty-five years old (14). The line refers more immediately to Toussaint Louverture, another Haitian who died in a cold, foreign land, and who is implicitly introduced as another father figure for Laferrière.[5] The play of identity between Laferrière and his various father figures is continued throughout the book, notably in relation to Césaire and the deceased father, who has the same name as his son: Windsor Laferrière. One consequence of this name sharing is that when the nurse from Brooklyn Hospital telephones, she asks to speak to Windsor Laferrière to announce the death of Windsor Laferrière, so that just as the father "has just died," so in a sense the son dies too (61).

Laferrière travels everywhere with his copy of Césaire's *Cahier d'un retour au pays natal,* a work he had found "insipid" on his first reading more than forty years previously (62). Subsequently, he had been able to appreciate Césaire's anger and intelligence, but not the poetry, finding it to be "too prosaic" (62). Significantly, however, it is only when he is traveling by train from Montreal, when he is "finally going toward [his] father," that he suddenly distinguishes "the shadow of Césaire behind the words" of the poem, and sees how Césaire went beyond his anger to discover the "unknown territories" of language (62). It is anger that connects Césaire to the dead father. The poet's "piercing rage" (62) is associated with the father's own anger, which "inhabited him so strongly" (61). In both cases, Laferrière suggests, anger derives from the "desire to live in dignity" (62) and is only partially masked by the two figures' outwardly gentle nature.

The connection between Césaire, the father, and Toussaint is further suggested when Laferrière attends the funeral in Manhattan and sees his father up close for the first time, so close that he only has to stretch out his hand to touch the body, which he however does not do out of respect for the distance the father wanted to keep between them in his life (64).[6] The sight of the father in his coffin reminds him of the well-known passage in Césaire's *Cahier* in which the poet "claims the corpse" of Toussaint Louverture from the cold site of his death, much like Laferrière does in Manhattan for his own father. "What is mine," Laferrière writes, citing Césaire, "is a man imprisoned by whiteness" (65). Underlying these implied connections, too, is Laferrière's anxiety about his own fate and mortality: will he die, he seems to wonder, a lonely death in a cold place? He seems haunted by a visit he made to visit his father several years previously, when the father refused to answer the door to him declaring that he had never had a wife, children or country (68). Told that he is "cut from the same tree" as his father (69), Laferrière seems to ask himself if he is destined to come to a similar end. Is the son fated, even duty bound, to die like the father(s)?[7]

Driving far into the frozen Quebec countryside, he feels a slight panic at having lost his bearings in the snow-covered landscape. This "animal of the city" is lost and alone in a setting that he realizes is not and never will be his natural abode: "Only the local inhabitant could find his way here," he says (16). For all that, he seems compelled to drive further into the wilderness, further to the "luminous north," which has a contradictory effect on him, "blind[ing]" and "thrill[ing]" him at the same time (17). At this time, the excitement of living in a foreign land is diminished, and in a remarkable, piercing image, he expresses his feeling of being alone, caught between two contrasting worlds:

> I am conscious of being in a world
> completely unlike my own.
> The sun of the south crossing
> the ice of the north
> makes a temperate sea of tears. (ibid.)

The disjuncture between the place of birth and his current home is further evidenced by the short dream he has when he returns to Montreal. Taking a nap in the cold car, he immediately sees himself as a child wandering beneath the tropical sun, which is however "cold as death" (19). Dreams do little at this stage to comfort him or to diminish his sense of being lost. In this sense, he perhaps connects with his father, whose face he has trouble conjuring in his mind, but whose feeling of being lost and alone he feels acutely (20).

Slipping back into his dream world, this time in the pink bathtub, a "round womb filled with water" (26) in which this "marine animal" feels most at ease, he is overtaken by what he calls "this old fatigue, whose cause I pretend to not know," and is carried away to "unknown territories" (21). He does not explain what the cause of his fatigue is, but it seems to have something to do with his separation from home, the effects of which he has apparently long suppressed. He sleeps in the bath for "an eternity," this being he says the only way for him to return incognito to the country "with the huge piece of news" (21). The dream leads him to a deeper understanding of exile and the motivations for wandering far from one's home country. He discovers that "there is not in this life either north or south nor father nor son and that nobody really knows where to go" (22). These binary opposites collapse in the dream as he comes to understand the reasons for his own wandering: no matter what one does to rekindle the memory of one's earliest days, "one will never find again the taste of these childhood afternoons spent looking at the falling rain" (22). In contrast to the past, when he would throw himself in bed to forget the hunger that ate at his insides, now he says he sleeps to leave his body, to calm his thirst "for images of other times," and to find himself once again in the country that he "left one morning without returning" (22).

His bearings lost, the direction of his life called into question, he returns to the only act that he can come back to: his writing. Not that this is particularly comforting—he says he recommences writing "like others start smoking again. . . . With this impression of doing something that is not good for me but which I cannot resist any longer" (23). The writing does not come naturally or easily; words come out "in a great disorder" and he manages no more than a few sentences before collapsing with exhaustion (24). He looks for a way of writing that would require less physical effort and decides to leave his Remington 22 typewriter in favor of writing by hand. "It is always at the end of a highly charged cycle," he says, "that we return to what we think to be more natural" (24).

It is striking in this book that Laferrière refers to himself as an exile; previously he had rejected this label, saying that after the departure of Jean-Claude Duvalier in 1986 there were no more Haitian exiles.[8] The death of the father leads to a reevaluation of his condition, and a realization that he and his father are two of the absent ones that every family has in their group photos, departed relations pushed out by the Duvaliers, who "introduced exile into the middle class" (116). The real opposition in the world, he thinks, is not between nations, but between those who live in exile and those who have never faced a culture other than their own (41–42). The same morning that he learns of his father's death, he picks up the notebook he kept when he first left Haiti in 1976, and feels the hurt of living for such a long time far from home and family. "Between the journey and the return," he writes, "is caught this decayed time that can push you to madness" (27). Living so long "without reflection" leads to a point where he no longer recognizes himself in the mirror (27). He flashes back to the moment he left Port-au-Prince, and picks up the photograph his mother gave to him as he left, an image of the two together that is now his "only witness for measuring the time that passes" (28).

Now, the only place where he feels at home is in the hot water of the bath, bottle of rum to hand and, never too far away, the volume of Césaire's poems (33–34). Reading one page of Césaire to each drink of rum, he falls into a dream in which Césaire is superimposed onto his father: "The same weary smile and that way of crossing their legs that recalls the dandies of the post-war era" (34). The text gives a strong sense that, however little contact Laferrière had with his father, he has sought to imitate him; a revolutionary, he says while studying a photo of his father "is first of all a seducer," which perhaps is something of a commentary on aspects of the characters he often presents in his works. In these moments of unavoidable lucidity, Laferrière realizes that without exile he would not have written in the way he had done; indeed, he may not have written at all, which leads him to question whether one writes far from one's country to console oneself, and to be doubtful of whether writing is truly a vocation for any author in exile (34). Writing in exile, it is suggested, is a means of trying to make up for something that is lost, a substitute that never truly compensates for the time spent away from home.

It is not only in space that he feels disorientated; in time too Laferrière is lost, as his memories become confused and it seems as if an eternity has passed since the phone call. "The exile of time," he writes, "is more unforgiving than that of space" (77). Time no longer passes in a regular, predictable way, but is now a “compact mass with a density heavier than that of the earth” (37). Time spent away from one’s native village, he says, is a time that cannot be measured, and which is outside of the time inscribed in our genes (39). That is, exile interrupts the “natural” passage of time; its flow becomes idiosyncratic, less the rigid determinant of an individual trajectory than its unpredictable corollary. It is not however that he regrets completely his exile; indeed he realizes that it is only in leaving home that one can be saved from family, blood, and routine, and that those who have never left home become embedded in an “immobile time” that can in the long term have detrimental effects on the individual (42). Also, as he reflects later, the best thing he has done with his life is to have removed the Duvaliers from his existence, something he could only have done in exile (144). There is also at this point an increased fluidity between his conscious and unconscious selves, as he shifts from one state to the other, sleeping to avoid his daily obligations and to encounter in sleep images of his childhood that come to him “in waves” and with remarkable clarity. It is as if the images are calling him, shaking him out of the moment and demanding to be recognized and recovered. Also, as he writes later, he cherishes his dreams as the only things that remain from his previous life, especially the childhood times spent with his grandmother, Da (124).

Leaving

It is only through leaving Montreal that Laferrière can begin to recover these images, and to grieve for his father. The moment of leaving is a familiar one for him; however much one delays it, it remains there, “waiting at the door,” demanding his departure (39). Not all departures are the same, however; to really leave, he says, one must forget “the very idea of the suitcase,” for objects and material things do not belong to us, and the comfort they seem to offer is exposed as an illusion at the moment of leaving (42). The time of leaving reminds him of his arrival in Montreal; in both instances he has but a small suitcase with nothing in it, which further connects him to his father, who had lived in a small, “almost empty” apartment and had “stripped himself of everything” before his own final departure (67). As such, Laferrière’s departure seems to complete a circle that takes him back to the condition he was in when he arrived, and in this sense appears to remind him of his status as a migrant, not completely belonging to either place. If he belongs to anywhere it is to the doorway, the threshold that marks arrival and departure and the point to which he is constantly returned.

He has a clear plan for his return to Haiti: he will spend one night only in Port-au-Prince before traveling to Petit-Goâve to see his grandmother's home, where he spent a large part of his childhood, and to visit her grave. Interestingly then, he seems more drawn to visiting and reconnecting with his deceased relatives than his living family; it is as if his connection and identification with the dead is at this time stronger than that with the living. The dead carry memories of the past and his own childhood that are important to him as he grieves his father. Significantly, too, these visits will take place in the countryside, which is implicitly connected to the past, while the city is more directly related to the present. It is in the countryside that he plans to spend the rest of his time, speaking with the country people; those who he says have never opened a book in their lives (47).

This turn to the country is also influenced by a growing disillusionment with hypermodern, urban life. Crossing the Canadian countryside in a night train, he imagines the people in the pale light of their homes gathered round the television, and laments how the descendants of the early trappers have now become "elegant city dwellers soaked in perfume" (57–58). The "vegetal world" of the trappers and their "autumnal odor of rain, green leaves, and rotten wood" now seem "so distant," and he regret the concessions that have created the distance between the people and the land (58). When he returns to Haiti, he will take up once more the theme of nature and the land, and seek in the natural environment a form of personal salvation.

Return

Tellingly, when Laferrière returns to Port-au-Prince he chooses not to stay with family, but in a hotel that overlooks the city and the sea. He does so, he says, in order to not give his mother the illusion that they are living together again when he has lived away from her for so long (118). Thus, for all his tender reflections on his mother, he keeps a distance from her in a way that recalls the distance he maintains with his father at the funeral. In both cases, physical proximity cannot erase the distance that time and exile have created. He situates himself repeatedly on the hotel balcony in a way that recalls Baudelaire's "Le balcon" from *Fleurs du mal,* and which casts the city as a Baudelairean mistress, as in the poem, a "mother of memories," giver of pleasure and possessor of "languorous beauty." Tellingly, he reveals near the end of the book that "Le Balcon" was his father's favorite poem (285). Later, he observes the city under an almond tree from behind a low, pink wall; life, he says, is on the other side of the wall (91). In this way, Laferrière can be simultaneously in the city but apart from and above it, which in turn suggests his ambiguous position as a returning exile, something like a tourist in his own hometown. For all that he has missed the place, he is wary of being consumed by it and the memories it holds.

But he cannot completely resist the city for long and, declaring that he no longer wants to think, but only to "see, hear, and feel," he drinks in the "explosion of tropical colors, smells, and tastes" that the city offers up to him as a remedy for his hibernal malaise. When he sleeps here, his sleep is by turns both light and deep (83). When he does go down to the street, it is to him like taking a "bath in this human river" (85). The energy of the city and its many sensory stimulants appear to bring about changes in his style and tone, at least in the earliest sections that relate his return. Sentences and lines become shorter, a great array of images, sounds, and smells are evoked directly and presented in an apparently unmediated way, the effect of which is to gain a sense of how Laferrière's consciousness is invaded and newly inhabited by these lost elements. Such is their effect on him that he appears to almost forget for a while the death of his father, the reason for his return. For a time, it seems like he finds everything in Haiti to be good, while everything in Montreal is worthless, which, as he reflects, is nothing more than a rebalancing, for there was a time when he "hated everything" in Haiti (219).

At the same time, he is wary of presenting an image of exotic poverty, and is sensitive to the hurt that lies behind the laughs and smiles of the street. As he had done previously in *Pays sans chapeau,* he sees himself as a "primitive painter," noting the "primary colors" and the "naïve sketches" that run before his eyes (86). As for a primitive painter, however, his images do not necessarily depict the "real country," rather a "dream country" (88). Looking out from behind the hotel wall he views a beautiful scene with three young girls chatting animatedly before a pyramid of colorful fruits, realizes that it is like the image on the painting he has just bought, and wonders which one is imitating the other (91). Laferrière is aware that the image the city presents of itself does not always reflect directly the people's inner sentiments. "The first tear," he writes, "would overflow this river of pain they are laughing and drowning in" (86). That is, he is unsure of the degree to which the "real" scene is a product of the image projected in the painting, or vice versa. Does life imitate art, or does art imitate life, he seems to wonder, calling into question his own art and drawing attention to its limitations and possible contradictions.

Laferrière feels a sharp sense of disorientation, particularly on waking from sleep, when he feels lost, his body undergoing a process of adaptation that he cannot control. A series of images invades his being. Memories that he had repressed in Canada for fear of being crushed by nostalgia have in Haiti "a concrete presence" (150). Feeling that he can barely breathe, the memories come to him "in three dimensions," assailing his senses in a way that makes him think that each traveler creates unconsciously a "stock of images and emotions" that he looks for on his return (151). People, too, assail him with anecdotes and stories of how they or someone they know knew him before he left. They all seek to be recognized, Laferrière realizes, as a means of confirming they are still alive (154). The returning traveler is endowed with this gift—the ability to confirm the memories of those who have stayed and who have a quite different conception of time and place. The sharing and retention of memory is a human response to the passage of time, the common "old ancestral enemy" of both travelers and those who remain in the country (150).

While the traveler has an almost mystical capacity to reawaken and confirm memories, he is also irrevocably different; the time spent abroad has changed him in ways he becomes aware of only on returning. Laferrière is reminded of this when he goes to buy a newspaper and is asked to pay the monthly price for a single issue. The vendor's justification is that Laferrière lives in the hotel, and is "a foreigner just like any other foreigner" (157). The banal incident has a profound effect on Laferrière: it leaves him reeling, as if he had "a stone in the heart" (ibid.). "To be a foreigner in one's home town," he says, is the lot of an increasing number of people, who will with time become the majority (158). The vendor's statement strikes him as it upsets his own understanding of his relationship with Haiti. He has written so extensively about the city and the people, he says, to "remain part of it" (161). Having been thrown out by the dictatorship, he has sought ceaselessly to return to Haiti "through the window of the novel" (ibid.).

The return to the city and to his family leads him to reflect on his own condition before he left Haiti. In particular, his nephew, also called Dany, becomes a kind of mirror in which the author seeks his young self, seeing at times clear reflections and at others unrecognizable images that remind him of the passage of time. When he goes into the nephew's room, his eyes look for the "smallest detail" in order to "go back in time to find again the young man I was before that hurried departure" (103). More obliquely, Laferrière notes without commenting the death of a young, much-loved musician, whom his nephew knew "through having briefly shared the heart of a young girl," a situation that recalls almost exactly the one described by Laferrière in *Pays sans chapeau,* where the musician Manu and the writer figure Old Bones love the same woman.[9] The issue of how to represent Haiti in art is raised again when they watch the film *Ghosts of Cité Soleil,* by Asger Leth, the work that follows the lives of the two shantytown gangsters, the brothers Bily and Tupac. Laferrière wonders what his nephew must think of the culture of guns, drugs, and hip-hop, while he himself feels quite distanced from it, noting that "everyone remains immured in his time" (105). As the film plays out, the two brothers move toward their deaths, murders that are fated by the conditions they live in and moreover desired by the film maker, fulfilling the storyline and allowing the crew to leave with the images they sought. "Blood, sex, and tears," Laferrière notes. "All that the viewer wants. Generic" (106). Again, then, there is a play between the generic demands of the art form and the behavior of the Haitian subjects that makes it difficult to judge the extent to which the lives presented are real, or simply creations adapted to and determined by the requirements of the art form.[10]

His conversations with his nephew also allow him to reflect on his writing, as the nephew wants to be a "famous author," a product, Laferrière says, of "this rock star culture" (107). It is only before one becomes an author, Laferrière reflects, that one can think of celebrity, for as soon the writing begins, a "faceless archer" takes aim at the ego, and any glory comes much later, "too late," Laferrière says (107). His inability to offer solid advice to his nephew leads to a fevered exchange between the two Danys in which it is difficult to know who is talking, which underlines the idea that Laferrière in talking to his nephew is also in a sense talking to his younger self, imagining how he was himself before he began to write.[11] Because "nothing has changed one iota" since his own childhood, his nephew faces much the same issues as he did at the same age (144). Laferrière's replies to the nephew's questions reveal that the author must discover his own style and content, and indeed find out whether or not he can write on his own, a process that might take ten years or more (109–10). The underlying anguish that the nephew shares with his uncle is again a reflection of Laferrière's own life: to stay in Haiti or to leave (111). And again, the author does not feel qualified to offer advice on this, the most fundamental and serious of all the issues his nephew and many other young Haitians face. What is the point in leaving, the author wonders later, "if it is to come back thirty-three years later like me"? (198).

This novel contains some of the most direct political and social critiques of all Laferrière's work. His father's absence due to political exile and the author's sensitivity toward the daily hardships faced by his family seem to make him more pointed in his social and political observations. Climbing the hills high above the city, he goes to see the luxury villas that are inhabited only by domestic staff, their owners having abandoned them to live in New York, Berlin, Paris, Milan, or Tokyo. As he observes, it is not unlike colonial times, when the "real masters" of Saint-Domingue lived in Bordeaux, Nantes, La Rochelle or Paris (131). The owners have built these homes in the hope that their children return to run the family business after being educated abroad. When the children refuse to return, it is the parents who leave to be close to them (ibid.). The villas are then let out at very high rates to executives from NGOs,[12] whose mission it is, ironically, to rid the country of poverty and overpopulation (132).

Laferrière is particularly critical of well-intentioned "humanitarian organizations," who arrive in the country with their programs of Christian charity, and who quickly learn the "rules of the game": to be waited on by an army of domestics and to help themselves to some of the funds allocated for their projects so that one wonders if they do not have in their blood "the atavism of the colonialist" (ibid.). The foreign organizations condemn local corruption, living in luxury themselves, while pronouncing that they are there to help the "wretched of the earth" (132–33). Laferrière's reference to the colonial era is quite telling, as it seems that it shares with the contemporary period a sense of fatalism based on the unsustainable nature of the society. The end of the society, the notion of an impending apocalypse, never appears to be too far away, which creates a sense of resignation and a very limited idea of the future. This idea is underscored in Laferrière's recollection of what a German engineer told him. When one arrives in the city with its turquoise sea and blue mountains, the German said, one only wonders how long it will take to turn into a nightmare (133–34). While waiting, one must live with the "energy of he who awaits the end of the world" (134). Time is lived from day to day; "a day here lasts a lifetime," the author says, "One is born at dawn. You grow up at midday. You die at dusk. And tomorrow, you have to change bodies" (139). For the poor, constant hunger only intensifies the sense of living with the imminence of death; the poor person Laferrière says, "does not read, does not go to museums, does not dance. He awaits his death" (140). In other words, one lives forever on the edge of the abyss, abandoned to the fate of the city, and compelled to live as if the end is imminent. As an unnamed friend says later, in Haiti "you have to live intensely for you can die at any moment" (163). It is only the rich who can speak easily about death; the rest "do nothing but wait for this death that is never far away" (ibid.). Also, as Laferrière reflects, at fifty-five years old, more than three-quarters of the people he has known in Haiti are dead. The half-century is a "difficult barrier" to cross in such a country, where people die so quickly that one "should not talk of hope for life, but of hope for death" (221).

This idea of a general "hope for death" appears to be in essence the very root of apocalyptic thought, living, and culture in Haiti. Reading this work after the earthquake, one almost senses the inevitability of a major disaster, and the feeling that locals and foreigners alike knew that something almost had to happen, an ending almost had to come to draw a line under the unsustainable reality of pre-earthquake Haiti. Later, Laferrière watches on the television news a story of the deaths in a car crash of five young musicians and the subsequent suicide of the fiancée of one of the musicians, and reflects on the endless "apocalyptic images" that he sees in the city (188). "Sometimes I no longer understand anything about this country," he writes, "it is as if there is in us a suicidal virus" (224). One also senses that behind such events there is a desire for the end to come that manifests itself in recklessness or excess, in the careless driving and wild living of the young, both poor and rich, or even in the fatalistic architecture of the shantytowns, makeshift homes teetering on the steep hillsides, and the tragic emptiness of the mountain-side villas. In his structural assessment of post-earthquake Haiti, Joel F. Audefroy argues that construction methods are largely determined by cultural, political and economic forces. Audefroy in effect argues in favor of incorporating aspects of "vernacular architecture" in the reconstruction of Haiti, and notes how traditional building knowledge has degenerated, to the extent that relatively few edifices built of wattle and daub remained undamaged by the earthquake.[13] One might add that construction styles reflect one's relative sense of permanence and belonging, and that the shantytowns of pre-earthquake Port-au-Prince communicated something of their residents' tragic, apocalyptic understanding of their place in society and their precarious existences.

Furthermore, there is a sense that such apocalyptic living creates the conditions for dictatorship: a young student remarks to Laferrière that "only a dictator can save this country," adding that he would prefer "anything but this untenable situation" (205, 206). Or perhaps it is the dictatorship that creates the apocalyptic living. A wealthy doctor suggests as much in his story of corruption in the country, of how he has thrived through corruption, and of how in the present period it is the former enemies of the dictatorship that are now in power. "They are frustrated, famished," he says, "and they panic at the idea of not being able to steal everything before they die" (232). There is no past, present, or future in the country: the doctor says, "Money exists, not time" (232). In such a situation, neither the rich nor the poor, the young nor the old live as if their conditions of living are sustainable, as if they are not constantly on the edge of the apocalyptic abyss.

Natural Returns

The only escape from the apocalyptic city seems to lie in the countryside, in nature and the neglected and mistreated land that nevertheless appears to offer still hope for common and personal salvation. Even in the city, he learns that his mother's daily life is enriched and made bearable by her attention to the natural elements around her: the two birds that meet in her garden at the same time each day; the lizards that she has named after her dead or exiled siblings; and the wind, which she gives a name to and which helps get her to sleep for her afternoon siesta (215). With his own consciousness filled with the apocalyptic clamor and chaos of the city, even the slightest encounter with nature and the peasantry seems to awaken in him a quite different set of memories and possibilities. Driving high into the hills with an unnamed friend, he comes across a line of women descending the hills, their backs straight, the napes of their necks covered in sweat: "elegance under the exertion," he remarks (163). Similarly, when they encounter a broken down lorry, he notes how the men have taken the women down from the vehicle and are pushing it to the sound of a "grave chant" (163). The sights and sounds of women and men working are potent reminders of the peasantry's capacity for self-sustenance and cooperation, which moreover seem to echo the practices of the *coumbite,* the common working practices that Roumain evoked so memorably in *Governeurs de la rosée.* In turn, Laferrière appears to evoke the memory of the *lakou* system, which was instituted in the early postrevolutionary period as a profoundly egalitarian system set up to counter the state's attempts to re-impose a plantation economy and which "emphasized self-reliance through working the soil" (Dubois 108). In Laferrière's text, there is a suggestion that the best (indeed, only) chance of continued existence for the peasantry, and perhaps the whole country is through such agrarian self-sufficiency. He seems to implicitly agree with the idea expressed by Fanon that for colonized peoples "the most essential value, because the most concrete, is first and foremost the land: the land which will bring them bread and, above all, dignity" (*The Wretched of the Earth* 9). More generally, too, Laferrière addresses the long-standing issue experienced by many Caribbean authors of "rootlessness, of not belonging to the landscape; dissociation . . . from the act of living" (Brathwaite 29–30). Given that he has lived for so long outside of Haiti, Laferrière perhaps feels a compounded sense of separation from the landscape, and this may be why he in this work depicts the "environment as an active agent" in his own personal story, and in that of the nation (Prieto 154).[14] He does so in a way that echoes Edouard Glissant's argument that in the Caribbean, "the individual, the community, the land are inextricable in the process of creating history. Landscape is a character in this process" (*Caribbean Discourse* 7).

The higher he climbs into the mountains, the more the sights and sounds of the country overtake him. He imagines himself living in an isolated mountainside home writing a five-volume historical novel, quite different from the more episodic books of the everyday that he writes in and of the city (164).[15] His immediate writing style is also affected; the long, complicated stanzas in prose of the later chapters on the city are replaced by shorter, more concise lines in which simple images, sounds, and scents suggest a clearing of his consciousness and a different perspective on Haiti and his relation to it. Stopping to buy some carrots and onions, he is "giddy" with the heavy smell of the earth (ibid.). "Everything grows here," he remarks, "the earth is good. The wind spreads the seeds" (165). Images of peasants along the riverside, their feet in the water, straw hats on, each one with a fighting cock under his arm and a bottle of alcohol in the back pocket, heading for the Sunday cockfight, suggest a timelessness that contrasts with the disorientating temporality of the city (164). For him, the "unchanging décor" of the sky, the sea, the sun, and the mountains is one of the few constant elements in Haiti, one that would be the same if he were to return in a hundred years (193). Invited by a woman to take a coffee under a mango tree close to the river, Laferrière feels the soft air caress his skin, hears the music of the wind in the leaves, and concludes that life in the country is "weightless" (170). Such is the effect on him that he wonders why people gather in the city, with its unsavory smells, its heat and dirt (165). For his own part, he realizes that he has difficulty breathing when the air is too pure and the life too easy, so keen is his "urban instinct" (ibid.).

In effect, Laferrière carries out more than one return in the novel. The return to the city is followed by that to the country, a return within the broader homecoming that takes him to places and people he had long forgotten, but which seem vital to him as he mourns his father and seeks to reorientate himself in relation to time and place. It is also a return to himself, to a lost feeling of self-recognition, and being recognized by others. Having lived so long "without reflection" (27), he seems to cherish the sense he gets in the countryside of being recognized. He jokes that even the animals begin to recognize him and thinks that maybe that is what a country really is: somewhere where "you think you know everyone and everyone seems to know you" (165).

Laferrière's most extensive excursion into the countryside is, perhaps ironically, made possible by the corrupt wealthy doctor, who was a friend of his father, and who allows him the use of his car and chauffeur to drive "in complete security" in the countryside (232). Tellingly, just as the doctor makes this offer, Laferrière falls asleep, noting that he is going to "confront the monsters of his childhood" (233). His trip into the countryside is also therefore something of a journey back to the "pays rêvé," the dream country that is related to the real, physical place of the hinterland and to the lost world of memory and childhood.[16] In the countryside too, dreams are a prominent element in people's lives, in that they are retold and shared over the first morning coffee, "making of the day a simple extension of the night" (235).

Significantly, too, he decides to take with him on the journey his nephew, his younger double, so that he is in a sense taking his younger self back with him to the forgotten places of childhood. In doing so, he allows himself to see the country simultaneously through the eyes of the young man and from his own, mature perspective, which creates a fascinating play of time and point of view and which to some extent allows him, in speaking to his nephew, to dialogue with his own younger self.

The journey brings into sharper focus the issues that lie at the heart of Laferrière's uncertainty. He seems reticent to revisit the world that he left, and appears almost fearful of the effects it will have on him. He is particularly anxious about the potential effect the journey will have on his own, broader trajectory; specifically, whether it will in some sense mark the end of his wandering. "If one returns to the point of departure," he wonders, "does that mean that the journey is over?" (238). "As long as you are moving," he adds, "you do not die" (239). These anxieties are countered by the perspective of those who have never left their native village, and who, he says, "await the traveler's return to judge whether it was worthwhile to leave" (239). This is the essence of his self-questioning: the unresolved (and perhaps irresolvable) question over whether the journey is worth that which is left behind in the place of birth.

The roads they take are dusty and bumpy (240). Metaphorically, as in *Pays sans chapeau*, the dusty road is the route of tradition that he consciously left behind both as a person and an author, a kind of dead end that he eschewed in favor of following his own, unpredictable trajectory.[17] On this journey, the dust gets into the car motor, causing it to overheat, and they spend the night in a roofless house, "walking through the Milky Way," where Laferrière believes he recognizes his grandmother in a star he had never seen before, not far from the Great Bear (241). In this case, then, the dusty road leads him to a dead-end and a forced stop, but also to an unexpected encounter, and the earliest sense of recognition and recuperation of the people and places that he has been separated from by time and exile.

In the dusty villages they stop by he finds further everyday things to marvel at. In one small locality, he notes that "everything is a miracle. First of all, the simple fact of existing" (244). Ironically, he becomes, as the city newspaper vendor had labeled him, something of a tourist in his own country: the world of the dust-covered people, he reflects, "is not ours" (238); he and a painter he visits exist "in two parallel universes" (247), while he has the impression that in this country you do not pass from one village to the next, but from one world to another (245). He in a sense passes from one dimension to another when he and his nephew swim naked in the sea until nightfall, the effect of which is to create a sense of liberation and of being suddenly free in time:

> I felt
> that I was
> a man lost
> to the north when
> in that warm sea
> under that pink sunset
> time suddenly became liquid. (246)

There are echoes here of his hot baths in Montreal, only in this case the sea is unconfined and almost maternal in the way it allows him to feel once more a sensation of warmth and liberty that he had long forgotten and most likely doubted he could ever feel again.

The trip into the country, in addition to being a journey back to his previous, pre-exile self, is just as importantly a means of encountering and remembering his father who again (like the nephew), is a kind of double of the author. This multisided play of identities is emphasized when Laferrière visits François, an old friend of his father (and of the wealthy doctor). François knows immediately that the father has died, judging Laferrière to be the "spitting image" of his father (249). To François, it does not matter where the father died, for to him, "You don't die anywhere. You die" (ibid.). The image that François presents of the father is of a young intellectual, gifted and charismatic, in other words not too different from the young Laferrière. François's description of the father, and his immediate recognition of Laferrière emphasize the importance of recognition to the author, even by those who have never seen him, and further suggests that in mourning his father he tries in a sense to save the father and to incorporate him and his memory into his own being and consciousness. In effect, Laferrière seeks to recognize the father as part of himself, as an element of his own being that has always been there, but that he has been unable to recognize until now. As he journeys through the country his own identity becomes less uniquely that of the individual who has lived in exile for more than thirty years than that of a composite being, made from other people, places, and times.

Perhaps the most important of these other people that have become part of him is the author's grandmother, Da. Laferrière stops at Petit-Goâve to visit her grave and 88 rue Lamarre, where he spent his childhood with her. He initially has trouble recognizing the home, but once he does his memories return and he reflects that those times "will never end" (256). Time in general has a different value in the countryside. People seem more attached to the places they live in, and more in tune with the "natural" passage of time. Many of the country people "remain immobile," while Laferrière spends his life "running" (258). When he arrives in another small, dusty village, the simple life of the people makes him feel that he has fallen into another time, that ten years separate him from Port-au-Prince, which he has just left. In many ways, the gap in time seems greater than ten years; the more they journey into the country the more they sense that life there has a quite different rhythm, dictated by a historical and cultural memory that incorporates slavery, the U.S. occupation of 1915–1934, and the long-standing struggles with the Haitian state (269). His dialogues with his nephew reveal something of his understanding of exile and belonging. Young Dany asks him what it is like to live abroad, and Laferrière replies that it has become the same as living in Haiti, that he has "lost the notion of territory," and it is not clear whether or not he regrets the way that time and exile have recast his conception of place (258). It does appear, however, that his idea of place and landscape has much in common with that of Glissant, particularly the latter's call for an "aesthetics of the earth" that has little to do with an "obsolete mysticism" of place and which eschews "territorial thought" (*Poetics of Relation* 150, 146). For both figures, an aesthetics of the earth "rises to the challenge of appreciating beauty even when the land and sea have been ravaged by colonial violence," and "in the context of waste and rupture can enable a regenerative response" (De Loughrey and Handley 27). In Laferrière's case, such regeneration is both an intimate, personal affair and an attempt to re-present as beautiful just such a site of apparent waste and rupture, in accordance with the role he assigns himself in his writing of a "primitive writer," an author who works, much like a "primitive" or "naïve" painter along what Benson calls "the unbridgeable chasm that seems to lie between the beauties of the painted [or written] tropical paradise and the wretchedness of a failing ecosystem" (Benson 62).[18]

Paradoxically, Laferrière's relationship to the land and the sights of the countryside is more immediate and fresh than that of the country people, but this only reminds him that he is "no longer from the region" (275). He sees and appreciates natural things, such as the beauty of the sunrise, which the local people no longer remark upon. It is nature rather than a specific territory that he wants to lose himself in, as he writes:

> I would like to lose
> all consciousness
> of my being
> so that I might
> melt into nature
> and become a leaf,
> a cloud
> or the yellow of the rainbow. (275–76)

However, the final connection with nature and with his dead father must be, he realizes, a personal affair, and he lets the driver and young Dany go back to the city while he continues alone to his final destination, his father's native village of Baradères (278). He does so in the back of a lorry full with other passengers and their animals. The effect of this final stage of the journey is unexpectedly soothing as he shuts out all thought to let himself be "cradled" by the crowd, where "the barrier between men and animals is very thin" (279). The truck has something of the feel of Noah's Ark, a suggestion reinforced by the heavy rain that they encounter as they reach the native village. The movement from drought to rainfall may also be an oblique reference to the narrator's own process of mourning, his ability to shed tears now that he is alone in his father's place of birth. Paradoxically, too, it is now that he is alone with people who do not know him at all that he starts to feel at home, and that he gives up his thoughts and consciousness to feel himself as a natural being.

Strangely, too, it is in the back of the lorry that he meets the person in the book with whom he can identify the most. An older woman, who has lived with her son in Brooklyn while her husband stayed in Haiti, is returning to bury her husband, whose coffin is at the back of the lorry. In a further echo of the narrator's own situation, a woman says of the grieving son that he is the "spitting image" of his dead father (280). As the narrator recognizes, he is in more or less the same situation, except he has no corpse with him "and almost no memory of the deceased" (ibid.). This journey without a corpse is, he says, to take his father back to his native village, a place the narrator is discovering for the first time (ibid.). "A ceremony so intimate," he says, "that it concerns only me. Father and son, for once, together alone" (281).

Stripped of his "urban airs," he becomes more aware of a deep, almost primitive element of being, the forgotten feelings and sacred chants that "only resurface at our funerals" (282). "We have two lives," he says, remarking how the young boy is discovering a part of his family and himself he has never known: "one that belongs to us. The second that belongs to those who have known us since childhood" (ibid.). In his father's native village, the narrator seems to be liberated from both of those lives: no one here knows him or asks him about his past and his future (284), and sleeping under the stars in his father's place of origin, he feels suddenly "so light" (285). Feeling that the sky is as close as the banana leaf he rests his head on, he finds finally in natural things his own nature.

It is in this natural state, divested of his thoughts and preoccupations, that he can finally imagine his own father's nature, his early life and motivations. He is drawn to the local cemetery, which he accesses through a banana plantation that is traversed by a stream, natural phenomena that he passes through to be able to think about his father (286). The starry night expands his sense of time and space; he thinks of his father as a child running "only yesterday" in the rain of Baradères (287). The vastness of the universe at night is both a metaphor for the mystery of his father's being and memory and a measure of the infinite grief a single death can bring about. The narrator sits on another person's tomb to think of and pay homage to the father that he never knew. His father, he reflects, again no doubt with his own life in mind, could have remained in his native village and never have known such a "strange destiny" (ibid.). He imagines how his father's journey must have started in the grass paths and rocky byways that lead to the main road, and how these routes led him to Port-au-Prince, and then to Havana, Paris, Genoa, Buenos Aires, Berlin, Rome, and finally New York (288). He imagines too that his father's character was unchanging, and that the adolescent must have foreseen on a starry night in Baradères at the beginning of his journey all the routes that he would take in his life, and even his son's life, which would be "an extension of his own and so like his own" (289). They each had their own dictator—Papa Doc for the father, Baby Doc for the son—and their own exile, "without return" for the father, and with this "enigmatic return" for the son (ibid.). The narrator's final act for his father is to give him a return, not of his body, but of his soul and spirit, those elements that allowed him to live in solitude for so long. For the narrator, there is a natural, circular movement in life that starts in a small place then leads out into the "vast world," and returns finally the "point of departure" (290).

Baradères is not however the narrator's final stop on his journey. He leaves there by sea in a sailing boat filled with merchants in a scene that recalls his arrival in the village. In both cases, the simple yet sophisticated lives of his fellow passengers give the journey an almost biblical quality; these are fisher people, merchants connected by the sea, trade and ancient family ties. His destination this time is the small coastal town of Abricots, the place thought of as "paradise" by the Arawaks (297), and where he sees in the natural world, the trees touching the sea, the red fish wriggling in the fishermen's boats, the children devouring sweet mangoes, the "languorous life of the time before Columbus" (ibid.). Unsure of whether he is in a "real time," he steps into this world he has long dreamed of, reposing in this pre-Columbian haven for three months to cure himself of the rhythms of urban life, to no longer think of his existence as a constant alternation between polar opposites, winter and summer, north and south, and to discover at last "spherical life," as he puts it (ibid. 298). Cradled by the "old Caribbean wind," he sleeps with a smile on his face, like he did when he was a child living with his grandmother, a time that "has finally come back" (299, 300). Thus returned by and through nature to this previous sense of himself and his place in the world, he pronounces finally the phrase that expresses the secret wish—or fear—of every traveler or exile: "It is the end of the journey" (300).[19]

Memory and Forgetting in *Yanvalou pour Charlie*

The motifs of exile, return, the city, the hinterland, memory, recognition, and identity are also prominent in Lyonel Trouillot's *Yanvalou pour*

Charlie, another remarkable, internationally acclaimed novel published in the year before the earthquake. The novel focuses primarily on a stratum of Haitian society that is not often presented in literary works: the professional middle class, represented in this case by Mathurin D. Saint-Fort, a young and ambitious commercial lawyer whose life in the city revolves around work and associated social events. In some senses, the novel could be about any similar young professional living in any city of the world. In a country with a notoriously high unemployment rate, everyday working life is not often adopted as a literary theme, but in this novel Trouillot focuses precisely on the quotidian, routine world of steady work, the ambitions and petty jealousies of office work, and the indignities involved in giving oneself entirely to one's career. The case of Mathurin is especially acute as he was not born into this class; rather he comes from a humble background in the country, which he has forced himself to forget and renounce in order to be accepted into the urban professional classes. The tension in the novel revolves around this denial of memory and origins. Remarkably for Trouillot, who like Laferrière is very much an urban-centered author, the novel builds to a reconsideration of nature and the hinterland as enriching elements, vital to the construction of a viable individual and collective identity. Just before the earthquake, then, Trouillot as much as Laferrière was reevaluating the hinterland and its associated culture, which had for so long been associated with outdated notions of indigenist authenticity, but which reemerge here quite remarkably and unexpectedly as sites of possible salvation for the alienated urbanite.

The tropes of memory and forgetting are signaled from the opening lines, which state: "I come from a very small village. That is one of the things that I have forgotten" (11). For a man such as Mathurin, who has struggled to get to get to the position where he can now climb the social ladder, "memory is a luxury, not a necessity" (11). The culture of the office is based on artifice; his colleagues Francine and Elisabeth are one-dimensional figures, the former given to complaining, the latter self-interested and ambitious, seeking to become the director of an NGO (12). The boss has no professional merits, and has inherited the practice. He and his wife own several homes and live in the one farthest from the city. The model of urban and suburban planning is much like that remarked on by Laferrière in *L'énigme du retour:* suburbs are built by the middle classes, until the shantytowns encroach too closely, and the rich move ever higher up the mountainside (12). Not truly belonging to this class, Mathurin views it from an ironic distance, caustically presenting the bourgeois manners and petty concerns of the boss and his wife, chiefly the wife's panics over living apart from the lower classes (13). His social circle is limited to others like him, those who participate in "this culture of [social] climbing" (14), and who are at once "almost rich" and "almost poor," not fully belonging to any social class (19). One important effect of the professional culture is to blur the distinction between truth and fiction: the boss lies routinely to convince potential clients, the only important thing being "victory" (15). Also, Mathurin has evolved to have "neither points of view nor prejudices"—values and opinions are some of the things that he has forgotten (17). It is only when he retires to his home that he can "forget everything" about the office and sit alone with a glass of whisky and his guitar (16). The guitar becomes a kind of aide-memoire for him, a connection to the village he came from, the memory of which he has had to repress. In effect, Mathurin, like Laferrière's narrator figure, is in exile, uprooted from a place and culture that he fears returning to, and alienated in a city that requires such forgetting in order to survive and thrive there. As he writes: "I come from nowhere" (23).

The novel suggests however that the two worlds—the city and the country—cannot be definitively separated and the past cannot be completely forgotten. The illusions and vanities of the urban present are shattered by the irruption of the rural past in the shape of Charlie, an adolescent from Mathurin's village who appears at the office seeking help. Charlie's appearance has the effect of upsetting Mathurin's hard-fought yet fragile sense of himself, "reawakening the dead and good feelings," and bringing back into his consciousness "stories of the village, murder, dirty money, love and poverty" (24). The most "dangerous" thing that Charlie brought into Mathurin's life was political in nature, "the adoption of something that could resemble a cause, with arguments for and against, reflections and a point of view on realities outside of my own" (ibid.). This is dangerous as it risks bringing Mathurin out of his apolitical cynicism, and fatally weakening the foundations of his life in the city.

When Charlie enters the office, he appears as a "thing," a "curiosity," a forgotten, emaciated being in dirty clothes, a "foreigner" from a different place and almost a different time (25–26, 27). He also takes with him Mathurin's previous self, the return of which is announced when he calls Mathurin by his other forename, Dieutor, the name the lawyer has repressed for its connotations of the countryside and which the only girl he has loved, Anne, used to call him (32). As he reflects, among the urban professional classes, "nobody likes the countryside" (39). There is also a fascinating level of communication that opens up between Charlie and Mathurin: the lawyer hears things that the boy does not speak aloud, phrases and thoughts in which lie truths that Mathurin cannot avoid. "You want to lie to me but you cannot," Charlie says without speaking. The words that Mathurin hears in Charlie's silences are, he realizes, his own words, "those that I have killed, like my memory" (36). For all that he resents the sudden appearance of Charlie in the office and the way it shatters his professional identity, Mathurin does not deny Charlie, and chooses to not have him ejected back onto the street. To Charlie's question "Is it you Dieutor?" he replies in the affirmative, which suggests that he is almost relieved to be recognized for what he is, or was before (38). The potential damage to his professional image is compensated by Charlie's recognition of his former self. Almost like a ghost from his past, Charlie revisits Mathurin, reminding him of all that he has forgotten and "opening the door of return" (28). As in Laferrière's novel therefore, return becomes an imperative for the exiled urbanite, and the protagonist is shaken out of the modern present to go back to a time and place whose memory has long been suppressed. "Without being invited," Mathurin writes, "Charlie, in his quest for a future, imposed on me a memory" (33).

As in Laferrière's work, the return and the memory are closely connected to questions of mortality. One senses that death is something Mathurin has run away from in moving to the city. His memories of the village are colored by death and the everyday tedium of village life, notably the road death of a child and the passing of his mentor, Gédéon (44). His first memory of death relates to an old man he saw walking in the street as a hurricane struck the village, his guitar round his shoulder. The man lived alone, and would disappear for weeks at a time to return to play spinning tops and strum his guitar on the beach. Mathurin and his father were the last to see him; he walked into the sea one day and never returned. "My first death," Mathurin writes, "had no body" (34). This experience seems to make Mathurin fearful of music and art; his father explains to him that artists are susceptible to that kind of fate. Having begun to play the guitar himself, he became fearful that when the wind blew death would come looking for him too. Encouraged by his mentor, the old man Gédéon, he persists with the guitar however, and begins to visit the local cemetery, learning the names on all the tombs, and taking his love Anne there to hear the music of the drums (35). This encounter with death seems to create a range of associations between death, music, art, and love that he lives with still. Playing his guitar alone at night in the city, he can feel again the intensity of his youthful emotions, while retaining a distance from them, living for his career and eliminating from his life anything unrelated to his social advancement.

Charlie's arrival in the office upsets the fragile equilibrium Mathurin had established, and he is pulled, half willingly, half reluctantly into Charlie's world, and by extension the neglected world of the peasantry. On the first night Charlie sleeps on his sofa and his presence is enough to trigger in Mathurin dreams of the country. Waking up the next day with in his mouth "the odor of the country," he reflects that it was the "first time for ages that I spent a night in my village" (50). Charlie literally takes him by the hand back into that world; on seeing a policeman, Charlie grabs Dieutor's hand to cross the road, a practice common to peasants, and which marks the two out as country people in the city (41). The physical contact between the two complements the emotional rapprochement that takes place almost immediately. Dieutor's identity becomes fused with that of Charlie; the two become a double act, inseparable, their fates intertwined. More broadly, the author suggests that the fate of the country cannot be separated from that of the city, that the two sites are complementary, and specifically that the city can potentially be saved by incorporating something of the memory and culture of the country.

This play of identity is something like that in *L'énigme du retour,* particularly the way in which the urban individual's discrete identity is dismantled in the encounter with elements from his past; and the model that emerges of a composite being, of an individual made up of others. In a sense, too, Charlie becomes a surrogate for Mathurin's deceased half-brother, Ismaël, the product of his father's liaison with a peasant woman, who died at five years old without Mathurin ever knowing him. The death of Ismaël has a profound effect on Mathurin, and leads directly to his decision to leave the village and to abandon everyone and everything associated with it, including his father and mother, Anne, and its music, drums, and dances (58). His great fear is to become like his father, and for Anne to be like his mother. In other words, his decision to leave is motivated more by his knowledge of what he does not want to become than by a clear idea of what and whom he wishes to be. In choosing law, as his mentor Gédéon tells him, he is choosing an "actor's profession" that will help him bring about change in his life. At the same time, as Gédéon cautions, "every actor takes off his mask one day and in doing so becomes a stranger to himself" (60). The presence of Charlie forces him to take off the mask of Mathurin and to reveal once again Dieutor, who has become, as Gédéon foresaw, a stranger.

Charlie

The play of identities in the novel is emphasized in and enacted by the narrative style, the alternation between first-person narrators, chiefly Dieutor and Charlie.[20] The latter's narrative style is marked by his verbosity—he says they speak a lot at the shelter, "It's our drug" (77)—and by his verbal tics, notably the word *sorry* that he repeats at regular intervals, especially just as he begins to speak, as if he has to apologize for his very being. Indeed, as he says, "when you are nobody's sons and when you no longer have a country, you always have to apologize for yourself for being wherever you are or simply for being alive" (76). Charlie also apologizes for telling his story, as he realizes that listening to other people's stories is always a dangerous activity, pulling the listener into the world of the storyteller and potentially disrupting the listener's life. As he says, "All the ills of the world come from the stories we tell" (79). He moreover plays the role of apologist for the country, the provincial areas that people like him have abandoned in favor of the city. "Nobody likes the country," he says, "except for holidays and old beliefs. If it were not so, people would remain there" (65). The province and the country are interchangeable concepts for him, both being neglected, almost invisible phenomena; as he says, "they are words that you can't always put an image to" (ibid.). In essence, people go to the city to be saved or to save; Charlie and Dieutor are in the former category, while Father Edmond, who runs the homeless children's shelter that Charlie lives in, is in the latter.[21] It is almost like a self-perpetuating industry: the church and other charitable organizations require a constant supply of the desperate and needy to keep the industry going. The criminal activities of Charlie and his small band of accomplices have led to their dismissal from the shelter, and at this point Charlie seeks out Dieutor's help "in the name of the old beliefs" (69).

Charlie's friends have much in common with him, in that they come from rural backgrounds, their families rent apart by poverty. The city and the country are like different worlds with quite different values and beliefs. Charlie's retention of the "old beliefs" of communal help is as out of place in the city as his friend Filidor's Vodou beliefs, his conviction that in every square inch of the countryside there roams an army of the dead (ibid.). An emotionally fragile child, Filidor is haunted by the gods, and tries unsuccessfully to free himself of them by believing in the one God of

Father Edmond. The Christian catechism does little to quell the influence of the Vodou gods in Filidor, and the shelter is "invaded" by the country divinities (71). There is a suggestion that Filidor's emotional troubles have an identifiable cause: his homosexuality, which manifests itself in the shelter in his relationship with Gino. In their different ways, both Christianity and Vodou seem to encourage Filidor's neurosis, seeing in his sexual difference the influence of malignant spiritual forces. Nathanaël, the band's leader, is emotionally quite different, dismissing all divinities, and being "fearful of nothing" (ibid.). Free of the fears that haunt the rest of the group, Nathanaël is seen by Charlie as "a leader, a real boss who has no boss, and always ready to help you out" (72). Nathanaël is also the most politically motivated of the group and, encouraged by his love for the young bourgeois militant Yanick, he talks of equality and of changing the world (ibid.). It is Nathanaël who is sensitive to the love between the Filidor and Gino, and who calls for an end to their mistreatment, saying that "there is not enough love in the world" and that "you have to take it wherever you find it" (81). There is a distinctly romantic side to Nathanaël's politics, which is most evident in his clinging to the symbol of the star he sees one evening on an old cinema poster. The star inspires Nathanaël to devise a plan whereby the others, if they follow him, will each be able to buy their own star (82). His own wish is for something of an ideal world, one in which "everything goes well," and which offers "a star for each living person" (86). The political arrangement he establishes among the group of four is strikingly democratic, in that he always listens to the others' opinions, and every decision is taken by the group (81). There is a primitive sense of order and communal togetherness among the group; and when they decide together to leave the shelter at nights they act like a pack, each one is but part of the broader group, dependent on the others for survival.

Charlie is less politically motivated than Nathanaël; his ideals are based on his pragmatic understandings of what makes the society work. "It's quite simple," Charlie says. "What makes the difference between people? Money. With money you can buy what you want" (83). The group stole money to put it aside and decide what to do with it later, as a kind of security for the future (ibid.).

Father Edmond, like Charlie, is something of a storyteller, and it is through hearing the priest's stories that Charlie realizes there is a danger in listening to other people's tales. "Nobody ever tells a story for nothing," Charlie says (79). In the priest's case, every story has a moral at the end, and sometimes there are two morals that contradict each other.

For instance, Father Edmond tells the story of Jesus in order that the children might be like him, while telling them that nobody will ever be the same as Jesus. In Charlie's mind, Jesus is like Pelé or Maradona: you might want to play like them, but know you will never be as good (ibid.). Father Edmond's hopes for the boys are limited to their living a humble, respectable life, not bothering anyone else, his biblical model being Joseph (ibid.). But biblical stories of humility and respectability seem ill suited to the lives of the urban poor. Charlie has seen older boys who have left the shelter determined to live the life of Joseph and look for their Mary to found their own home. The story rarely ends well, however, as a "Joseph without tools" and a Mary "made ugly and ever more jealous by poverty" do little but create a great number of "little Jesuses all destined for the way of the Cross" (84). The Joseph gets angry and begins to beat his wife and children. Alternatively, if you are not a Joseph, you might become another biblical figure, Barabbas, an insurrectionary, a robber or kidnapper hooked on cocaine (ibid.). These are again the Chimères, the apocalyptic urban gangster figures, their own identities and narratives borrowed from other places and grotesquely contorted by the extreme nature of urban living in Haiti. The urban poor have in effect two choices: to live in endless misery or in a momentary "glory" that ends in a "bloodbath" (85). The Chimères' true glory comes only after death, when they are presented on the television news, their faces mutilated, and their only means of identification their clothes and chains, the latter no doubt constituting a symbol of the ongoing, unending enslavement of the poor.

What is interesting about Charlie's group is that they seek for themselves, at least initially, a third way; neither Joseph nor Barabbas, they want to live "far from the parables something like a normal life" (ibid.). In some ways, however, their vision combines elements of the two other narratives: to achieve the normal life they desire they must carry out robberies, not for a moment of glory but to live in the future the kinds of lives they speak of among themselves. The future is in this sense a story, almost a fantasy for them in a life that forces them to live forever with the pressing demands of the present and the inescapable consequences of the past. It is a story that relies on money for its realization, for as Charlie says "to be the person you want to be, you need to have some cash in reserve" (86). As he does in his other works, notably *Bicentenaire,* Trouillot deliberately plays on issues of morality and ethics, suggesting that the group is justified in carrying out its robberies.[22] As Charlie reflects, they throw the stolen wallets over the walls of the houses of the rich so that they could be returned to their owners by "someone who had sufficient means to be honest and sufficient time to be kind" (88). Such qualities are implicitly the preserve of the rich; and a quite different set of values applies to the poor. It is Nathanaël who largely determines the ethics of the group, as it progresses from pick pocketing to burglaries. In effect, to have any chance of living a decent, ethical life, one has to carry out unethical actions.

It is also Nathanaël who upsets the initial reason for being part of the group—to accumulate money so that they can each live the life they want to. Nathanaël the romantic is seduced by two related dreams, his two personal "stars": that of a possible social order based on "perfect equality" (94); and that of ever being loved by Yanick, the young bourgeois militant who encourages his belief in social utopia. As Charlie reflects, "everything was going well, until the day [Nathanaël] started to take seriously the ideas that circulate on the outside" (92). In a practical sense, Nathanaël's romantic ideals lead to a split in the group and a decision to divide up two years early the money they had accumulated. They moreover lead to Nathanaël using a pistol during the band's final burglary, much to the others' anger. The pistol becomes a symbol of Nathanaël's political convictions, and also of his love for Yanick and of the extremes he will go to in order to impress her. His ultimate act in this regard is to kill a businessman, again to impress Yanick, whom Charlie regards as false, barely believing in the things she reads in her books (99). To Charlie, Nathanaël and Yanick's rhetoric evokes only fear, the same emotion he feels when Father Edmond reads the story of Moses and the Pharaoh. "It's nice," Charlie says, "but people don't stop dying, and the war, even when it is over, continues in another way and the people still don't stop dying and nothing changes" (94). If preaching religion or politics did any good, Charlie argues, Father Edmond would already have transformed the city into an earthly paradise, people would no longer come to live in a lifeless city, and the people who "get themselves killed" would finally feel at home (ibid.). Crucially, Charlie is aware of the political arguments, but believes that they are not relevant, that they are "not things for our time" (ibid.). The specifics of the contemporary period can find no resolution in the old political narratives, which are to Charlie, little other than "madness" (95). He sees no point in Nathanaël's study group, given that "they all think the same thing" and that "the great plans always end up failing" (96). For Nathanaël and his fellow militants, studies lead to action, while for Charlie it is the opposite: action is primary, and learning secondary (ibid.). As such, Charlie's position is not so much apolitical as post-political, belonging to an age in which ideas of communal salvation have seemingly lost any capacity they may previously have had to alter society.

Nathanaël

The section of the novel entitled "Nathanaël" is apparently narrated not by the character himself but by a third-person narrator. It is not entirely clear why this is so, but it seems to suggest that his voice is somehow compromised by or lost in political rhetoric. Also, a good part of the section focuses on characters other than Nathanaël, which perhaps reflects his democratic principles or again, less positively, the way he in a sense sacrifices himself to those principles. It could be that the third-person narrator is in fact Nathanaël and that this is the mode best suited to his persona. No characters are named in this section, which has a more detached, allegorical feel. The section recounts the movement toward Nathanaël's sister's home, the place where the accumulated money has been hidden, and where it will now be split up between the group members. The band is now itself divided into smaller factions: Dieutor and Charlie; Filidor and Gino; and Nathanaël and the bourgeois militants. For Dieutor it is a journey into the heart of the city's misery, the world he believed himself to be insulated from, but which he is now drawn to, and forced to confront. It is a hellish, apocalyptic world, with no streets, only narrow passages that wind between the slums. The land they walk on is itself uncertain, shifting: made up of bottles, cans, cartons, and fruit peelings, it is an "uneven" land that sinks or hardens according to the elements it is made up of (103). Their destination is the very end of the slum, another composite place, where the mud meets the sea, the urban detritus has replaced the sand, and the city almost overflows into the water.

The journey has something of the classical quest narrative, in that it changes the travelers markedly. Specifically, Dieutor and Charlie's identities become doubled, enmeshed, the one melting into the other. This is signaled first in the clothes they wear: Charlie wears his Sunday best, new shirt, pants, and sneakers bought for him by Dieutor, while Dieutor also wears "somber" clothing, shirts, pants, and sneakers that he found in an old chest and which he chose to make him look "poor" (105). The near-matching clothes they wear are signs of a broader rapprochement that has taken place in the intervening few days that they have spent together: Dieutor has become increasingly paternal toward Charlie, whose presence has evoked in Dieutor forgotten melodies that he plays on his guitar, most notably a *yanvalou* that Anne loved to listen to and which now "haunts" him (ibid.). But their relationship is fragile, literally on an uncertain footing, crossing a land that "mutates" incessantly (ibid.).

Also fragile now is the relationship between Charlie and the rest of the band. The sub-group of Filidor and Gino are said to be no longer sure that they really know anyone (107). Like Charlie and Dieutor, Filidor and Gino form a couple, only the latter's bond is far tighter: they are "an old couple, they complete and support each other, equal in affection, different in size and abilities" (ibid.). They are moreover an amalgam of the city and the country: Filidor has always stood out in the city for the unusual shape of his head, while Gino is a child of the city, who has developed a quite particular set of competencies that allow him to survive in the city. Unlike the others, Gino decided himself to enter the shelter, after having assessed the living conditions it offered and comparing them to those on the outside. His great skill is in planning and calculating, while Filidor's talent is for running, specifically running from misfortune (108). When they feel fear, they instinctively move closer to each other, like animals in a threatening environment. It is their togetherness that guarantees their survival; alone they would no doubt perish.

While Gino and Filidor complement each other in every way, Charlie and Dieutor make a more haphazard couple, literally out of step with each other. Having trouble finding the "rhythm of their footsteps," they are a team "in search of itself" (109). There is however an unspoken, shared desire to truly find the other and to fall into the other's rhythm, which is what they gradually begin to achieve the more they advance together toward the end of the slum. At the same time, their friendship, or "something that does not yet have a precise name" develops (112). Tellingly, neither one no longer feels the need to say sorry (114). Dieutor has more trouble adapting to the slum, the images, sounds, and smells of which shock him. It is a place within Haiti, but which seems foreign to him, almost otherworldly, especially in the way that animals (poultry, dogs, rats) and humans live in close proximity. In this sense, the distinction between animal and human existence seems minimal; each species is reduced to scraping a living in a degraded, lifeless place. The foreign nature of the slum is emphasized in the different language that Dieutor hears there, the words that he heard first in Charlie's mouth and which he now hears all around him in the shantytown. He is radically out of place, a "foreigner, far from himself" (113).

Also out of place in the slum is the woman first identified as Nathanaël's sister. Nathanaël is noticeably protective of her, and insists that the band should not use her to provide information on the rich people she cleans for (89). She is one of the few visitors who come to the shelter, and appears particularly demoralized. Living in one of the poorest shantytowns, she is a ghostly figure who looks far older than her twenty-nine years; with her scarred face and "clothes from another time" (91) it is "like she is dead" (92). The scar was inflicted by her lover, "because of her child," who turns out to be Nathanaël, whom she took to the shelter for protection before taking the time to have her wound treated (115). She lives now with a sense of shame, and has no memories; the only thing she remembers is her monthly visit to the shelter (116). She resents not the man who inflicted her scar, but life for closing the factory she worked in, and for making the neighborhood a "tomb" (125). Through the sister/mother character the text identifies how living in the slum distorts identity and being. The scar on her face is a "war wound in an unfinished war" (132); it is moreover a visual sign of the rupture in her life, her severed relationship with her son, who is aware of the truth but who still calls her sister, in a further example of role-playing and the adoption of false identities (123). Something like Dieutor/Mathurin but in a more desperate way, she is forced to adopt a false identity and to lose virtually all of her memories to survive in the city.

The issue of false identity is further raised in the case of the third group that makes its way through the slum. This group is the "most disparate" of the three, and is composed of a girl (Yanick) and two boys (Nathanaël and Yanick's brother, Franck). Although it is Nathanaël who leads the way, he is in reality "the one that follows" (119). He feels that in pursuing Yanick he has betrayed his idea that one should take love where one finds it, and is now looking for it "elsewhere" (ibid.). In contrast to Nathanaël and the rest of the band, Yanick and her brother have learned everything from books, been brought up protected, "overprotected" by parents (120). Like Nathanaël however and unlike Charlie, learning for Yanick precedes action; she has learned in books about the place that she now crosses and that "to construct, one must destroy" (ibid.). The sense that she is playing a role is emphasized in the fact that she has chosen the name Yanick (her real name being Johanne; her brother's real name is Andy). Yanick is the name she uses for her secret meetings with her fellow militants, a persona that she adopts in these circumstances but which she drops when around her parents. Having revolted first in her books, she sees now in Nathanaël a "real poor person," a kind of character from her books made real. "It is for people like him that she adopted the cause," the narrator says, "without knowing them" (120–21). She particularly likes that he has killed for the cause, knowing that he did it for her. She is less comfortable with the reality that, outside of her books, the real poor would have desires and feel love. It is her play of identity that prevents her from reciprocating Nathanaël's love. Underneath Yanick, Johanne is still there, and Johanne "cannot love" the boy that Yanick is following through the slum. She can only love another like her; a volunteer like her who fights for others. She cannot love the "subject of the cause," and will explain to him one day the "difference between humanism and true love" (121). In this sense, the play of identities and masking cuts across all social classes, distorts relationships between people, and confuses individuals' sense of themselves. The effects of these distorted identities vary however according to the social status of the person affected: in Yanick's case, her "real" identity is something she can slip in and out of at ease without compromising her status; Dieutor/Mathurin's life is radically upset by the irruption of Charlie and his past into his life; while the sister/mother lives forever on the scar, as it were, between her two, incomplete identities.

To the mother, Yanick and her brother come from "another world" (122). Her maternal instincts make her suspicious of the bourgeois militants, and she senses a danger for her son, whose headaches have intensified since he killed the businessman, an act he carried out to "help out" the group, when Franck could not pull the trigger (126, 127). It is Franck's fear that brings about the event that finally tears the original band apart. When Gino appears with a sack of money and a gun, Franck becomes nervous. Gino fires his gun, knowing it is loaded with blank cartridges, to "put the fear up the two jokers who claim to change the world" (131). Franck's response is to fire back with his own pistol, missing Gino but hitting Charlie, fatally wounding him. This exchange of fire seems to say something about politics and social class relationships. The act of defiance by the poor and the challenge to the pretensions of the bourgeois militants makes a sound like a real bullet, but it is a blank that is purposely aimed to hurt no one, only to shake the middle class out of its complacent assumptions and to truly recognize the poor on their own terms. The reaction to such a challenge is heavy-handed and concerned only with self-preservation. Unable to interpret the meaning of Gino's shot, Franck's reaction is to fire indiscriminately, to destroy the very object of his and Yanick's political activism. The discord between the two classes hurts finally only one side, while the rich can return safely to their homes and alternate identities. Crucially, following the shootings, Yanick no longer recognizes herself, and does not know which of the two names to call her brother; he "looks like both at the same time" (135).

Nathanaël, too, can no longer sustain his identity as a brother and breaks into a violent fit of tears and anger that only his mother can face, as she too is finally able to play that role (138). Cradling him for once like a child, she becomes the mother of Nathanaël, who also gives up on the identities he has adopted to fill the void created by his ruptured relationship with his mother and falls into the sleep of a child, without headaches and without stars (142).

Anne

The final section of the novel is entitled "Anne," though it is not narrated exclusively by Dieutor's former love. It opens with his voice, reflecting on Charlie's final hours and the effect it has had on him. More accurately, it is no longer exclusively Dieutor's voice, but a composite entity that incorporates elements of Charlie's verbal style. "I have careless moments," Dieutor says "in which his voice continues to speak inside of me, and sometimes, without doing it deliberately, his words come out of my mouth" (148). The change in voice indicates a deeper change in his identity, which itself has become infused with aspects of Charlie's character. Dieutor returns to his professional and social world, and is all the more detached from and cynical about it. Not truly belonging to the urban bourgeoisie, he identifies the hypocrisy and petty jealousies that seem to abound in that world, and at times voices his real thoughts, which are echoes of what Charlie would have said, and are uttered much to the embarrassment of his colleagues and associates (ibid.). In a sense, he is already too old to change his life and being completely: as he says, "One's nature does not change once you have reached thirty" (150). In another way, however, he has changed, and this is signaled in his voicing Charlie's words unexpectedly and in writing and receiving letters. He has learned, he says, that "nothing is immobile. Time displaces everything. Even places"(ibid.).

It is through letters that the voice of Anne is communicated. Her letters appear like missives from another time, the world that Dieutor has largely forgotten, but which has continued to exist in his absence. It is Dieutor who instigates the communication, apparently moved by the death of Charlie to reconnect to some extent with his past and the people and places he has left behind; "everything is mixed up in me," he says on reading the letters, "everything is intertwined" (159). The image Anne presents of the village suggests a place divided by long-standing resentments, between the "main street" and the "secondary streets," and between the inhabitants of the village and the people living on the other side of the canal (151). The latter site is associated with the "former plantations and drums," and is considered by the people of the village to be related to the peasantry (ibid.). The old hierarchies are still in place, and communication with the outside is difficult; letters are rarely delivered to the addressee. But it is the epistolary form that Anne prefers, as it gives the two parties "time to reflect" as they wait to receive their replies (152).

Anne has followed a quite different path to Dieutor; trained as a teacher, she lives a modest life and dreams of building a secondary school. She has only visited Port-au-Prince twice, but realized that she is "not made for life in the cities" (154). The great mystery for Anne concerns exile, and why some leave their places of origin and others stay. Through her letters to Dieutor she gains a sense of traveling, "of visiting an elsewhere," which leads her to reflect that perhaps the real journeys are the "little visits from one person to another" (168). Although she has lived in the same place, she is no less susceptible to the effects of time. "Here, without budging," she says, "I have seen the present chase away the past" (161). The things that Dieutor left behind are no longer there, and "it is not distance that has killed them, but time" (162). This is important, as it reminds the exile Dieutor that the exile brought about by time can be as significant as that of place, and that no matter where one lives, one is never immune to feelings of exile and loss. As Anne says, too, underscoring one of the novel's central ideas, time has the inevitable effect on people of distancing them from the people they were and of forcing them into a "play of roles" that characterizes the present time (163). Time affects not only people, but also the land, in that it can no longer sustain the people that live and work on it. "The land no longer has the means to be the servant of man, his nurturing mother," Anne writes (161). As in Laferrière's *L'énigme du retour,* the countryside is dry, covered in dust, and inhabited by people who are themselves dust-covered, and appear as ghostly figures, rendered gray by the all-consuming dust. The drought and the condition of the land have a direct effect on the culture of the village, as the old rhythms have lost their vigor: "the drums cough and the drummers get tired quickly" (162). The old dances, too, are being lost to time, and the yanvalou and congo of Anne's childhood seem "distant" (ibid.). The yanvalou is particularly important, as its name means "I salute you, oh land," and is as such a means of celebrating and remaining connected to the land (163).

As in Laferrière's novel, too, the hinterland undergoes a radical reevaluation by Trouillot who, to this point, has been very much an author of the city. The hinterland in *Bicentenaire,* for example, is connected to the voice of the mother figure, whose folk proverbs and maxims seem decidedly out of place and of little use to her sons living in the city. In *Yanvalou pour Charlie* as in *L'énigme du retour* there is a remarkable and unexpected turn away from the city and toward the country. Port-au-Prince for Anne is a "city without its own traditions or truth, a city of masks in which people pretend to be that which they are not and become beasts that devour everything in their paths" (167). This turn to the country in Dieutor's case is motivated by his sense of loss, and his need to mourn Charlie and his own half-brother, Ismaël, whose identities become confused as Dieutor thinks of them. Like Laferrière's narrator, Dieutor comes back to the countryside to mourn, to return the deceased to their place of origin. He also makes the journey for the old man Gédéon, the one who taught him to play guitar, for Anne, and for the land itself, to "salute it" in Charlie's name (173). He will give Charlie's money to Anne for her school project, and visit what he calls "the real countryside," across the canal from the village, to participate in the dance (174). It is in the dance, the yanvalou, that Dieutor will pay homage to Charlie, and that Dieutor will pay tribute to his own star, which is the land itself, the "land whose surface is so badly shared out," and that has been "broken up in unequal portions" (ibid.). The drums will speak to him, asking who Mathurin and Dieutor are, and he will reply in both cases that they are him. The drum will ask him who Charlie is and he does not yet know which one, Mathurin or Dieutor, will keep quiet, or which one will speak of Charlie "to the rhythm of the drums" (175). Thus, it is finally through his return to the countryside, to "folk" culture, to dance, and to rhythm that he will seek to reconcile the two parts of his identity, mourn the deaths that haunt him, revisit the memories that he has sought to escape, and crucially, celebrate the land, that neglected, fundamental element without which neither he nor his country can hope to survive.

It is difficult to overstate how unexpected and significant this turn to the country is by these two prominent authors. As Raffy-Hideux writes, the greater part of their work is characterized by "an overrepresentation of the urban space at the expense of the rural space" (349). In addition to being decidedly urban authors, Laferrière and Trouillot had both been markedly reticent, even skeptical about the celebration of "folk" elements in Haitian culture. In Laferrière's other novel of return, *Pays sans chapeau,* the protagonist Old Bones ironically derides the celebration in Haitian ethnography of peasant culture. He does this through his interactions with the ethnographer J. B. Romain, who says that in his analysis of Haiti, he is still "back in Africa," and that in order to understand Haiti,

"We must go to the roots of things" (124). It is the notion of roots and nationalist authenticity that Old Bones most objects to, as he makes clear to the ethnographer: "I must tell you, Professor, that the word *roots,* no matter where it comes from, makes my hair stand on end. If we can do it, why can't the Germans do the same?" (209). Yet Romain insists that the role of Haiti's artists is to produce "propaganda . . . it's all just advertising" (ibid.). In effect, beyond his preoccupation with literary style, this critique of nationalist ethnography has been Laferrière's "cause," and he has consciously chosen not to write in the tradition of ethno-nationalist authors like Roumain and Alexis. One consequence of this is that he has until now avoided the "dusty road" that leads to the countryside and its associated values of cultural roots and authenticity. In *L'énigme du retour,* however, he does take the dusty road and finds in nature and community elements that he had to some extent neglected and which he embraces as a means of mourning his father and reorienting himself in time and space.

If anything, Trouillot has been even more direct in his critique of Haitian cultural nationalism and even more resolutely an author of the city. In his *Rue des pas perdus* (1998), as I have shown, he presents an elderly madam figure who declares that Haitian history is a "corset, a stifling cell . . . an apocalyptic calypso," and that Haiti is an "epic failure factory[,] . . . an abyss for tightrope walkers" (1). Crucially, she blames these failures on intellectual culture, specifically the ethnographic tradition. All contemporary ills began, she says, "with the wind," with gusts of "folkloric-tropical-negritudinal rubbish" (3). Again, this skepticism over nationalist ethnography apparently led the author to largely abandon the countryside and to present the city in all its chaos as the primary site for understanding contemporary Haitian life. His turn to the country and to the folk culture embodied in the yanvalou is perhaps even more remarkable than Laferrière's similar turn. Together these authors suggest a renewed interest in the rural and in nature, and the beginnings of a revived interest in "folk" culture and customs as a counter to the apparently unending, apocalyptic chaos and intractable problems of urban life. It is probably too much to say that these two works signal a sustained, general reengagement with nature and folk life in Haitian literature, but these are two very important authors and one senses in these works from 2009 a turn not so much to the past as to a future in which the apparently timeless culture of the countryside could be properly integrated. In effect, the turn to nature would become one of the most prominent shared themes of the earliest post-earthquake writings.[23]

The final cruel irony of Laferrière's and Trouillot's anti-apocalyptic reengagement with nature is it that took place on the eve of the earthquake, an apocalyptic event that would demonstrate once more the destructive capacity of natural forces and Haiti's particular vulnerability to them.

IN REINTERPRETING nature in the ways described, these two novels echo the interest in early Haitian and broader Latin American and Caribbean writing in nature as part of the "foundational narratives" of emerging nations (Anderson 18). As Dash writes, in nineteenth-century Haiti, literary representations of nature and the land were closely associated with notions of cultural authenticity and constituted "the source of a national ethos" (*The Other America* 48). In many cases, paradise was a key site in the national imaginary proposed by early writers, who were "deeply influenced by the Romantic sublimation of national landscapes" (Anderson 18). These were utopian landscapes that sustained and nurtured national imaginaries and which had little place for natural disasters, or could not foresee the many environmental disasters that would ravage many parts of the region in the twentieth and twenty-first centuries.

Laferrière and Trouillot write of nature in the middle of disaster—the state of permanent catastrophe that Hurbon describes—and find yet in the tropical environment traces of the nurturing qualities that appeared so abundant and infinite in the nineteenth century. They also in effect write against the wider historical discourse about tropical environments, one that has since colonial times presented nature as a source of danger (for the European), and an explanation for issues of poverty and disease. To blame, fatalistically, or even apocalyptically, the environment for social and economic problems in effect obscures the many and complex detrimental effects of European interventions in the Caribbean. In Bankoff's terms the predominance of Western cultural ideas is not restricted to the domain of literature or the social sciences; it is, he says, also evident in the "theoretical underpinnings of the natural sciences that renders unsafe those same regions of the globe as 'marginal environments' through a discourse of disease, poverty and hazard" (28).

Also, particularly in Trouillot's case, there is an interest in the issue of mass urbanization, and the slums that result from it. The neighborhoods that Trouillot writes of are in effect part of what Mike Davis calls the "planet of slums"—the late-twentieth-century growth in shantytowns and the consequent "rapid urbanization of poverty" (*Planet of Slums* 17, 156). By personalizing the experience of slum dwellers, Trouillot suggests something of the lived experience of this displaced and dispossessed, and often anonymous and invisible group. The inner lives of the poor are presented as complex, their needs, desires, and instincts as "natural" as those of any other sector of society. As such, Trouillot's novel serves to critique the colonially rooted discourse of disaster that would place "marginal" people as integral parts of their peripheral, unseen environments, and interpret their poverty as a "natural" product of living in an environment that is itself prone to hazards and disasters. As the 2010 earthquake would show, there is little that is "natural" or inevitable about the damage and suffering caused by particular events, and that just as slums, in Davis's phrase "begin with bad geology" (ibid. 122), so "slum-dwellers" begin with and are defined by bad economics, bad history, and bad politics.

As Mark Anderson argues, a major earthquake destabilizes the idea of the constancy and solidity of the land, and with it is apparently ruptured the "natural" connection between the land and identity, for such an event "sweep[s] the ground from beneath our feet and reduc[es] to rubble our literal and conceptual edifices" (1). It is perhaps surprising, then, that the return to nature and the land, announced in the pre-earthquake novels of Trouillot and Laferrière, has been one of the most marked tendencies of post-earthquake writing. For example, in his earthquake chronicle, Laferrière writes of the enduring vitality of natural phenomena. He notes that birds "do not seem concerned by the situation" (*Tout bouge autour de moi* 39). Also, he remarks that whereas hurricanes sometimes inflict more damage on nature than on human life, "Earthquakes destroy that which man has patiently built while leaving the flower intact" (ibid. 44). In describing earthquake survivors as a "forest of remarkable people" Laferrière effectively associates the people with nature, and suggests their lasting and essential connection to the land. Similarly, in his own earthquake chronicle, Rodney Saint-Éloi remarks on the enduring qualities of nature in the lilacs he sees following the earthquake, which remind him of his childhood, and as such are markers of memory and identity that endure while human creations crumble and disappear (*Haïti Kenbe la!* 132–33). The final paradox for both humans and natural phenomena is that strength and vitality are most tangible in a period of catastrophic destruction, and that it is at a moment of apocalyptic breakdown, when time itself seems to stop, that one senses, through ephemera, something of the infinite passage of time.

Conclusion

THE CARIBBEAN is a space defined by and conceptually inscribed in time: pre- and post-Columbian; colonial and postcolonial; pre- and post-emancipation; pre- and postrevolutionary; pre- and post-independence; and in Haiti's case, pre- and post-occupation, pre- and post-Duvalier, and now perhaps, pre- and post-earthquake. In each case there is a radical and violent irruption in time that is not erased by the apparent movement into the "post-" period, but which instead continues to define time like an inescapable shadow so that any sense of a future truly liberated from the past (however that may be conceived of) remains hanging, suspended, in abeyance. The concept of history as a teleological movement from past to present to future appears redundant and untenable in a region where each time period seems to overlap, turn in or even back on itself, in ways that render time's relationship with history one of the contemporary Caribbean's most pressing philosophical, and political, issues. In David Scott's terms, the once self-evident notion of the natural convergence between time and history requires radical revision, for history itself has in a sense stalled, in the Caribbean and in the broader world. For Scott, history no longer unfolds in a process of "discrete but continuous, modular change," or as a "linear, diachronically stretched-out *succession* of cumulative instants" (*Omens* 5). The future no longer overcomes the past, and the present is not experienced as a "state of expectation and waiting for the fulfillment of the promise of social and political improvement" (ibid.). The primary causes of the sense of historical blockage are the end of the era, again in the Caribbean and elsewhere, of "revolutionary socialist possibility" and the coming to prominence of "the new utopia of liberal democracy, its dogma of human rights, and the disciplining and governmental technologies to urge and enforce its realization"(4). As Scott writes, in the moment where history has appeared so resistant to change, "time has suddenly become more discernible, more conspicuous, more at odds, more palpably *in question*" (12, Scott's emphasis). The apparent end of the prospect of a discernibly different and improved political and social future in the Caribbean had led Scott to write previously that "we live in tragic times" (*Conscripts* 2). The narrative of Caribbean history, and therefore of time, has shifted from the romantic anticolonial model of change and overcoming to one of tragedy, which Scott prefers as a mode of interpreting the stalled present (8). In terms of time, to read Caribbean history as tragedy is to question whether the past can be truly disentangled from the present. In place of the "seemingly progressive rhythm" of time, tragedy presents "a broken series of paradoxes and reversals," unpredictable, nonlinear movements in time and history that confuse any sense of the distinctiveness of past, present, and future (13).

As this book has shown, in Haiti it is not so much the tragic as the apocalyptic mode that has been employed by many artists and authors as a means of narrating the present, in which the past reappears, having never truly been surpassed. In some regards, the differences between the tragic and the apocalyptic reflect those between Haiti and other Caribbean independent states—that is, differences more of degree than nature, of being further advanced, or immersed, in an unchanging sense of the present as blocked, impassable time. In Frank Kermode's terms, modern versions of apocalyptic narrative are means of interpreting historical crises—the uncertainties of modernity, wars, and conflict as much as rapid technological change. The "sense of an ending" is for Kermode undiminished in the modern era "and is as endemic to modernism as apocalyptic utopianism is to political revolution" (28). The apocalypse narrative in its modern forms still carries for Kermode "notions of a decadence and possible renovation, still represents a mood finally inseparable from the condition of life, the contemplation of its necessary ending, the ineradicable desire to make some sense of it" (187). For Kermode, this desire to "make some sense" of the desired and "necessary" ending to life and to the world is related to prophecy. Apocalyptic prophecy in particular is connected to the desire for the end of an era, spans of time that would come to a close, and from which one would either move into another time span or face the end of time itself. Prophetic narratives of the end of time are related to a "need for means of measuring historical time" and to a sense of ongoing crisis, which is to Kermode but "a way of thinking about one's moment, and not inherent in the moment itself" (187, 101). In Scott's reading of Kermode, he remarks that Kermode attunes us to the "*artifice* of temporality by which we arrange or order our experience," and that human experience of time is not given, but depends to a large degree on how we envisage or narrate the ending of our story (*Omens* 68, Scott's emphasis). A key phase in apocalyptic time is that of transition, which is again for Kermode a human invention, a "fiction" that is "our way of registering the conviction that the end is immanent rather than imminent" (101). Notions of time, prophecy, transitions, and preordained endings are therefore ways of making sense of moments of crisis, which are themselves but inventions related to time and to one's attempts to understand it, especially when history and its narrative of temporal change and progress have been superseded by the coming to prominence of time, and the ways one attempts to see in it, prophetically, beginnings and endings. These are some of the ideas I take up in this concluding chapter, most notably the notion of prophecy and what its conspicuous presence in certain works of contemporary Haitian writing means for our understanding of time in a time of catastrophe.

Prophets of the Past

Two months before the earthquake of January 12, 2010, the author Frankétienne finished writing his latest play, *Melovivi ou Le piège*. A work set in a "devastated, ruined space with no escape, following a disaster," its two characters are named simply A and B and speak "so that they do not die" in the post-apocalyptic world in which they exist (17). "There is no space," one says, while the other adds, "There is no time," before they say together "There is no longer anything. Nothing more but nothingness" (20). On January 11, 2010, Frankétienne was rehearsing the play, and following the disaster he declared that it was a "visionary" work, an idea echoed in the preface to a new edition of the play, which declares that Frankétienne is a "prophet," and his text "was the only clairvoyant seismograph" to foresee the disaster (Hadjadj 9). In effect, premonitions of disaster run through Frankétienne's work, from *Mûr à crever* (1968), in which he writes that "literature is moribund," to *Rapjazz* (1999), which presents Port-au-Prince in terms that seem to prefigure a disaster to come: "My city undressed/my city its hat removed/my city its roof removed/my city dethroned/my city broken up" (Hadjadj 11).

To refer again to Kermode, prophetic narratives such as those in Frankétienne's work may be read as ways of ordering time, especially in a time of crisis and catastrophe, which again, to quote Kermode, are artificial concepts, ways of thinking about one's moment, "and not inherent in the moment itself" (101). Frankétienne is in fact far from alone in evoking prophetic narratives in his work. Indeed, in a significant number of prominent works of Haitian writing from the past twenty years, the coming of an apocalyptic event seems to have been foreseen or prophesied. One could perhaps say that literary prophecies were fundamentally important to the very founding of the Haitian state, particularly if one believes one biographer's assertion that Toussaint Louverture read and was inspired by the Abbé Raynal's famous prophecy of black freedom in the Caribbean. "All that the negroes lack," Raynal wrote, "is a leader courageous enough to carry them to vengeance and carnage." To his own question, "Where is he, this great man, that nature owes to its vexed, oppressed, tormented children?" he replied prophetically, "He will appear, do not doubt it. He will show himself and will raise the sacred banner of liberty" (qtd. in Dubois, *Avengers* 58). According to C. L. R. James, Toussaint the slave read these words and saw himself as the prophesied "black Spartacus" (25). While it is difficult to verify if Toussaint was indeed moved in this way by reading Raynal, it does suggest the possibility that apocalyptic prophecy was a fundamental source of inspiration for one of the leaders of the revolution. More broadly, it is possible to think, as Terry Rey has done, of other revolutionary figures such as Makandal, Boukman, and Biassou as charismatic leaders "whose preaching, possession, and prophecy stirred the enslaved of Saint-Domingue to ferocious assaults on Napoleon's legions and ultimately to victory" (343). Rey's analysis of one lesser-known revolutionary leader, Romaine-la-Prophétesse, further suggests the importance of charismatic prophecy to the success of the revolution, and that Marian prophecy was a key component of the "Kongo prophets" to whom Rey relates Romaine's own religious thought (344). Indeed, one might say that the "national narrative" of Haiti is to some degree founded on prophecy, presentiments of apocalyptic overcoming, and that Haiti itself is a kind of prophecy, a marker in time that anticipates and forewarns of the future, an idea that I will return to later in this conclusion. In the contemporary period, prophetic statements and apocalyptic visions of the future appear in important novels and plays, and seem to indicate something of a mystical apprehension of a catastrophic event to come, and not only in the better-known example of Frankétienne's *Melovivi ou Le piège*. In what follows, I will consider two less known and perhaps less obvious examples of this apparently prophetic, visionary element in contemporary Haitian literature, before reflecting further on their presence and significance.

Both examples come from novels already discussed in previous chapters. The first is from Gary Victor's *A l'angle des rues parallèles,* one of the key texts in the recent appearance of the apocalyptic strain in Haitian writing. First published in March 2000, the novel, as I have shown, sets out an apocalyptic vision of Haiti under the rule of an unnamed Lavalas president who is controlled by the omnipotent Elu, the Elected or Chosen One, himself a prophetic figure driving the country toward complete political and social breakdown. It is when the novel presents the grave natural and environmental effects of history that its prophetic element becomes most apparent. Recounting the story of how a Haitian official had gone to have his respiratory problems treated in Cuba, where fecal matter was found on his lung tissue, Eric observes that the environment has been degraded "to the rhythm of our own debasement" (76). The land is "filthy and miserable" (82). The environment is "taken hostage" by people's recklessness, but "avenges itself in a thousand ways," in a way that suggests that nature has itself a kind of conscience that will eventually exact revenge for its mistreatment (76). Indeed, in what might be read retrospectively as something of a prophetic insight, Eric recalls first the day of the solar eclipse—an example of what Kermode would call a millenarian marker of time and history—which revealed to him "how we were mired in a medieval, backward culture . . . which is completely incapable of letting us enter into modernity" (98–99). Soon, he feels, the city will "empty itself of all human presence," and he senses a "force emerging from the depths of the land," "the unnamable" as he calls it, announcing the final stages of the general societal breakdown (99). There is therefore inscribed in Eric's reading of nature an apocalyptic narrative whereby that which nourishes and sustains can equally be a force that brings destruction. Read in hindsight, the passage appears to have a prophetic quality in its apprehension of a natural disaster emerging from the earth that would announce a final apocalyptic collapse.

The second example is from Lyonel Trouillot's *Rue des pas perdus,* which is as I have argued another important contemporary novel that presents distinctly apocalyptic themes. The particular prophetic passage involves the unnamed postal worker, who, on the night of the atrocities, takes his lover Laurence to the home of his friend Gérard, the intellectual and apocalyptic prophet, a "myth merchant" (27), who foresees the atrocities that the night will bring and a future "foreign occupation" (28). In a final, remarkable prediction, Gérard prophesies an apocalyptic event that would finally come to pass more than a decade later. "Thousands will die," he says, "until the earth cracks wide open" (28).

What, then, to make of such a prediction in a novel published twelve years before the earthquake of 2010, indeed of the very similar prophecy in Victor's novel? Is it mere coincidence, or is there a sense in Trouillot's case in particular that the author is negotiating through his different narrators his own conflicting visions of reality? The postal worker's rationalism is set up to temper Gérard's irrational, mystical apocalyptic vision. One certainly senses that Gérard is mad, and yet his madness seems to contain truths and an awareness of how things are and will be that apparently cannot be imagined by a rational mind. Laurence appears to be susceptible to Gérard's mystical predictions, and it is, as stated before, the narrator's rationalism that seems out of place. One might say also that this clash of discourses is suggestive of an inner confusion on behalf of the author, who seems to hesitate between the rational and the mystical, and indeed to see in Gérard's ravings a foreshadowing of the future—striking glimpses of further apocalyptic moments to come.

One could no doubt offer other similar examples of apparently prophetic passages in recent Haitian literature, or indeed of works of visual art that may be read as prophecies. How can this prophetic, apocalyptic element in Haitian writing in particular be accounted for? The first explanation might be that of coincidence, that the written work just happened to present an event that finally took place. Also, one might argue that the prophesied event, in this case a cataclysmic earthquake, is not exactly unheard of in Haiti or the broader Caribbean, and that it was inevitable that such a destructive event would eventually come to pass. There is moreover the possibility of reading a work retrospectively and identifying a pattern of events that apparently leads back to the prophecy, seemingly proving its veracity. The identification of such a pattern has the advantage of creating a kind of order, of diminishing the sense that life is subject to overwhelmingly random events over which the individual has no control. Such a reading is potentially comforting in that it suggests that destiny is at play, and that the event was fated, part of a broader natural or divine pattern that has its own inherent meaning. Thus, as in Kermode's theory of apocalyptic prophecy, the foretelling offers a model of time that counters the overwhelming sense of disorder and crisis in the present, and the feeling of meaninglessness that these concepts often entail.

These interpretations explain to a certain extent the attraction of apocalyptic prophecies to artists and individuals more broadly, though in the specific cases cited above they do not seem to answer fully some pertinent questions. Specifically, why should prophecy be an element in contemporary Haitian writing; in other words, why Haiti, why now?

Further potential explanations relate again to issues of time and narrative. The word *prophecy* is derived from the Greek verb προφημι (*prophemi*), which means "to say beforehand, foretell." The key component of any prophecy is therefore time: that the prophetic vision should anticipate and occur *before* the prophesied event. Prophecy may appear implausible if one considers time and history to be largely linear in nature, a forward movement with an identifiable beginning and ending, and related to *chronos,* the idea of sequential, successive time. However it seems that in Haiti—or at least in much Haitian literature—there are other conceptions of time and history at play, quite different from the linear model, and closer to the concept of *kairos,* the idea of cyclical, spontaneous, or indeterminate time. Specifically, time is often judged to turn in circular or cyclical movements so that the idea of progressing through time in a linear fashion seems barely appropriate to an understanding of time and history in Haitian writing. As one character in René Depestre's novel *Hadriana dans tous mes rêves* puts it: "In our country, for sure, history repeats itself more than it does anywhere else" (100). In much post-Duvalier Haitian literature in particular time is often repetitive and circular, and history is lived as a constant return to indeterminacy and uncertainty, as Émile Ollivier suggests: "As we are in what we might call an eternal return, it seemed to me that Haiti existed in a circular time. . . . The history of this country, from independence to today, . . . has been an endless series of banditry, corruption, and chaos" (Lambert 155).[1]

Michel-Rolph Trouillot's critique of Western historicity—that is historical authenticity or fact—is useful in developing this idea of time and in ultimately relating it to the question of prophecy. Trouillot argues that many Western historians are conventionally "tied . . . to the assumption that history requires a linear and cumulative sense of time that allows the observer to isolate the past as a distinct entity" (*Silencing the Past* 7). The key concept here is the notion of the past as a "distinct entity," separate from present time. Such a conception of the past allows the historian to treat it as a period that is gone, finished, having occurred at an earlier point in time, which has moved on in a linear manner and changed, bringing in a new and different period. As Trouillot argues, however, "the past does not exist independently from the present." "The past—or, more accurately, pastness," he says, "is a position," and "in no way can we identify the past *as past*" (15, Trouillot's emphasis). Consequently, the constitution of people as collective subjects "goes hand in hand with the continuous creation of the past," and as such subjects "do not succeed such a past: they are its contemporaries" (16). Moreover, history, or historical narrative can have a future-oriented, prophetic function:

Trouillot cites the case of the Hawaiians who read their encounter with Captain Cook as "the chronicle of a death foretold" (26).

While Trouillot does not address the quite prevalent idea in much Haitian literature that time and history are lived as essentially circular and repetitive rather than linear phenomena, his work does seem informed by the temporal paradoxes that constitute to a large extent the particular conception of historicity that characterizes many works of contemporary Haitian writing. In calling into question the notion that the past is ever a "distinct entity," in arguing that collective subjects are involved in the "continuous creation" of the past and that as such they are its contemporaries, and in suggesting that historical narratives may also have prophetic functions, he echoes and gives a theoretical grounding to the nonlinear sense of time and history that characterizes much post-Duvalier Haitian literature.[2] In effect, Trouillot echoes and gives a Caribbean perspective on broader anthropological thought on time, perhaps most pertinently Lévi-Strauss's theories of cyclical time, and its relation to ritual, whereby the past is reenacted in the present in order to create a sense of order and historical continuity in times of crisis. Lévi-Strauss draws a contrast between "mechanical" time, which is "reversible and non-cumulative" and "historical" time, which is "'statistical'; it always appears as an oriented and non-reversible process" (286). In certain strands of anthropological thought cyclical time is often related to non-Western societies and considered in contradistinction to the presumed linear time of modern industrial societies. Cyclical time evokes the idea of constant return, "a world in which the difference between past and future can be dispensed with, because what has been recurs and what is to come has already been, a world in which destiny is synonymous with origin" (Adam 518). Trouillot's own thought suggests something of the repetitive, cyclical nature of Caribbean time, but in contrast to Lévi-Strauss he and the other Haitian authors analyzed in this book ascribe this understanding of time less to the effects of timeless ritual than those of repetitive, often catastrophic history.

Amy Wilentz offers a fascinating, complementary reading of historical narratives in Haiti when she suggests that Haitians, and particularly the political classes, "appear to be following a script as they make decisions" (87). Wilentz argues that when Haitians think of powerful outside political powers such as the United States, France, or the United Nations, "they see the racist, imperial face of Napoleon at the turn of the nineteenth century" (ibid.). Also, when faced with what Wilentz calls foreign "do-gooders" contemporary Haitians "remember the on-again, off-again relationship between the rebel slave leaders and the friendly-seeming directorate of the French Republic" (88). Any Haitian politician who "let[s] down his guard" in his dealings with foreigners "will be taken to be collaborating with forces that are bent on destroying the slave descendants' hard-won sovereignty and liberty" (ibid.). He will be seen "in eighteenth-century terms: as a monarchist, a loyalist, a traitor to the revolution" (ibid.). Therefore, according to Wilentz, Haitian history lives still in a form of collective historical narrative, "and its habits march directly into the thoughts of everyday people as well as professionals and officials" (ibid.). If history repeats itself, Wilentz suggests, it is at least in part because the terms of the nation's engagement with politics return constantly to those of the revolutionary period.[3] As she writes, "After enough time in Haiti, everything . . . seems like déjà vu" (228).

By extension, Trouillot and Wilentz are also useful in understanding the presence and function of prophetic passages in certain contemporary Haitian literary works, for if time is understood not as a linear progression from one discrete period to the next but as a far more complex phenomenon in which the past is not finished but undergoes continuous creation and indeed can become the future, prophecy is taken out of the realms of mystical revelation and can be considered as a function of a particular, and quite valid, understanding of time. There may also be a connection here to the ongoing experience of disaster, in that disaster, as Susanna Hoffman argues, disorders not only space but also time (124). As Hoffman suggests, disaster disrupts the historical teleology leading to modernity, and when, as in the case of Haiti, disaster recurs regularly, a society can become entrapped in cyclical, repetitive time (132). In short, prophecy is possible and indeed quite credible because the past is not considered to be finished, and for that reason the future becomes more predictable: the past is much like the future and the future resembles closely the past.

Thus when characters in Lyonel Trouillot's *Rue des pas perdus* or Gary Victor's *A l'angle des rues parallèles* prophesy catastrophic events to come they seem to do so with an awareness of such events in the past, which is not truly past, and which will in some sense become the future. What is interesting too is that these authors seem to combine in their works two distinct functions and forms of prophecy, identified by the anthropologist Paul Friedrich as "poetic prophecy" and "prophetic poetry." Poetic prophecy is founded initially in the realms of folklore and anthropology as cultural creation and lived experience but is examined by Friedrich for its poetic qualities, while he analyzes the prophetic poetry of figures such as T. S. Eliot or William Blake chiefly in terms of its visionary nature and ecstatic inspiration (qtd. in Mould 209). In certain Haitian literary works, these forms and functions fuse creatively so that one has a quite distinctive blend of sophisticated, modern poetics and a prophetic sensibility that is grounded in the everyday, and that sees in the mire of the present intimations of the future. In effect, these works imply that culture more broadly has a transformative, prophetic quality, an idea suggested by Dubois when he writes of the African slaves of Saint-Domingue who were at the "bottom of the social pyramid" but nonetheless "profoundly influenced the society's culture and therefore its future," and of Jacques Roumain's belief that "cultural work could open the way for societal change" (Dubois 21, 308).

Prophecy in these regards may be considered as an important, perhaps defining element of Haiti's "disaster narrative." Anderson writes that when disasters recur over time, as in the case of Haiti, this can lead to the formation of a tradition of disaster narratives that "engenders its own aesthetics, allowing it to transcend its moment" (22). Over time, the repetition of plotlines and tropes relating to disaster "creates a powerful, self-sustaining disaster narrative" that in Haitian writing at least inheres in the distinctive apocalyptic thread this book has explored, a key aesthetic and thematic element of which is the prophetic trope that Victor and Trouillot invoke (Anderson 22).

Anderson in effect indicates the second aspect of the act of prophecy, which has to do with the narrative or the *telling* of the time to come. The Greek definition carries two elements, one relating to time, and the other to enunciation: "to *say* beforehand, to fore*tell.*" This definition indicates something of the power of language and its ability to shape the future. It also echoes Paul Ricoeur's insistence that the most effective means of engaging with the endless paradoxes of time is through narrative (both literary and historical), and not speculative thought. Speculation on time is to Ricoeur "an inconclusive rumination to which narrative alone can respond" (6). If narrative does resolve what he calls the aporias of time, it does so, he insists, "in a poetical and not a theoretical sense of the word," and "emplotment . . . replies to the speculative aporia with a poetic making of something capable, certainly, of clarifying the aporia . . . but not of resolving it theoretically" (ibid.). Narrative is for Ricoeur related to the human, and time only becomes "human time" to the extent that it is "organized after the manner of a narrative; narrative, in turn, is meaningful to the extent that it portrays the features of temporal experience" (3). There is therefore in Ricoeur's thought what Scott calls "a constitutive circle that continuously joins together temporality and narrativity," whereby human time is made through narrative and narrative is constituted by and through time (*Omens* 3). Prophecy is one such means of "emplotting" time, and of clarifying poetically something of the nature of time, without offering a final theoretical resolution. For Ricoeur, prophecy amounts to extrapolating from "the configurations and concatenations of the past in the direction of what is still to come," and consists of speaking about the future "in terms appropriate to the past" (144). Just as therefore, there is a constitutive circle that connects time and narrative, so the notion of future time is made from the structures and narratives of the past and the conceptualization of the past is itself formed at least in part by an idea of future time. Ricoeur's work on time indicates something of the capacity of narrative to imagine and thereby bring into being the human future. It also serves as a reminder of Kermode's notion of the artifice of temporality, and is an important reference for Scott in his imaging of Caribbean time, notably his argument that how one lives in the present "depends very much on our projection of the *ending* of our story" (*Omens* 68). Indeed, the idea of the self-fulfilling prophecy is, for example, predicated on the apparent power of language and narrative to bring about the future. Left unsaid or untold, the prophecy has little if any power to determine the future. The attraction of the prophecy narrative, particularly in a place characterized by longstanding disorder, is again that it offers order and meaning, even if that meaning is related to an apocalyptic collapse. In Scott's terms, the apocalyptic ending projects a version of the future that determines in large part the experience of the present. Also, as I have argued elsewhere in the book, the apocalypse is in some important senses desired, conceived in and brought about by words, be they those (little-read yet no doubt representative of a broader understanding of time and history) of Haiti's novelists, or of the various churches, particularly the Protestant evangelicals, those groups spiritually invested in the apocalyptic downfall of Haiti and its indigenous systems of belief which, ironically, have little or no conception of the apocalypse. More broadly, as John May has suggested in his study of the apocalypse in the Americas, so-called "primitive peoples" have no myths of "future cataclysm" as they tend to think that the world regenerates itself cyclically. Crucially, however, he does also argue that there "is a millennialism . . . developing among contemporary primitives that is built upon cataclysm and the expectation of a new age; and all of these myths are antiwhite and antichristian, representing a revolt against the failure of missionaries to live their religion" (6).

This, in turn, may begin to explain some of the apparent attraction of the apocalypse to contemporary Haitian authors. The certain desire for an apocalyptic ending should not in this sense be read as the hope for an absolute end of time. Rather, it seems to be a wish for an ending to the particular historical cycle in which Haiti seems to have been caught for decades, if not centuries. Colonialism and its legacies imposed a different kind of apocalypse, one that contains only death and disaster, without the salutary promise of renewal. Conversely, what we see in Haitian narratives of the apocalypse, or indeed now of the post-apocalypse, is less a desire for self-destruction than a profoundly felt wish for rebirth and an escape from a conception of time and history that seems to be lived, tragically, as an end time without end.

IN THIS regard, Haiti's national history should perhaps not be seen as an isolated instance, but as an extreme case upon which broader historical, economic, and social forces have had a particular impact. Repetitive history is not unique to Haiti, as Žižek indicates in his discussion of September 11 and the global crisis of 2008, events that he frames in terms borrowed from Marx, drawing on Hegel, according to which "great events and characters of world history occur, so to speak, twice[,] . . . the first time as tragedy, the second time as farce" (qtd. in Žižek, *First as Tragedy* 1). No strangers to such historical repetitions, Haiti and the broader Caribbean, as Michel-Rolph Trouillot insists, "have always been modern, differently modern, contradictorily modern, otherwise modern, yet undoubtedly modern" (*Global Transformations* 45). History has in a sense thrust modernity onto the Caribbean, as Kaussen argues: "By virtue of the Atlantic slave trade, slave revolution, peasant revolts, mass migrations, organized labor, and other social movements, Caribbeans from the beginning have been full participants in global modernity" (*Migrant Revolutions* 18).[4] The politics of small states such as Haiti are often a reflection of international conditions "acting as vectors for domestic political situations" (Bellegarde-Smith 176). Such a relationship "advances the feeling of powerlessness of the small state, since the crucial economic and financial decisions affecting it are made abroad in a decreasing number of loci of power" (ibid.). As such, Haiti may be seen as a state that not only has a particularly acute experience of contemporary international economic and political conditions, but also as one that is itself a kind of prophecy, a nation that anticipates the apocalyptic denouement that commentators such as Žižek now predict for the Western world.[5] As Erica Caple James suggests, "Haiti's challenges at times prefigure what the world at large is facing: manifest anxieties over political, economic, social, and ontological insecurity" (295).

Amy Wilentz pursues a similar idea in her post-earthquake work *Farewell, Fred Voodoo: A Letter from Haiti.* Switching from her reflections on the past of Haiti, she turns toward the end of the book to a consideration of the future: "what we are all seeing in Haiti," she says, "is . . . , perhaps, a look forward in keeping with Haiti's exceptional and counterintuitive modernism" (303). Haiti was, she continues, "before its time with its unique (one could say premature) revolution[,] . . . with its guerilla-style freedom-fighting rebellion against the U.S. occupation[,] . . . with its time as a practice ground for later U.S. foreign policies of regime change" (303). Perhaps, she argues, "Haiti today is in the throes of another modern convulsion. Sometimes it pays to look at it in fast-forward instead of in fast-reverse" (303). Following the earthquake, Haiti appears like a "postapocalyptic dystopia; its deforested countryside and overpopulated, crumbled urban landscape, with its smoke and stench, seem like plausible sets from one of the darkly pessimistic movies of the early years of the new millennium" (303–4). Wilentz's fear is that Haiti represents the apocalyptic future of the rest of the world: "trees uprooted, water gone, the soil sinking into the sea, the land filling up with plastic waste and too many people, epidemics surging, and everyone starving and dying" (304). Moreover, she wonders whether the foreigners who come to Haiti to "repair [and] save" it "are all unconsciously hoping that in trying to save Haiti, they'll be able to save themselves, setting the scene for a future rescue of humanity" (ibid.).

It is telling that Wilentz uses terms that refer to popular film, to Haiti as a "scene" on which a possible global apocalyptic future is acted out, and where it is difficult to distinguish the "good" from the "bad." It is also significant that she evokes the "darkly pessimistic movies" that have proliferated during the early years of the twenty-first century, in that many of these films present that most distinctively Haitian apocalyptic figure—the zombie.[6] Writing of the "unending stream of zombies traipsing through U.S. popular culture," Dubois argues that early films such as *White Zombie* (1934) "helped spawn an entire genre, which fixed Haiti in many minds as a place of dark ritual and wandering undead" (*Aftershocks* 298). Such generic representations of the zombie figure tended, however, to obscure the deeper symbolism of the *zonbi* in Haitian folklore, meanings that pertain to the social and political reality of the individual, and which can be related to the broader contemporary world. As Dubois says, the "*zonbi* is a powerful symbol with a specific, haunting point of reference. It is a person devoid of all agency, under the complete control of a master: that is, a slave" (ibid.). Wilentz makes a similar point when she writes "There is something about a zombie . . . that speaks to us at the beginning of the twenty-first century. The zombie is something we all fear becoming. . . . He's dead but he's walking; he has to work after death. He's the living dead, an ancient figure, but he's also the inanimate animated, like the robot of industrial dystopias" (96). The zombie, Wilentz says, "works for free. You feed him very little," and as such he is like "Apple's Chinese factory workers; or like the refugees in Haiti's earthquake camps; or like guest workers in European countries"—so many of the world's "plausible zombies," contemporary revenants of the slave figure, "deadened, soulless, egoless, empty-eyed" (ibid. 96–97).

In this sense, the zombies that are portrayed in contemporary film, television, computer games, and other media carry connotations of a population under control, living unfree lives, and apparently unable to change its apocalyptic destiny. They thus have a political meaning, or at least suggest that politics has failed them, or indeed that they have failed politics, abandoned it in favor of a fatalistic, apocalyptic perception of humanity's future. Such a vision of the global future is expressed not only in contemporary popular culture, but also in more marginal movements, such as the UK-based Dark Mountain Project, which published a manifesto in 2009 that envisioned the inevitable end of a historical epoch. "It is our civilisation's turn," the manifesto reads, "to experience the inrush of the savage and the unseen; our turn to be brought up short by contact with untamed reality. There is a fall coming. Now a familiar human story is being played out. It is the story of an empire corroding from within."[7]

The apocalyptic strand in Haitian and Caribbean cultures can ultimately be read as the dystopian counter-narrative to Glissant's well-known belief that "the whole world is . . . becoming creolized" (*Traité du tout-monde* 194), that the historical processes that have shaped the Caribbean are now reshaping the rest of the world. It also counters to some extent the qualities attributed by Nesbitt to "Caribbean critique," writings that he says "cry out in insubordination and aversion to the state of their world . . . and that seek to articulate the promise that another world is possible[,] . . . a radically new and suddenly possible mode of existence" (*Caribbean Critique* xi, xiii).[8] The lived reality of disaster in the Caribbean virtually effaces any sense of "another world," a notion that implies a future deliverance from the apocalyptic past and present. This is, again, what the 2011 *Small Axe* visual art statement means when it refers to the "paralyzing *futurelessness* of catastrophe" (134, emphasis original). If, as Michel-Rolph Trouillot, suggests, the "lessons learned from the Caribbean are applicable elsewhere" (*Global Transformations* 45), and if Haiti in particular has a prophetic function, we are left finally with the unnerving prospect that what we see there now is but a presage of a broader catastrophic collapse, a window onto all of our apocalyptic futures.

Notes

Introduction

1. See Elisabeth Kübler-Ross, *On Death and Dying* (New York: Simon and Schuster, 1969).

2. See the various essays collected in the excellent volume edited by Elizabeth M. DeLoughrey, Renée K. Gosson, and George B. Handley, *Caribbean Literature and the Environment: Between Nature and Culture* (Charlottesville: University of Virginia Press, 2005). See, for example, Antonio Benítez-Rojo's argument that the Caribbean "plantation machine" was "one of the most powerful and devastating to the environment of any the world has seen." "Sugar and the Environment in Cuba," 33–50, 40.

3. Stuart Hall writes in similar terms of the "global/multicultural" city, and of the tendency of the privileged classes to organize themselves into "gated enclaves" (40).

4. See Deborah Jenson, "From the Kidnapping(s) of the Louvertures to the Alleged Kidnapping of Aristide: Legacies of Slavery in the Post/Colonial World," *Yale French Studies* 107 (2005): 162–86. See also the November 19, 2012, *Miami Herald* report on kidnappings in Haiti and the comment by Reginald Delva, secretary of state for national security, that "Haitians can take a lot of things, even an assassination. . . . But kidnappings remind us of slavery, and people can't handle that." Jacqueline Charles, "Haiti Kidnapping: Shrouded in Secrecy," *Miami Herald,* November 19, 2012, http://www.miamiherald.com/incoming/article1944731.html.

5. Dash traces the beginnings of this modern apocalyptic thought to the pre-Negritude journal *Légitime Défense* ("Postcolonial Eccentricities" 37).

6. See James Arnold's description of Césaire's work as "the apocalypse of negritude" (201).

7. See also Joseph on the apocalyptic strain in the music of Bob Marley (50).

8. As Dash says, Benítez-Rojo's use of an apocalyptic tone in a passage that declares the Caribbean to be profoundly un-apocalyptic "is evidence of how

easy it is to become enmeshed in ideological prescriptiveness" ("Postcolonial Eccentricities" 35).

9. See Celia Britton's discussion of the opposition between apocalypse and chaos in Benítez-Rojo's work, whereby "chaos dissolves the confrontations and binary oppositions of Western thought into a fluid, all-inclusive, endless process based on rhythmic plurality and varying repetition" (*Sense of Community* 114).

10. See also Régine Joseph's argument that the "apocalyptic vision . . . declines in mid-twentieth-century French Caribbean literature to give way to a new aesthetic," which she describes as "post-apocalyptic writing" ("Ruins of Dreams" 42).

11. See Martin Munro, *Different Drummers: Rhythm and Race in the Americas,* 148–49.

12. Unless otherwise noted, all translations from the French are my own.

13. As Dash argues, Fanon adopted a more apocalyptic tone in his later work *Les Damnés de la terre,* in which Fanon "visualizes the aggressivity of the colonized in terms of purifying violence" ("Postcolonial Eccentricities" 34).

14. Letter to author, 8 May 1999.

15. See also Celia Britton's analysis of Maximin's *L'île et une nuit,* and her argument that Maximin "insistently undermine[s] the notion of apocalypse" (*Sense of Community* 113).

16. See also Régine Joseph's argument that "understanding how the apocalyptic aesthetics emerged and evolved in the French Caribbean requires that we focus on Haiti, not Martinique. For it is in Haiti that French Caribbean writers have had a sustained two-hundred-year-old response, the longest to the modernist call to end the problem of colonialism" ("Ruins of Dreams" 41). Joseph also discusses the apocalyptic elements of pre-Duvalier Haitian history, including the civil war, the coups d'état of the nineteenth century, the American occupation, and the 1946 Revolution (58–63).

17. There is another interpretation that proposes that the Duvalier period marked a break with the apocalyptic radicalism of Jacques-Stephen Alexis, René Depestre, and others, which announced a "new literature of doubt . . . that does not envision final solutions nor transcendental discourse" (Joseph xix). It is true that the "grand narratives" of the past were supplanted by a more "ambivalent literary practice," but at the same time apocalyptic aspects of the social and political contexts in Haiti only intensified under the Duvaliers, and the literature produced during and after that period largely reflects that apocalyptic reality, without however offering apocalyptic solutions (ibid.).

18. In addition to Katz's book, see for example, Amy Wilentz, *Farewell, Fred Voodoo;* Paul Farmer, *Haiti after the Earthquake;* Laurent Dubois, *Haiti: The Aftershocks of History;* Jeremy Popkin, *You Are All Free: The Haitian Revolution and the Abolition of Slavery;* Mark Schuller, *Killing with Kindness: Haiti, International Aid and NGOs.*

19. I will explore this issue further in chapter 2.

20. Trouillot is most interested in the ways in which "peasant culture and values" impact upon Haiti's urban communities (*State against Nation* 83). See also 114–18 on the "Cultural Guerilla War." On the importance of literature for "our lesson in politics," see Braziel, *Ghosts* xxii.

21. See, for example, Susan Bassnett's essay "Seismic Aftershocks: Responses to the Great Lisbon Earthquake of 1755" on the various interpretations of the Lisbon earthquake of 1755, which range from religious questions on the existence of God to Enlightenment-inspired rationalist understandings.

22. See also David Scott's reading of the collapse of the Grenada Revolution as "merely one significant *episode* in a larger story of generations of conflict in what is now imagined and represented as the cyclical pattern of a general history whose generative logic is catastrophic" (*Omens* 74–75).

23. See also Jonathan Katz's argument that suggests that disasters are also godsends for donor countries, who he says, let President René Préval carry the blame for the lack of reconstruction (207). Raoul Peck's 2013 film *Assistance mortelle* presents a scathing critique of humanitarian and development aid in Haiti. For a critique of "military humanitarianism" in post-earthquake Haiti, see Jennifer Greenburg, "The 'Strong Arm' and the 'Friendly Hand.'"

24. See also Hurbon's critique of the "privatization of the State," in "De la privatisation de l'État ou les embûches de la reconstruction." *L'Observatoire de la reconstruction* 5 (November 2012): 2–4.

25. See in this regard the excellent Haiti Memory Project, an online archive of testimonies about the earthquake (http://haitimemoryproject.org). The project, somewhat unlike Hurbon "assumes that the earthquake is a point-zero in the lives of individual Haitians and in Haitian history; it is a moment that divided time into 'before' and 'after.'"

1. The Duvaliers and Apocalyptic Memory

1. Kaussen writes that noirisme was a response not only to the failure of liberal politics to make a lasting impression in Haiti, "but also to the failures of the U.S.'s liberal colonial project in Haiti (based on the free market, individualism, and the promise of social mobility) and to the ways it reinforced as well as negatively transformed traditional Haitian hierarchies of racial difference" (*Migrant Revolutions* 71).

2. See, for example, Denis et al., *L'avenir du pays et l'action néfaste de M. Foisset* 1–3.

3. *Les Griots* (July–September 1939): 3.

4. See also Robert Fatton Jr.'s argument that "Haiti's predicament is not rooted in the absence of a nation, but rather in the ruling class's incapacity to construct an 'integral' state . . . capable of organizing both the political unity of the different factions of the ruling class and the 'organic relations between . . . political society and civil society'" ("Haiti: The Saturnalia of Emancipation" 115).

5. Caple James also writes critically of the "political economy of trauma," whereby "the activists' pain and suffering became commodity 'fetishes' . . . , powerful products of material and symbolic value created through the transformation of raw materials that circulated in both terror and compassion economies. . . . In terror economies the extraction of pain and suffering was a tool to augment the illegitimate power of the de facto regime. In the compassion economy products of transformed suffering circulated in humanitarian markets alongside the aid dispensed to Haiti to assist with its transition" (26).

6. Chancy further proposes that Caribbean historical novels share a common goal with their European predecessors: "the desire to ground their texts in the historical moment to which their present is tied, while also giving voice to the popular within those nation-states they seek to illustrate (or question) in their works (*Sugar* xi.)

7. Caruth, drawing on Freud, considers the ways in which traumatic events "seem to repeat themselves for those who have passed through them" (1). In many cases, she writes, "the experience of a trauma repeats itself, exactly and unremittingly, through the knowing acts of the survivor and against his very will" (2).

8. Earlier novels that deal with the Duvalier period include Roger Dorsinville, *Mourir pour Haïti, ou, Les croisés d'Esther* (1980), and *Les vèvès du créateur* (1989), and René Depestre, *Le mât de cocagne* (1979). More recent works include *Un alligator nommé Rosa* by Marie-Célie Agnant (2007). See also Braziel's extensive analyses of Duvalierist state violence in the work of Edwidge Danticat and Dany Laferrière in her *Duvalier's Ghosts.*

9. Sorel is later renamed Gracieux by the community. For clarity, I will refer to him as Sorel throughout this section.

10. Although Chauvet's novel is nominally set in 1939, during the government of Sténio Vincent, it is clearly a damning critique of the Duvalier regime during which the book was written.

11. Amy Wilentz points out, "One reason Papa Doc had his Tonton Macoute death squads wear sunglasses, along with their denims, was to hide their eyes. This, he hoped, would frighten the population" (97).

12. Caple James suggests that the U.S. occupation of 1915–34 "revived the practices of the plantation slavery period: brutality and sexual coercion and violence" (54).

13. For a discussion of Mars's earlier works, see Vitiello.

14. In interview, Mars talks of her "natural disposition" for writing about sensuality: "There is a fine line," she says "between pain and satisfaction, between disgust and dependency, between fear and pleasure, between guilt and devotion" (Ménard 232).

15. David Nicholls challenges this description, and argues that "Duvalierism was not totalitarian in the way that fascism was" (214).

16. The figure of Simone Duvalier will be discussed in more detail below.

17. Dash writes: "Haitian novelists never managed to produce outstanding treatments of political dictatorship. This subgenre produced far more accomplished novels in Spanish, as we see in the work of Alejo Carpentier, Gabriel García Màrquez and Miguel Angel Asturias" ("Exile and Recent Literature" 458).

18. On the Aristide commission, see Caple James, 99–100, 200–204.

19. United States Institute of Peace, "Truth Commission: Haiti," http://www.usip.org/publications/truth-commission-haiti.

20. On the Guatemalan Historical Clarification Commission, see Hayner 82–83. On the South African Truth Commission, see Christie.

21. On the novel's water imagery and intertextual links to Roumain's *Gouverneurs de la rosée,* see Jean-Charles. See also, Sourieau.

22. As another victim says of her torturer later in the novel, "No one will ever have that much of your attention. No matter how much he'd changed, I would know him anywhere" (132).

23. Braziel proposes that the preacher "though a Protestant, bears a striking resemblance and is an allusive parallel to the Catholic priest, Jean-Bertrand Aristide" (*Ghosts* 221).

24. Braziel argues that, "through the figure of Anne . . . Danticat reinscribes and transmutes Chauvet's emotional themes—*amour, colère, folie*" (*Ghosts* 222).

25. Marie-Célie Agnant's novel *Un alligator nommé Rosa* (Montreal: Les Éditions du Remue-ménage, 2007) also focuses on a figure based on Simone Duvalier, and is largely set in a hospital.

26. Simone Duvalier died in a Paris hospital in December 1997.

2. Utopian Ends

1. See Naomi Klein, *The Shock Doctrine: The Rise of Disaster Capitalism* (London: Penguin Books, 2007).

2. Kaussen identifies "a model of utopia and revolutionary action" in Chauvet's character Claire, in the novel *Amour* (*Migrant Revolutions* 168).

3. "Pourquoi Aristide doit-il partir?," *AlterPresse,* February 17, 2004, http://www.alterpresse.org/spip.php?article1166. The Haïti Alter Presse website is an invaluable and underused source of contemporary articles on the circumstances surrounding the departure of Aristide.

4. Chapter 3 will consider in more depth the history of the Chimères and their representation in film and literature. See Amy Wilentz's judgment on the Aristide presidencies: "Broadly speaking, he could not reconcile the irreconcilable, and, pushed to the very edge by the forces arrayed against him, he fell that second time—and again, change did not happen" (47).

5. For more on this contradiction, see Martin Munro, "Whose and Which Haiti? Western Intellectuals and the Aristide Question," *Paragraph* 36.3 (2013): 408–24.

6. The president seems to be an allegorical representation of René Préval, who was in office from 1996 to 2001.

7. See Hanétha Vété-Congolo's argument that in the novel "Gary Victor uses extreme provocations to show the cataclysm that awaits Haitian society if safeguards are not put in place following the example of his spokesman, Eric" (134).

8. Later, the earth begins to tremble again, and this is attributed to the dead poet exacting revenge on the Chosen One (183).

9. Dennis Lim, "Taking a Man, Then Removing His Myth," *New York Times,* 13 November 2009, http://www.nytimes.com/2009/11/15/movies/15lim.html.

10. Amy Wilentz writes of how Aristide had built near his birthplace in Port-Salut "a fortress palace along the lines of a Grecian temple-cum-medieval dungeon," a "colossal structure" that Peck may be alluding to in his use of the Citadelle as a setting for the film (234).

11. There may be a comment here on African American figures such as Danny Glover, who has long planned a film on Toussaint Louverture and who has been an ardent supporter of Jean-Bertrand Aristide.

3. The Chimères and the Haitian Antihero

1. Richard Sanders argues that the term *Chimère* was used to demonize all of Haiti's poor. Here, I use it to refer more specifically to the armed militia. Richard Sanders, "Epithets without Borders," *Press for Conversion!,* November 2008, http://coat.ncf.ca/our_magazine/links/63/63_14.htm.

2. See also Garland's critique of the "documentary" elements of the film, and his argument that it is a "Trojan horse of conservative ideology fitted out with the form and style of the ghetto film" (181).

3. Deibert writes that Tupac had learned English in free courses given after the U.S. troops arrived in 1994 (166).

4. See Braziel's critique of the film as "a film and art commodity [that] hideously and odiously violates the people that it cinematically, shamelessly, ruthlessly, and unapologetically exploits" (*Ghosts* xxiv).

5. Tony Smith, "As Police Flee, Rebels Tighten Grip in Haiti's Heartland," *New York Times,* February 21, 2004, http://www.nytimes.com/2004/02/21/world/as-police-flee-rebels-tighten-grip-in-haiti-s-heartland.html.

4. Religion, Nature, and the Apocalypse

1. Lahens uses the idea of the apocalypse later in the book when writing of the human and material destruction. "All that was missing," she writes, "were the trumpets of the Angel of the Apocalypse" (69).

2. See also Chris Bongie's argument (drawing on Nietzsche) that secular modernity is effectively "a 'problematic' time of waiting, from which solutions appear absent, and in which reaction has taken the place of action. What is called for, as a way out of the unenviable position, is a volcanic 'eruption' (*Ausbruch*) that will propel us beyond the confines of the waiting world that we find ourselves humanely, all-too-humanely, inhabiting" (345).

3. Jonathan Katz writes of the thousands of missionaries who continue to arrive in Haiti, and who have since the earthquake sought to teach Haitians "self-reliance." The irony for Katz is that "Haitians not only tended to harbor a faith more fervent and deeply tested than that of the missionaries, but also self-reliance beyond anything the visitors were likely to imagine" (135).

4. Although I refer at times to the narrator as Laferrière, it is important to not conflate entirely the author with his narrator, even in a work as apparently autobiographical as this.

5. A photograph of the Haitian poet Davertige, another "dandy," also reminds him of his father (77).

6. He writes later that he was only four or five years old when his father left Haiti (74).

7. Laferrière seems to distance himself from his father's fate later when writing of the briefcase the father left for him to collect. Unable to open the case, Laferrière is relieved, saying that what his father did not know is that "destiny is not transferred from father to son. That case belonged only to him. The weight of his life" (74).

8. See Munro, *Exile and Post-1946 Haitian Literature,* 178–79.

9. See ibid., 194–96.

10. He later reflects that, with its beating sun, dusty streets, and two brothers ready to kill each other over a woman, the film is a western, and that "death has finally found here its aesthetic form" (219–20).

11. As he says later of his nephew, "I was once in his place" (143).

12. For a case study of the failure of international aid in Haiti, see Arthus. See also, Mark Schuller, "Cholera and the Camps."

13. See Joel F. Audefroy, "Haiti: Post-Earthquake Lessons Learned from Traditional Construction."

14. See also Prieto's argument that in much Caribbean writing there is an interest in environmental and evolutionary "adaptiveness," which "emphasizes the importance of unpredictable mutations, ecological niches, and biodiversity" (*Literature, Geography* 155–56).

15. He later reflects that what he needs is a small room with a window with a view of the "green countryside." "There," he says, "I will be able to write the novel that I have long thought about" (228).

16. See Munro, *Exile and Post-1946 Haitian Literature,* 186–87.

17. See ibid., 196–201.

18. On Laferrière as a primitive writer, see Munro, *Exile and post-1946 Haitian Literature,* 187, and J. Michael Dash, "Afterword: Neither France nor Senegal" (229).

19. See Lucy Brisley's conclusion, "The 'enigma' of return . . . is that rather than finding his home, he finds himself: home is no longer a territory but a state of being" (116–17), and Gabrielle Parker's idea that "whereas the conundrum of

the exile is put forth directly, it refers more obliquely to its underlying subject: the writer himself" (73).

20. The similarities between these two are further suggested in Charlie's ambition to play classical guitar (80).

21. Charlie was sent to Father Edmond by his mother, who said she was leaving Haiti on a clandestine voyage to the Bahamas (68).

22. See Munro, *Exile and Post-1946 Haitian Literature,* 98–99.

23. See, for example, Laferrière's *Tout bouge autour de moi* and Lahens's *Failles.*

Conclusion

1. See also, Glissant's argument that "our conception of time is not the linear time of the West. [It is a] time in spiral that corresponds to neither the linear time of the Westerners, nor to the circular time of the Pre-Columbians . . . but is a sort of product of the two" ("Le Chaos-Monde" 122–23).

2. Jonathan Katz suggests a similar idea of cyclical, self-repeating history in Haiti, when he writes, "It's as if the island was built with a kind of reverse *deux ex machina:* No sooner does a story begin to find resolution than something arrives to thoroughly unresolve it" (265).

3. Wilentz further argues that "often it is actually those who do remember history who are doomed to repeat it, while those who have no idea or who've forgotten can sometimes escape a reprise" (142).

4. See also Kaussen's argument that "Haitian urbanization and migration in the occupation period predict aspects of our own era of globalization, its ills—but also its possibilities" (*Migrant Revolutions* 28).

5. See, for example, Žižek's *Living in the End Times.*

6. On the zombie figure in Haiti, see Ramsey, 170–73, and Laënnec Hurbon, *Le barbare imaginaire* and "American Fantasy and Haitian Vodou." At the time of writing, a brief list of recent manifestations of apocalyptic themes in popular culture would include the Batman film *The Dark Knight Rises* (2012), the French television series *Les revenants,* the song "Radioactive" (2012) by the band Imagine Dragons, and Janelle Monáe's track "Dance Apocalyptic" (2013). See also the various "survivalist" magazines and websites, for example: http://survivalist.com.

7. The Dark Mountain Project, "The Dark Mountain Manifesto," http://dark-mountain.net/about/manifesto.

8. The utopian nature of "Caribbean critique" is further suggested in Nesbitt's description of how it has been "compelled to articulate the critical project not as an absolute idealism but as a materialist politics that would destroy and re-invent the very foundations of a slave-holding, colonial world dedicated to the most violent bestialization of human beings, while striving to remain faithful to the imperatives of the ideas of equality, justice, freedom, and truth that inform the struggle" (xii).

Bibliography

Adam, Barbara. "Perceptions of Time." In *Companion Encyclopedia of Anthropology,* edited by Tim Ingold, 503–26. New York: Routledge, 1994.

Alexis, Jacques-Stephen. *Compère Général Soleil.* Paris: Gallimard, 1955.

———."Du réalisme merveilleux des Haïtiens." *Présence Africaine* (1956): 245–71.

———. *Les arbres musiciens.* Paris: Gallimard, 1957.

Altizer, J. J. *History as Apocalypse.* Albany: SUNY Press, 1985.

Anderson, Mark D. *Disaster Writing: The Cultural Politics of Catastrophe in Latin America.* Charlottesville: University of Virginia Press, 2011.

Aristide, Jean-Bertrand. *Dignity.* Translated by Carrol F. Coates. Charlottesville: University of Virginia Press, 1996.

Aristide, Jean-Bertrand, and Christophe Wargny. *Jean-Bertrand Aristide: An Autobiography.* Translated by Linda M. Maloney. New York: Orbis Books, 1993.

Arnold, A. James. *Modernism and Negritude: The Poetry and Poetics of Aimé Césaire.* Cambridge, MA: Harvard University Press, 1981.

Arnold, David. "Introduction: Tropical Medicine before Manson." In *Warm Climates and Western Medicine: The Emergence of Tropical Medicine,* edited by David Arnold, 1–19. Amsterdam: Rodopi, 1996.

Arthus, Wien Weibert. "The Alliance for Progress: A Case Study of Failure of International Commitments to Haiti." In *The Idea of Haiti: Rethinking Crisis and Development,* edited by Millery Polyné, 135–63. Minneapolis: University of Minnesota Press, 2013.

Audefroy, Joel F. "Haiti: Post-earthquake Lessons Learned from Traditional Construction." *Environment and Urbanization* 23.2 (2011): 447–62.

Averill, Gage. *A Day for the Hunter, a Day for the Prey: Popular Music and Power in Haiti.* Chicago: University of Chicago Press, 1997.

Bakun, William H., Claudia H. Flores, and Uri S. ten Brink. "Significant Earthquakes on the Enriquillo Fault system, Hispaniola, 1500–2010: Implications for Seismic Hazard." *Bulletin of the Seismological Society of America* 102.1 (2012): 18–30.

Bankoff, Greg. "Rendering the World Unsafe: 'Vulnerability' as Western Discourse." *Disasters* 25.1 (2001): 19–35.

Bassnett, Susan. "Seismic Aftershocks: Responses to the Great Lisbon Earthquake of 1755." In *Sites of Exchange: European Crossroads and Faultlines*, edited by Maurizio Ascari and Adrian Corrado, 177–88. Amsterdam-New York: Rodopi, 2006.

Bell, Madison Smartt. *Toussaint Louverture: A Biography.* New York: Vintage, 2007.

Bellegarde-Smith, Patrick. *In the Shadow of Powers: Dantès Bellegarde in Haitian Social Thought.* Atlantic Highlands, NJ: Humanities Press International, 1985.

Benítez-Rojo, Antonio. *The Repeating Island: The Caribbean and the Postmodern Perspective.* Translated by James Maraniss. Durham, NC: Duke University Press, 1997.

———. "Three Words Towards Creolization." Translated by James Maraniss. In *Caribbean Creolization: Reflections on the Cultural Dynamics of Language, Literature, and Identity*, edited by Kathleen M. Balutansky and Marie-Agnes Sourieau, 53–61. Gainesville: University Press of Florida; Kingston: University of the West Indies Press, 1998.

Benson, LeGrace. "Haiti's Elusive Paradise." In *Postcolonial Ecologies: Literatures of the Environment*, edited by Elizabeth De Loughrey and George B. Handley, 62–79. New York: Oxford University Press, 2011.

Bongie, Chris. *Islands and Exiles: The Creole Identities of Post/colonial Literature.* Stanford, CA: Stanford University Press, 1998.

Brathwaite, Edward. "Timehri." In *Is Massa Day Dead?*, edited by Orde Coombs, 29–30. New York: Anchor, 1974.

Braziel, Jana Evans. *Artists, Performers, and Black Masculinity in the Haitian Diaspora.* Bloomington: Indiana University Press, 2008.

———. *Duvalier's Ghosts: Race, Diaspora, and U.S. Imperialism in Haitian Literatures.* Gainesville: University Press of Florida, 2010.

Brisley, Lucy. "On the Vicissitudes of Nostalgia: Dany Laferrière's *L'énigme du retour.*" In *Dany Laferrière: Essays on His Works*, edited by Lee Skallerup Bessette, 94–121. Toronto: Guernica, 2011.

Britton, Celia M. *Edouard Glissant and Postcolonial Theory: Strategies of Language and Resistance.* Charlottesville: University of Virginia Press, 1999.

———. *The Sense of Community in French Caribbean Fiction.* Liverpool: Liverpool University Press, 2009.

Brown, Vincent. *The Reaper's Garden: Death and Power in the World of Atlantic Slavery.* Cambridge, MA: Harvard University Press, 2008.

Buteau, Pierre, Rodney Saint-Eloi, and Lyonel Trouillot, eds. *Refonder Haïti?* Montreal: Mémoire d'encrier, 2008.

Button, Gregory. *Disaster Culture: Knowledge and Uncertainty in the Wake of Human and Environmental Catastrophe.* Walnut Creek, CA: Left Coast Press, 2010.

Caple James, Erica. *Democratic Insecurities: Violence, Trauma, and Intervention in Haiti.* Berkeley: University of California Press, 2010.

Caruth, Cathy. *Unclaimed Experience: Trauma, Narrative, and History.* Baltimore, MD: The Johns Hopkins University Press, 1996.

Césaire, Aimé. *The Collected Poetry.* Translated by Clayton Eshleman and Annette Smith. Berkeley: University of California Press, 1983.

Chancy, Myriam J. A. *Framing Silence: Revolutionary Novels by Haitian Women.* New Brunswick, NJ: Rutgers University Press, 1997.

———. *From Sugar to Revolution: Women's Visions of Haiti, Cuba, and the Dominican Republic.* Waterloo, ON: Wilfrid Laurier University Press, 2012.

Chéry, André. *Le chien comme métaphore en Haïti: Analyse d'un corpus de proverbes et de textes littéraires haïtiens.* Port-au-Prince: Henri Deschamps, 2004.

Christie, Kenneth. *The South African Truth Commission.* Basingstoke: Palgrave MacMillan, 2000.

Cosentino, Donald. "Baby on the Blender: A Visual History of Catastrophe in Haiti." *Small Axe* 36 (2011): 134–54.

Danticat, Edwidge. *The Dew Breaker.* New York: Alfred A. Knopf, 2004.

Dash, J. Michael. "Afterword: Neither France nor Senegal: Bovarysme and Haiti's Hemispheric Identity." In *Haiti and the Americas,* edited by Carla Carlagé, Raphael Dalleo, Luis Duno-Gottberg, and Clevis Headley, 219–30. Jackson: University of Mississippi Press, 2013.

———. "Exile and Recent Literature." In *A History of Literature in the Caribbean,* vol. 1, edited by A. James Arnold, 451–63. Philadelphia: John Benjamins, 1994.

———. *Haiti and the United States: National Stereotypes and the Literary Imagination.* New York: St Martin's Press, 1997.

———. *Literature and Ideology in Haiti, 1915–1961.* Basingstoke: Macmillan, 1981.

———. *The Other America: Caribbean Literature in a New World Context.* Charlottesville: University of Virginia Press, 1998.

———. "Postcolonial Eccentricities: Francophone Caribbean Literature and the *fin de siècle.*" In *The Francophone Caribbean Today: Literature, Language, Culture,* edited by Gertrud Aub-Buscher and Beverley Ormerod Noakes, 33–44. Kingston: University of the West Indies Press, 2003.

Davis, Mike. *Ecology of Fear: Los Angeles and the Imagination of Disaster.* New York: Metropolitan, 1998.

———. *Planet of Slums.* New York, Verso: 2006.

Dayan, Colin. "Rituals of Belief, Practices of Law." *Small Axe* 31 (2010): 193–99.

Deibert, Michael. *Notes from the Last Testament: The Struggle for Haiti.* New York: Seven Stories Press, 2005.

DeLoughrey, Elizabeth, and George B. Handley. "Introduction: Toward an Aesthetics of the Earth." In *Postcolonial Ecologies: Literatures of the Environment,* edited by Elizabeth DeLoughrey and George B. Handley, 3–39. New York: Oxford University Press, 2011.

Denis, Lorimer, François Duvalier, Michel Aubourg, and Léonce Viaud. *L'avenir du pays et l'action néfaste de M. Foisset*. Port au Prince: Imprimerie de l'État, 1949.

Depestre, René. *Hadriana dans tous mes rêves*. Paris: Gallimard, 1988.

Deren, Maya. *Divine Horsemen: Voodoo Gods of Haiti*. New York: Chelsea House, 1970.

Desmangles, Leslie. *The Faces of the Gods: Vodou and Roman Catholicism in Haiti*. Chapel Hill: University of North Carolina Press, 1992.

Desmangles, Leslie, and Elizabeth McAlister. "Religion in Post-earthquake Haiti." In *Haiti Rising: Haitian History, Culture, and the Earthquake of 2010*, edited by Martin Munro, 70–78. Liverpool: Liverpool University Press; Kingston: University of the West Indies Press, 2010.

Drayton, Richard. "The Problem of the Hero(ine) in Caribbean History." *Small Axe* 15.1 (2011): 26–45.

Dubois, Laurent. *Avengers of the New World: The Story of the Haitian Revolution*. Cambridge, MA: Harvard University Press, 2004.

———. *Haiti: The Aftershocks of History*. New York: Metropolitan Books, 2012.

Dupuy, Alex. *The Prophet and Power: Jean-Bertrand Aristide, the International Community, and Haiti*. Lanham, MD: Rowman and Littlefield, 2007.

Duvalier, François. "Message du Docteur François Duvalier, Président à vie de la République, à l'occasion du cyclone Inès et de la prochaine compétition électorale à la veille de l'an X de la revolution duvaliériste." Port-au-Prince, n.p, 1996.

Edmondson, Belinda. *Caribbean Romances: The Politics of Regional Representation*. Charlottesville: University of Virginia Press, 1999.

Etienne, Yolette. "Haiti and Catastrophes: Lessons Not Learned." In *Tectonic Shifts: Haiti Since the Earthquake*, edited by Mark Schuller and Pablo Morales, 27–34. Sterling, VA: Stylus Publishing, 2012.

Fanon, Frantz. *Peau noire, masques blancs*. Paris: Seuil, 1952.

———. *The Wretched of the Earth*. Translated by Richard Philcox. 1961. New York: Grove, 2004.

Fatton, Robert Jr. "Haiti: The Saturnalia of Emancipation and the Vicissitudes of Predatory Rule." *Third World Quarterly* 27.1 (2006): 115–33.

———. *Haiti's Predatory Republic: The Unending Transition to Democracy*. Boulder, CO: Lynne Reiner, 2002.

Foucault, Michel. *The History of Sexuality*. Vol. 1, *An Introduction*. Translated by Robert Hurley. 1978. New York: Random House, 1990.

Frankétienne. *Melovivi ou Le piège, suivi de Brèche ardente*. Paris: Riveneuve, 2010.

Gallagher, Mary. "Concealment, Displacement, and Disconnection: Danticat's *The Dew Breaker*." In *Edwidge Danticat: A Reader's Guide*, edited by Martin Munro, 147–60. Charlottesville: University of Virginia Press, 2010.

Garland, Christopher. "The Rhetoric of Crisis and Foreclosing the Future of Haiti in *Ghosts of Cité Soleil.*" In *Haiti and the Americas,* edited by Carla Carlagé, Raphael Dalleo, Luis Duno-Gottberg, and Clevis Headley, 179–98. Jackson: University of Mississippi Press, 2013.

Garraway, Doris L. "Empire of Freedom, Kingdom of Civilization: Henry Christophe, the Baron de Vastey, and the Paradoxes of Universalism in Post-revolutionary Haiti." *Small Axe* 39 (2012): 1–21.

Garrigus, John D. "Pre-revolutionary Saint-Domingue." In *Haiti Rising: Haitian History, Culture, and the Earthquake of 2010,* edited by Martin Munro, 115–25. Liverpool: Liverpool University Press; Kingston: University of the West Indies Press, 2010.

Glissant, Edouard. *Caribbean Discourse: Selected Essays.* Translated by J. Michael Dash. Charlottesville: University of Virginia Press, 1989.

———. "Le chaos-monde, l'oral et l'ecrit." In *Ecrire la parole de nuit: La nouvelle littérature antillaise,* edited by Ralph Ludwig, 111–29. Paris: Gallimard, 1994.

———. *L'intention poétique.* Paris: Seuil, 1969.

———. *Introduction à une poétique du Divers.* Paris: Gallimard, 1996.

———. *Poetics of Relation.* Translated by Betsy Wing. Ann Arbor: University of Michigan Press, 1997.

———. *Traité du tout-monde.* Paris: Gallimard, 1997.

Greenberg, Jennifer. "The 'Strong Arm' and the 'Friendly Hand': Military Humanitarianism in Post-earthquake Haiti." *Journal of Haitian Studies* 19.1 (2013): 95–122.

Gribben, Crawford. *Evangelical Millennialism in the Trans-Atlantic World, 1500–2000.* New York: Palgrave MacMillan, 2011.

———. "Rapture Fictions and the Changing Evangelical Condition." *Literature and Theology* 18.1 (2004): 77–94.

Gugelberger, George. "Introduction: Institutionalization of Transgression: Testimonial Discourse and Beyond." In *The Real Thing: Testimonial and Latin American Discourse,* edited by George Gugelberger, 1–19. Durham, NC: Duke University Press, 1996.

Gutiérrez, Gustavo. *Essential Writings: Making of Modern Theology.* New York: Orbis, 1996.

———. *A Theology of Liberation: History, Politics, and Salvation.* New York: Orbis, 1971.

Hadjadj, Fabrice. "Frankétienne sismographe." In Frankétienne, *Melovivi ou Le piège suivi de Brèche ardente,* 9–13. Paris: Riveneuve, 2010.

Hall, Stuart. "Cosmopolitan Promises, Multicultural Realities." In *Divided Cities: The Oxford Amnesty Lectures 2003,* edited by Richard Scholar, 20–51. Oxford University Press, 2006.

Harris, Wilson. *Carnival.* London: Faber and Faber, 1985.

Hayner, Priscilla B. *Unspeakable Truths: Transitional Justice and The Challenge of Truth Commissions.* 2nd edition. New York: Routledge, 2011.

Hoefer, Anthony Dyer. *Apocalypse South: Judgment, Cataclysm, and Resistance in the Regional Imaginary.* Columbus: The Ohio State University Press, 2012.

Hoffman, Susanna M. "The Monster and the Mother: The Symbolism of Catastrophe." In *Catastrophe and Culture: The Anthropology of Disaster,* edited by Susanna M. Hoffman and Anthony Silver-Smith, 113–42. Santa Fe, NM: School of American Research Press, 2002.

Hurbon, Laënnec. "American Fantasy and Haitian Vodou." In *Sacred Arts of Haitian Vodou,* edited by Donald Cosentino, 181–97. Los Angeles: Fowler Museum, 1995.

———. *Le barbare imaginaire.* Paris: Cerf, 1988.

———. "Catastrophe permanente et reconstruction." *L'Observatoire de la reconstruction* 6 (2012): 8–10.

———. "Current Evolution of Relations between Religion and Power in Haiti." *In Nation Dance: Religion, Identity and Cultural Difference in the Caribbean,* edited by Patrick Taylor, 118–27. Bloomington: Indiana University Press, 2001

———. "La désymbolisation du pouvoir et ses effets meurtriers." *Chemins critiques* 5.1 (2001).

Huxley, Francis. *The Invisibles.* London: Hart-Davis, 1966.

James, C. L. R. *The Black Jacobins: Toussaint L'Ouverture and the San Domingo Revolution.* New York: Vintage, 1963.

Jean-Charles, Régine Michelle. "A travers l'Atlantique noire: L'imagerie de l'eau dans les textes haïtiennes." In *Écrits d'Haïti: Perspectives sur la littérature haïtienne contemporaine (1986–2006),* edited by Nadève Ménard, 163–76. Paris: Karthala, 2011.

Joseph, Régine Isabelle. "Ruins of Dreams: Marie Chauvet and Post-Apocalyptic Writing in Haiti." PhD diss., New York University, 2010.

Katz, Jonathan M. *The Big Truck That Went By: How the World Came to Save Haiti and Left Behind a Disaster.* New York: Palgrave Macmillan, 2013.

Kaussen, Valerie. *Migrant Revolutions: Haitian Literature, Globalization, and U.S. Imperialism.* Lanham, MD: Lexington Books, 2008.

———. "Violence and Methodology: Reading Aristide in the Aftermath of 2004." *Small Axe* 30 (2009): 148–60.

Kermode, Frank. *The Sense of an Ending: Studies in the Theory of Fiction.* 1967. Oxford: Oxford University Press, 2000.

Kovats-Bernat, J. Christopher. *Sleeping Rough in Port-au-Prince: An Ethnography of Street Children and Violence in Haiti.* Gainesville: University Press of Florida, 2006.

La Capra, Dominick. *Writing History, Writing Trauma.* Baltimore, MD: The Johns Hopkins University Press, 2001.

Laferrière, Dany. *L'art presque perdu de ne rien faire*. Montreal: Boréal, 2011.
———. *L'énigme du retour*. Paris: Grasset, 2009.
———. *J'écris comme je vis*. Lyon: La Passe du Vent, 2000.
———. *Pays sans chapeau*. Paris: Le Serpent à plumes, 1999.
———. *Tout bouge autour de moi*. Montreal: Mémoire d'encrier, 2010.
Laguerre, Michel S. *The Military and Society in Haiti*. Knoxville: University of Tennessee Press, 1993.
Lahens, Yanick. *La couleur de l'aube*. Paris: Sabine Wespieser, 2008.
———. *Failles*. Paris: Sabine Wespieser, 2011.
Lambert, Fernando. "Émile Ollivier, écrivain d'Haïti du Québec." *Notre Librairie* 133 (1998): 154–59.
Landes, Richard. *Encyclopedia of Millennialism and Millennial Movements*. New York: Routledge, 2000.
Laroche, Maximilien. "La Lutte du héros contre sa victimisation." *Tanbou*, Spring 1994. http://www.tanbou.com/1994/Spring/Lutte.htm.
Leth, Asger. *Ghosts of Cité Soleil*. Nordisk Film, 2006.
Lévi-Strauss, Claude. *Structural Anthropology*. 1963. Harmondsworth: Penguin, 1972.
Márquez, Gabriel García. *One Hundred Years of Solitude*. New York: Harper, 2006.
Mars, Kettly. *Saisons sauvages*. Paris: Mercure de France, 2010.
Maximin, Daniel. *L'île et une nuit*. Paris: Seuil, 1995.
May, John. *Toward a New Earth: Apocalypse in the American Novel*. South Bend, IN: University of Notre Dame Press, 1972.
McAlister, Elizabeth A. "From Slave Revolt to a Blood Pact with Satan: The Evangelical Rewriting of Haitian History." *Studies in Religion/Sciences Religieuses* (2012): 1–29.
———. *Rara!: Vodou, Power, and Performance in Haiti and Its Diaspora*. Berkeley: University of California Press, 2002.
McAlister, Melani. "What Is Your Heart For? Affect and Internationalism in the Evangelical Public Sphere." *American Literary History* 20.4 (2008): 870–95.
Ménard, Nadève. "Kettly Mars: La sensualité au coeur de la vie." In *Écrits d'Haïti: Perspectives sur la littérature haïtienne contemporaine (1986–2006)*, edited by Nadève Ménard, 229–33. Paris: Karthala, 2011.
Ménil, René. *Antilles déjà jadis: Précédé de Tracées*. Paris: Robert Laffont, 1981.
Métraux, Alfred. *Le vaudou haïtien*. Paris: Gallimard, 1958.
Meyer, John M. *Political Nature: Environmentalism and the Interpretation of Western Thought*. Cambridge, MA: MIT Press, 2001.
Moïse, Claude, and Emile Ollivier. *Repenser Haïti: Grandeur et misères d'un mouvement démocratique*. Montreal: Editions du CIDIHCA, 1992.
Mould, Tom. *Choctaw Prophecy: A Legacy of the Future*. Tuscaloosa: University of Alabama Press, 2003.

Moylan, Tom. "Realizing Better Futures, Strong Thought for Hard Times." In *Utopia Method Vision: The Use Value of Social Dreaming*, edited by Tom Moylan and Rafaelle Baccolini, 191–222. 2nd edition. Bern: Peter Lang, 2009.

Moylan, Tom, and Rafaella Baccolini. *Utopia Method Vision: The Use Value of Social Dreaming.* Oxford: Peter Lang, 2007.

Munro, Martin. *Different Drummers: Rhythm and Race in the Americas.* Berkeley: University of California Press, 2010.

———. *Exile and Post-1946 Haitian Literature: Alexis, Depestre, Ollivier, Laferrière, Danticat.* Liverpool: Liverpool University Press, 2007.

Najman, Charles. *Haïti, la fin des chimères?* Dominant 7, 2004.

Nesbitt, Nick. *Caribbean Critique: Antillean Critical Theory from Toussaint to Glissant.* Liverpool: Liverpool University Press, 2013.

Nicholls, David. *From Dessalines to Duvalier: Race, Colour and National Independence in Haiti.* Basingstoke: MacMillan, 1981.

O'Leary, Timothy D. *Arguing the Apocalypse: A Theory of Millennial Rhetoric.* Oxford: Oxford University Press, 1994.

Parker, Gabrielle. "'Returns to the Native Land': Dany Laferrière's Unresolved Dilemma." In *Dany Laferrière: Essays on His Works,* edited by Lee Skallerup Bessette, 72–93. Toronto: Guernica, 2013.

Patterson, Orlando. *Slavery and Social Death: A Comparative Study.* Cambridge, MA: Harvard University Press, 1982.

Peck, Raoul. *L'homme sur les quais.* Velvet Film, 1993.

———. *Moloch Tropical.* Velvet Film, 2009.

Peck, Raoul, and Clyde Taylor. "Autopsy of Terror: Conversation with Raoul Peck." *Transition* 69 (1996): 236–46.

Petty, Sheila. *Contact Zones: Memory, Origin, and Discourse in Black Diasporic Cinema.* Detroit, MI: Wayne State University Press, 2008.

Prieto, Eric. *Literature, Geography, and the Postmodern Poetics of Place.* New York: Palgrave Macmillan, 2013.

Raffy-Hideux, Peggy. *Les réalismes haïtiens contemporains: Récit et conscience sociale.* Paris: Honoré Champion, 2013.

Ramsey, Kate. *The Spirits and the Law: Vodou and Power in Haiti.* Chicago: University of Chicago Press, 2011.

René, Jean Alix. *La séduction populiste.* Port-au-Prince: Jean Alix René, 2003.

Rey, Terry. "The Virgin Mary and the Revolution in Saint-Domingue: The Charisma of Romaine-la-Prophétesse." *Journal of Historical Sociology* 11.3 (1998): 341–69.

Richman, Karen. "Religion at the Epicenter: Agency and Affiliation in Léogâne after the Earthquake." In *The Idea of Haiti: Rethinking Crisis and Development,* edited by Millery Polyné, 111–32. Minneapolis: University of Minnesota Press, 2013.

Ricoeur, Paul. *Time and Narrative.* Vol 1. Translated by Kathleen McLaughlin and David Pellauer. Chicago: University of Chicago Press, 1984.

Roumain, Jacques. *Gouverneurs de la rosée* (Paris: Éditeurs francais réunis, 1944).
Saint-Éloi, Rodney. *Haïti Kenbe la!* Neuilly-sur-Seine: Lafon, 2010.
Schuller, Mark. "Cholera and the Camps: Reaping the Republic of NGOs." In *The Idea of Haiti: Rethinking Crisis and Development,* edited by Millery Polyné, 181–201. Minneapolis: University of Minnesota Press, 2013.
———. *Killing with Kindness: Haiti, International Aid, and NGOs.* New Brunswick, NJ: Rutgers University Press, 2012.
Scott, David. *Conscripts of Modernity: The Tragedy of Colonial Enlightenment.* Durham, NC: Duke University Press, 2004.
———. *Omens of Adversity: Tragedy, Time, Memory, Justice.* Durham, NC: Duke University Press, 2014.
Shemak, April. "Re-membering Hispaniola: Edwidge Danticat's *Farming of Bones.*" *Modern Fiction Studies* 48.1 (2002): 83–112.
Smith, Matthew J. *Red and Black in Haiti: Radicalism, Conflict, and Political Change, 1934–57.* Chapel Hill: University of North Carolina Press, 2009.
Sourieau, Marie Agnès. "La mémoire engourdie de terreurs: *The Dew Breaker* d'Edwidge Danticat." *Journal of Haitian Studies* 11.2 (2005): 94–104.
Spivak, Gayatri Chakravorty. *Death of a Discipline.* New York: Columbia University Press, 2003.
Suk, Jeannie. *Postcolonial Paradoxes in French Caribbean Writing: Césaire, Glissant, Condé.* Oxford: Oxford University Press, 2001.
Sylvain, Patrick. "The Violence of Executive Silence." In *The Idea of Haiti: Rethinking Crisis and Development,* edited by Millery Polyné, 87–109. Minneapolis: University of Minnesota Press, 2013.
Trouillot, Evelyne. *La mémoire aux abois.* Paris: Hoëbeke, 2010.
Trouillot, Lyonel. *Bicentenaire.* Arles: Actes Sud, 2004.
———. *Street of Lost Footsteps.* Translated by Linda Coverdale. Lincoln: University of Nebraska Press, 2003. Originally published as *Rue des pas perdus* (Port-au-Prince: Editions Mémoire, 1996).
———. *Yanvalou pour Charlie.* Arles: Actes Sud, 2009.
Trouillot, Michel-Rolph. *Global Transformations.* New York: Palgrave, 2003.
———. *Haiti: State against Nation—The Origins and Legacy of Duvalierism.* New York: Monthly Review, 1990.
———. *Silencing the Past: Power and the Production of History.* Boston: Beacon Press, 1995.
Vété-Congolo, Hanétha. "Lorsque la folie seule fait taire le silence: Pour le développement, *Le livre d'Emma* et *À l'angle des rues parallèles.*" In *Écrits d'Haïti: Perspectives sur la littérature haïtienne contemporaine (1986–2006),* edited by Nadève Ménard, 119–35. Paris: Karthala, 2001.
Victor, Gary. *A l'angle des rues parallèles.* La Roque-d'Anthéron: Vents d'Ailleurs, 2003.
"The Visual Life of Catastrophic History: A Small Axe Project Statement." *Small Axe* 34 (2011): 133–36.

Vitiello, Joëlle. "Douceurs et violences dans l'écriture de Kettly Mars." In *Écrits d'Haïti: Perspectives sur la littérature haïtienne contemporaine (1986–2006)*, edited by Nadève Ménard, 376–83. Paris: Karthala, 2001.

Walcott, Derek. *Omeros*. New York: Farrar, Straus and Giroux, 1990.

———. *What the Twilight Says*. London: Faber and Faber, 1998.

Wilentz, Amy. *Farewell, Fred Voodoo: A Letter from Haiti*. New York: Simon and Schuster, 2013.

Žižek, Slavoj. *First as Tragedy, then as Farce*. London: Verso, 2009.

———. *Living in the End Times*. London: Verso, 2010.

Index

Recent Books in the New World Studies Series

Jeff Karem, *The Purloined Islands: Caribbean-U.S. Crosscurrents in Literature and Culture, 1880–1959*

Faith Smith, editor, *Sex and the Citizen: Interrogating the Caribbean*

Mark D. Anderson, *Disaster Writing: The Cultural Politics of Catastrophe in Latin America*

Raphael Dalleo, *Caribbean Literature and the Public Sphere: From the Plantation to the Postcolonial*

Maite Conde, *Consuming Visions: Cinema, Writing, and Modernity in Rio de Janeiro*

Monika Kaup, *Neobaroque in the Americas: Alternative Modernities in Literature, Visual Art, and Film*

Marisel C. Moreno, *Family Matters: Puerto Rican Women Authors on the Island and the Mainland*

Supriya M. Nair, *Pathologies of Paradise: Caribbean Detours*

Colleen C. O'Brien, *Race, Romance, and Rebellion: Literatures of the Americas in the Nineteenth Century*

Kelly Baker Josephs, *Disturbers of the Peace: Representations of Madness in Anglophone Caribbean Literature*

Christina Kullberg, *The Poetics of Ethnography in Martinican Narratives: Exploring the Self and the Environment*

Maria Cristina Fumagalli, Bénédicte Ledent, and Roberto del Valle Alcalá, editors, *The Cross-Dressed Caribbean: Writing, Politics, Sexualities*

Philip Kaisary, *The Haitian Revolution in the Literary Imagination: Radical Horizons, Conservative Constraints*

Jason Frydman, *Sounding the Break: African American and Caribbean Routes of World Literature*

Tanya L. Shields, *Bodies and Bones: Feminist Rehearsal and Imagining Caribbean Belonging*

Stanka Radović, *Locating the Destitute: Space and Identity in Caribbean Fiction*

Nicole N. Aljoe and Ian Finseth, editors, *Journeys of the Slave Narrative in the Early Americas*

Stephen M. Park, *The Pan American Imagination: Contested Visions of the Hemisphere in Twentieth-Century Literature*

Maurice St. Pierre, *Eric Williams and the Anticolonial Tradition: The Making of a Diasporan Intellectual*

Elena Machado Sáez, *Market Aesthetics: The Purchase of the Past in Caribbean Diasporic Fiction*

Martin Munro, *Tropical Apocalypse: Haiti and the Caribbean End Times*